Covering Violence

Covering Violence

A Guide to Ethical Reporting About Victims and Trauma

William Coté and Roger Simpson

Journalist Profiles by Migael Scherer

Columbia University Press

New York

Columbia University Press
Publishers Since 1893
New York   Chichester, West Sussex

Library of Congress Cataloging-in-Publication Data

Coté, William E. (William Edward)
    Covering Violence : a guide to ethical reporting about victims and trauma /
William Coté and Roger Simpson.
        p. cm.
    Includes bibliographical references and index.
    ISBN 0-231-11450-8 — ISBN 0-231-11451-6 (pbk.)
    1. Disasters—Press coverage. 2. Violence—Press coverage. 3. Victims—Press
coverage.   I. Simpson, Roger, 1937–   II. Title.

PN4784.D57 C68 2000
070.4'33—dc21

00-034627

Casebound editions of Columbia University Press books
are printed on permanent and durable acid-free paper.

Printed in the United States of America
c 10 9 8 7 6 5 4 3 2 1
p 10 9 8 7 6 5 4 3 2 1

Dedications

William Coté: To my wife, Donna, and to the memory of my parents, Maybelle and Mervin Coté

Roger Simpson: To Jeffrey Cantrell, whose love made the book possible

Contents

PREFACE   *ix*

ACKNOWLEDGMENTS   *xiii*

Introduction: Journalists and Violence   1

A Witness for the Community
Scott North   13

Slain Mother's Love Manages to Find Daughter
Scott North   18

1   Trauma: Assault on an Essential Human System   22

2   The Journalist's Trauma   42

3   Reporting at the Scene   56

Uncovering What's Already There
Rick Bragg   75

Piedmont Journal: Tried by Deadly Tornado,
An Anchor of Faith Holds
Rick Bragg   78

4   The Interview: Assault or Catharsis?   83

Focusing on the Humanity
Jeff Gradney   102

The Deep, Familiar Pain
Jeff Gradney   105

5   Writing the Story   107

6   Pictures and Sounds of Trauma   123

Photos That Connect
Lynne Dobson   145

The Test of Fire
Michele Stanush   153

7   Reporting on Rape Trauma   157

Charting the Course of Recovery
Debra McKinney   177

Malignant Memories: It's a Long Road Back to Recovery
from Incest
Debra McKinney   181

8   Reporting About Children   185

9   Using the Spotlight with Precision and Sensitivity   199

10 Oklahoma City: "Terror in the Heartland"   212

11 Conclusions   222

The Dart Award for Excellence in Reporting on Victims of Violence   235

A NOTE ABOUT TRAUMA TRAINING   237

BIBLIOGRAPHY   239

INDEX   245

Preface

We awoke to the powerful role of trauma in human experience in quite different ways. We had been newspaper reporters and had covered a wide range of news events, but we matured as journalists without knowing much about what the victims in our stories truly experienced. Our ignorance wasn't at all remarkable, though. Few of the reporters, editors, and photographers around us understood trauma, either.

William Coté first observed the effects of trauma as a young reporter filling in on the police beat at a small Michigan daily in the 1960s. He noticed startlingly different reactions among defendants, family, and friends in a court hearing on a murder case. Some people showed shock, despair, or fury. Others appeared calm or almost unconcerned. Newsroom colleagues with more experience shrugged their shoulders when he asked them to explain the range of responses.

Even after nineteen more years as a reporter and editor, Coté didn't truly understand many aspects of trauma. The veil began to lift in 1991 when, as a professor of journalism at Michigan State University, he directed a day-long seminar for students and working professionals, "Victims and the Media." Conceived by Dr. Frank Ochberg, a psychiatrist and former state mental health director, the seminar inspired MSU's new Victims and the Media Program. The key element of that program is educating students about trauma in the core newswriting and reporting courses that every journalism student must take. In the first course, students learn about the thorny topic through reading and discussion and watch videotapes of reporters interviewing professional actors portraying victims of violence.

In the next course, students interview survivors of shootings, rapes, and other trauma.

Roger Simpson came to see trauma as integral to journalism practice as he designed and taught an ethics course at the University of Washington in the 1980s. He regularly invited advocates for sexual assault survivors to speak to the ethics students. Those talks led to classes that examine how news coverage might affect the emotional injury that accompanies the physical assault. Over time he began to realize how much he did not know about the experience of surviving violent injury. A Seattle conference that brought journalists and the families of murder victims together in the late 1980s found survivors venting their anger and showed usually confident journalists to be more defensive than sensitive when confronted with the families' complaints. A key that might have helped everyone in that session was missing; few participants said anything about trauma.

Then, in 1993, Simpson attended a conference at the Virginia Mason Medical Center in Seattle where speakers showed how victims of violence experience trauma and what they endure as they recover. He pressed the School of Communications at the University of Washington to change its advanced journalism curriculum to make a permanent place for several hours of trauma training. Since the spring of 1994 nearly every journalism student at Washington has heard about emotional trauma and has practiced interviewing survivors (played by talented drama students).

Once we began to teach about trauma, we gained support from victims, from those in medicine and psychology who treat and study trauma, from medical centers, and from our colleagues. Vitally helpful reinforcement has come from students, past and present, and increasingly from journalists who recognize the traumatic stresses of their own work.

Among these allies is Migael Scherer, who contributed the profiles of journalists included in this book. Scherer came to this work in the early 1990s as a guest speaker in Roger Simpson's ethics course. As a survivor of a high-profile rape and a former high school journalism teacher, she was motivated by her firsthand knowledge of how news coverage can inflict unnecessary harm and—most alarming of all—discourage victims from reporting sexual assault to police. Soon she was working regularly with Simpson and by 1996 was a consultant to the Journalism and Trauma Program, developing a curriculum to cover these issues in ways that support the overall goals of Washington's journalism courses.

Students in the MSU and Washington courses navigate the trauma training with flair, beginning with reasonable fears and often concluding by sensing that their work in journalism will directly benefit from confronting the issues raised in awkward interviews of trauma survivors. Graduates—and we've talked to many—say they were indeed sent to photograph, interview, or write about trauma victims early in their first jobs and that the classroom "dry run" helped them to handle a trying assignment.

Reporters and photographers are coming to us often these days to attest to the need to address trauma and its effects on victims and on journalists. Twenty years ago few in the business thought that trauma had anything to do with the education of a journalist. These days many journalists know that trauma has a heavy hand on them and on those they interview and photograph.

As we have drilled our classes on trauma, we have found time to meet with press associations and newsroom staffs. We've asked journalists if they have any of the symptoms that are typical of someone suffering from trauma. We weren't surprised to find that many reporters show signs of emotional injury that are a lot like those of police and firefighters.

Our experience reflects the growing attention to trauma issues in journalism around the country. A newspaper ombudsman regularly conducts workshops for his and other staffs on how trauma affects victims. Journalists pour their pains and successes into narratives that truly show their sensitivity or their suffering. We know other journalism teachers who have included victims' concerns in their reporting courses for years. As we were writing this book, a program to help journalists deal with trauma at disaster and crash scenes was being planned. In January 2000 the Center for Journalism and Trauma, initially funded by the Dart Foundation, was established as a national resource center for the media at the University of Washington School of Communications.

The three of us have had the rare experience of seeing our field anew through a lens that was obscured for much of our lives. What follows is our sense of what journalism in the United States can be if reporters, editors, and photographers have a realistic sense of traumatic injury and recovery.

Acknowledgments

This book would not exist without the inspiration and insights of Frank Ochberg, M.D., a psychiatrist who has done more than anyone else to bring journalists and trauma experts into dialogue about their common interests. He guided Michigan State University and the University of Washington in implementing trauma education for their journalism students. He has been profoundly helpful to both of us in the writing of this book. He continues to make us proud of our efforts.

The Washington program has had the dedicated assistance of Migael Scherer since its inception. Her profiles of journalists in this book exemplify the fine writing for which she has won awards and a remarkable awareness of the authors' goals .

The Dart Foundation, Mason, MI, has provided the funds to transform the journalism and trauma education efforts in our schools and to enable us to immerse ourselves in both trauma science and newsroom response to traumatic events.

William Coté thanks his Michigan State associates: Former School of Journalism Director Stan Soffin and present Acting Director Stephen Lacy; Bonnie Bucqueroux, coordinator of the Victims and the Media Program; Prof. Sue Carter, co-chair of the Victims and Media Advisory Council; Kirk Haverkamp, who gave special help as a graduate assistant, and School of Journalism staff members. The Michigan Victim Alliance and officers Linda Harkness and Dan and Pat Anderson gave their time and advice willingly.

Bill Coté gives his loving appreciation to his wife, Donna. She married him even after she knew he was consumed with writing and teaching about covering victims of violence. She encouraged him greatly while he worked on this book.

Roger Simpson notes the support of former University of Washington School of Communications Director Ed Bassett, current director Anthony Giffard, and the contributions of colleague Kevin Kawamoto. Journalism faculty have infused the book with their own experiences and made their classrooms available for training: Kathleen Fearn-Banks, Michael Henderson, Don Pember and Doug Underwood. The book also reflects the uncountable ideas of graduate research assistants in the Journalism and Trauma Program: James Boggs, Cathy Ferrand Bullock, Jason Cubert, Elizabeth Koehler, Brennon Martin, Janice Maxson, Kristin Moran, Paula Reynolds-Eblacas, and Jill Wiske.

The book also reflects the contributions of those who have taught in the Journalism and Trauma program: E.K. Rynearson, M.D., and Jennifer Favell, Ph.D., on the staff of Separation and Loss Services of Virginia Mason Medical Center in Seattle, and former associates Cindi Sinnema and John Purrington.

Columbia University Press and its editors saw the need for this book. Executive Editor Ann Miller offered unwavering support. Outside peer reviewers, whose names are not known to us, helped us focus the work. Helen Benedict and Migael Scherer gave us counsel on the sexual assault chapter. Donna Gaffney helped us address children's trauma. We also thank copy editor Polly Kummel and editor Leslie Bialler.

For an early effort to address this topic, we solicited manuscripts from experts in the trauma field and in journalism, excellent work that we regretted having to put aside in favor of this co-authored book. For those contributions, we thank Bonnie Bucqueroux, Sue Carter, Steve Lachowicz, Kathleen Nader, Frank Ochberg, Edward Rynearson, Migael Scherer, and Hope Tuttle.

Finally, we want to note the special assistance of Joann Byrd, editorial-page editor, and Michael Barber, staff reporter, both with the *Seattle Post-Intelligencer*; Hope Tuttle, now with the office of the attorney general of the State of Washington; literary agent Elizabeth Wales; Patricia Dinning, a retired University of Washington staff member, and Bruce Shapiro of *The Nation*.

Despite the efforts of all these good people, only the two authors are accountable for the content of this book. Although we have, of course, collaborated on the entire project, Coté is primarily responsible for the introduction and chapters 1, 5, 6, 10, and 11; Simpson is primarily responsible for chapters 2, 3, 4, 7, 8, and 9.

Grateful acknowledgement is made to the following for permission to reprint material in copyright that accompanies the journalist profiles:

For Scott North's "Slain Mother's Love Manages to Find Daughter": Copyright © 1999 by the Herald (Everett, WA).

For Rick Bragg's "Piedmont Journal: Tried by Deadly Tornado, An Anchor of Faith Holds": Copyright © 1994 by the New York Times Co. Reprinted by permission.

For transcripts of Jeff Gradney's news reports: Copyright © KING-5 Television, a wholly owned subsidiary of A.H. Belo Corp., 1996.

For excerpts from "The Test of Fire" and photographs by Lynne Dobson: Copyright © 1994 The Austin American-Statesman.

For excerpts from Debra McKinney's "Malignant Memories": Copyright © 1993 The Anchorage Daily News.

Covering Violence

Journalists and Violence

In 1988 terrorists blew up an airliner over a small town in Scotland. In 1996 and 1998 jets exploded and crashed into the Atlantic, one near New York City and the other in Nova Scotia. In 1989 the Loma Prieta earthquake disabled the San Francisco area, killing dozens, injuring hundreds, and leaving untold others frightened by their vulnerability to nature's whims. In 1995 an American terrorist's bomb destroyed the federal building in Oklahoma City and took 168 lives. In 1998 an earthquake-generated tsunami killed more than two thousand people in Papua, New Guinea. Later that year a hurricane killed thousands and devastated the agricultural economies of Central American nations. On April 20, 1999, two high school students in Colorado went on a shooting rampage, killing twelve classmates and a teacher and wounding others before they killed themselves. The attack in Littleton was one of many school shootings, violent actions by young people that mirrored workplace shootings among adults. Before the year ended powerful earthquakes struck Turkey, killing many thousands of people.

International media armies converged on these places, fought for the most revealing words and pictures, and quickly moved on, leaving those events framed in our minds as fleeting actions, lasting only hours or days, and the images at their center only those of fear, anxiety, shock, and grief. In the frenzy some journalists broke the traditional rules of reporting: they pulled on hospital scrubs or firefighter's gear or claimed falsely to be a victim's relative to gain illicit entry to off-limits wards, areas designated as official crime scenes, and hotel areas set aside for families of the dead.

The few stories that got worldwide attention overshadowed the nearly daily confrontations between journalists and their audiences in U.S. towns and cities. A shooting, a car crash, or a rape afflicts friends, relatives, and neighbors as well as victims. If truth is the first casualty of war, privacy often is the first casualty of any devastating, unexpected event. Reporters, photographers, and editors—just doing their job—interview and photograph victims and relatives, moving their pain to the front page or the evening newscast where everyone can see it.

It isn't surprising that the public and the people in the stories complain about insensitive, callous, and excessive coverage. Anger drives people to throw rings of protection around children and other victims, defiantly shouting off or closing out the circling reporters. Journalists quickly become scapegoats for the discomfort that ensues from exposure to tragedy. Joann Byrd, editorial page editor of the *Seattle Post-Intelligencer,* told us that in three years as ombudsman of the *Washington Post,* she "probably fielded a couple thousand calls from people angered by coverage—in the *Post* or elsewhere—of trauma." Other calls for change in media coverage of violence come from religious, parent, or women's advocacy groups. There were signs at the close of the 1990s that the issue had the attention of some political leaders. Many of the harshest critics of the news media were subjects of news stories, at once victims of the violence that drew newshounds to the area and of the media invasion itself. But other thoughtful people ask simply why a wealthy industry can't do a better job of reporting violence.

The American journalist stands in a whirlwind, grasping venerated news values in a desperate search for shelter. The storm swirling about the journalist gains force as mass media inundate us with images and words about violence and disaster. Reporters and photographers go to the scene, see the effects of violence, and report to the public. Readers and viewers all too often complain about the media's exploitation of suffering people yet readily join in the country's gluttony for the violence-filled products of commercial entertainment. Media corporations, aided by dazzling technology that can set up live coverage from the devastation in minutes, build pain and injury into their news formulas, in the worst cases making sure that the first stories in the news program whack our emotions. The mass-mediated world promotes our penchant for violence and nature's capacity for destruction, while news consumers go about their chores and pleasures out of harm's way. An irony consistent with the end of the millennium was that crime rates had fallen across the nation for several years even as the media projected a picture of escalating crime and violence.

Journalists, more than ever before, express personal anguish about delivering the news of violence. Inside the newsroom is more alarm about this task than we have ever known. Today, journalists candidly voice the pains of news work, which once were disguised by a code of professionalism and a macho style that even the first women on the city desk felt compelled to adopt. We listened as a reporter on a small Washington State newspaper said, "Every day I get up and there's this river, this wild, raging river, and I take a deep breath, and I dive in and at the end of the day I claw out, and the next day I jump back in. I don't feel that I ever have time to think about what I'm doing." Rick Bragg, a *New York Times* reporter whose beat and talent land him regularly in tragedy's wake, writes about interviewing a minister in Alabama after a tornado destroyed her church and killed her daughter. "You hate this part, as a reporter, you hate to look into the eyes of a woman who has seen her child taken away forever," he says (1997:245). Journalists concede that they too suffer as they do their work—a thought that would have stunned the brash, cynical reporters of earlier eras. Their suffering goes beyond mere distaste for some chores. Reporters and photographers emerge from covering horrible events with their emotions battered by the sights and sounds of the story.

And then they ask the questions that their colleagues are often asking these days. How does a journalist usefully report violence to people engorged on violence? Why do the oldest kinds of stories—new only in the names and faces of the latest victims—now provoke anger at the messenger along with rapt attention? What are the personal and professional costs of trading in the injuries and hurts of other humans? Do such stories need telling? If the stories need telling, how can a reporter get a better purchase on their parts: the people, what they go through in violence and loss, how they recover, what the traumas of violence and disaster mean for them and for the rest of us.

Journalists are facing the social ferment around violence and looking for solutions. Like them, we've searched for a way out of the storm, a way to tell about life's worst experiences in ways that serve personal and social needs. We are both former reporters who now teach in journalism schools, and we are convinced that the answers for the besieged journalist are close at hand, in the traditional skills and values of reporting. We have tried to respect the goals that define journalistic excellence. Among these goals are searching responsibly for the truth, keeping the public interest in mind, caring for the people in the story and others close to them, respecting the voices of people at the center of an event, knowing that the storytellers also are at risk, and doing no harm.

Skilled reporters put the individual's struggle with fateful events at the center of their professional concern. The personal story is their raison d'être. Events, they believe, are best perceived through the thoughts, words, emotions, and actions of the people swept before them. But we also have come to see the double-edged character of those stories, that the focus on the personal both serves and provokes readers, viewers, and listeners. Through such stories we see how other people suffer and endure, and we sense some of our weaknesses. We recognize our penchant for voyeurism, the fragility of the shield of privacy that we hope will protect us in similar circumstances, and how easily fairness is sacrificed to a striking image: the tear or grimace that prods the emotions.

We have come to appreciate how much of the training of reporters and photographers, the day-to-day conduct of the business, and even the rewards of journalism reflect "assembly-line" thinking. On the news assembly line each person performs a set of tasks so that a finished product will emerge at a pre-set time—a television news program at 6 P.M., a newspaper on the porch at 5 A.M., a newsmagazine in the mail on the same day each week, or a bulletin on a Web site in minutes. The assembly lines of the news media squeeze both mundane and extraordinary events—even those that kill and maim people—into the same hourly, daily, or weekly production schedule. They push reporters to get more information at a faster pace, exposing the brutal surface reality of events but little of the truth about what will follow.

In these chapters we show how to supplement the assembly line with a quite different model of news gathering—one that is called for when either the emotions of close neighbors or the mass consciousness of the globe is shattered by a cataclysmic event. Our model traces the shock waves of the event. When something explodes or the earth shakes, it instantly affects those at the epicenter. Then the shock waves radiate outward in ever-larger circles from the detonation point. The waves may wound less severely at points far from the center, but they wound nonetheless.

Think of an event with the force to affect people far into the community and beyond. The bomb that destroyed the federal building in Oklahoma City in 1995, killing 168 people and wounding many others, is a good illustration. At the center people died or were wounded. The waves then struck families and friends—not with physical injuries but with emotional wounds. Firefighters, police, emergency workers, and Red Cross personnel, who arrived quickly and labored for days, suffered the same shock waves, their effects seen in extraordinary weariness, emotional vulnerability, or apparent emotionless dedication to harrowing duties. Then the waves struck further out in the community, taking a toll even on people who lost no friends or relatives. Journalists too suffered emotional wounds as they witnessed and recorded personal and community tragedies. In Oklahoma City journalists were in both of the latter two groups—hurt by their duties at the disaster scene and hurt by their compassion as part of the larger community. Newspeople who flew in to Oklahoma City from other parts of the country and the world were affected as well.

Half a century of research about trauma has yielded new thinking about its social, political, and economic consequences. Exposure to traumatic events is extensive; studies estimate that 40 percent to 80 percent of the population has experienced a traumatic event. In that number traumatic injury is common—perhaps a quarter of those exposed suffer long-term traumatic wounds. Many victims conceal their symptoms out of fear of the perpetrators or of social prejudice, their inability to obtain treatment, or their confusion about the causes of their symptoms. Sandra Bloom, a psychiatrist, sees trauma "as a central organizing principle in the formation, development, maintenance of human society" (1997:212). Trauma, in other words, is more central to human existence than we like to acknowledge. Indeed, one of its most insidious characteristics is the way it encourages us to deny it.

What we now know about trauma can make a difference in how journalists do their jobs and their relationships to the people they cover. We know that the interviews, the stories, and the photographs all have the potential either to add to the injury or to help in the recovery. To tell honest stories the journalist must know the basics of how violent acts and events affect people. We have written this book to support those who want to report about the victims of traumatic injury to help them and their communities in ways that do credit to journalism. We show how journalists can give the public vital information about calamities without further harm to the victims. The book is premised on the conviction that news can tie the victim and the public together constructively through the rigor of thoughtful reporting practices.

Ubiquitous Media Violence

Nothing is at all novel about modern culture's addiction to violence and its fascination with victims. Tales of assaults, murders, rapes, robberies, earthquakes, and floods appear in the earliest surviving publications. The first newspapers in virtually every country told of human and natural violence as readily as they reported on affairs of state and commerce. The oldest known preserved report of a current event in the Americas is a news booklet printed in Mexico City about a 1531 storm and earthquake in Guatemala. Early newspaper illustrations and, later, photography captured the sinister side of human nature along with its finer points.

That representations of violence have pursued humans through history leads to the speculation that horror—in the forms of art, stories, dramas, and plays—serves humans' struggle for survival, preparing our brains and bodies for the reality of a violent assault by another person or by nature.

But American society and the media may have gone over the top in their preoccupation with violence. Violent acts abound in television programming—not just dramatic shows but also children's fare, talk shows, and, most critically, the news. Prime-time television offers five to six violent acts each hour. Bad enough for adults but so-called children's programs are many times more violent. By the age of eighteen, the study shows, a typical American child will have watched thousands of murders and 200,000 acts of violence (Huston 1992:54, 136).

Whatever the merit of any particular cultural depiction of violence, Americans have for decades been exposed to endless hours of television and movie violence and the echoes of it in other media, including newspapers, magazines, and recordings. Visually exciting media violence is a relatively new part of our culture yet already so ubiquitous that some people spend more time with it in a day than with any other single activity.

Depictions of violence may not be the gravest part of the problem. Careful studies of television programs, for example, affirm that violent acts occur in a context that is neither realistic nor informative. Indeed, the acts appear to be calculated to induce fear. Perpetrators are rarely captured or punished—the 1994–1995 *National Television Violence Study* says that those who commit violence in prime-time drama go unpunished most of the time, usually repeat their violence, typically rely on guns to maim and kill, and often act as though violence was a humorous action. Few programs offer any warnings about violence or any useful information about its consequences.

Television's portrayals of victims are just as unrealistic. In 58 percent of all violent interactions depicted on dramatic television, the victim did not experience any pain. In only 13 percent of the situations did the victim show moderate or extreme pain. Although the *National Television Violence Study* did not consider the traumatic aftermath of violence, we know that few, if any, depictions suggest how trauma has injured the person or how long a reasonable degree of recovery requires. The context, the researchers warn, is important because it tells us what to expect in violent interactions.

Television news programs often commit many of the same errors. The emphasis is on crimes and events rather than punishment or other outcomes. The accused dominate the spotlight until the justice process ends. Victims fade from view or remain marginal figures for both the justice system and the media. Journalists trot out easy explanations or simplistic ironies to quickly summarize violent acts—small towns do not have murders, only poor parents abuse their children, immigrants kill because they cannot handle the fast-paced American culture, personal debts explain why people go berserk. Journalism often lacks the patience to wait for a fairer explanation or the humility to say none is obvious.

At the same time the frantic rhythm of violence plays across television news programs and across the front sections of newspapers. The news industry scrambles to feed a system whose hunger for news and information is expanding at an extraordinary rate. Explosions in the numbers of cable channels and the capacity of the Internet to make every person, organization, and corporation a news provider offset the fairly stable numbers of newspapers, magazines, and television networks. As long-time news media and the upstart cable and Web services fight for attention, violence is the currency of the competition.

Giving the Victim "Equal Space"

Edna Buchanan, Pulitzer Prize winner and former *Miami Herald* crime reporter, is noted for vivid newspaper stories and books that depict vicious murderers and other assorted lawbreakers. As a reporter she sometimes went to great lengths to spotlight particular criminals in hopes of locating or bringing them to justice. She warns against the temptation to give too much exposure to criminals, no matter how intriguing they are. "Writers have to work at not glamorizing them. Crooks may be colorful, quotable, and even likable, but they are not nice people." she says. "When you tell their stories, it always helps to give the victims equal space" (1987:14).

It's no simple matter to give the victims "equal space." Humane reporting doesn't simply call for equal time or column inches for victims in the news. It requires a new set of assumptions about the person who suffers trauma and new thinking about how to apply those ideas to the basic work of journalism. The most important of these is that the traumatized person has become a different person emotionally. If news practices take trauma into account, reporting their stories can help victims. That belief explains our commitment to teaching and writing about journalism and trauma. We don't contest the quest in the justice system and among mental health specialists and journalists to know more about what drives some people to act violently. Half a century ago that interest drove journalists to focus on criminals to the nearly complete exclusion of those they killed or injured. We share Edna Buchanan's desire for fair reporting about victims and have planned this book as a practical guide to reporting about those who endure violence in any form.

Benefits for the Public Interest

The public has a huge stake in the conflict between time-honored journalistic practices and new worries about people caught in the shock waves of disaster and violence. Better reporting about trauma can help readers and viewers gain empathy for the suffering of victims and enrich our awareness of the powerful role trauma plays in our collective lives. The news does not often illustrate or explain Sandra Bloom's contention that trauma is the organizing idea of our society. Yet so many public policy issues gain clarity when we take into account the implications of disasters, wars, and other kinds of human abuses.

The cutting edge of information about psychological trauma is the finding that it denies vital human values to those who suffer its effects. The immediate depredations (described in detail in chapter 1) of anxiety, unwanted memories, and numbness cost a person the vitality of life. Another devastating stage follows as the traumatized person moves into the margins and shadows of existence, unnoticed and little understood. If the ultimate benefit of the changes we propose here is greater awareness of how others suffer from trauma, our renewed capacity to offer collective care and support will perhaps be the greatest public benefit.

In recent years public health officials have labeled violence as an epidemic that warrants the kind of response that has been marshaled against cancer, alcoholism, and HIV-AIDS. In 1993 the head of the federal Centers for Disease Control and Prevention told the *New York Times:* "Violence is the leading cause of lost life in this country today. If it's not a public-health problem, why are all those people dying from it?" (Stevens 1994:23). Violent deaths deserve and receive the greatest attention from people concerned about public health, but the costs of trauma also need massive attention. Americans, wonderfully indulged with information about diets, vitamins, and aids to sexual potency, know virtually nothing about the risks of traumatic injury or the prevalence of people who carry telltale symptoms of trauma. When reporters' work is informed by trauma, the public stands to learn about the epidemic, about those afflicted by trauma, and about those who find ways to cope with and minimize its abrasive assault.

Additional Issues

This book identifies ways that journalists do—and can—act humanely toward victims while adhering to the traditional values of journalism. This guidance, we are well aware, may bump journalists up against contrary expectations about their work.

For example, approaching someone whose life has just shattered may lead a reporter to consider what some journalists call an unthinkable option in journalism—"Should I not do this interview at all?" Most of this book is based on the premise that journalists will interview victims or family members, but we believe that sometimes contact is not justified. We think the choice not to interview or photograph is a fundamental one. Journalists should make that decision with care after initial contact with the person and after consulting with editors or coworkers. Concern for the traumatized person should sometimes lead the news organization to find an alternative approach to the assignment. In other words, if the journalist's actions are likely to harm the traumatized person, the reporter should back off. Not all such choices fall neatly on one side of the ethical divide. Some intrusions— or decisions not to intrude—plague the journalist long after. It is critical, though, that a deliberate decision replace a knee-jerk assumption that reporters must interview all victims, photographers must shoot all injured people, and pen and film should capture all tears and screams.

When we make these points in conversations with reporters, we know almost to the word what we will hear next. "My editor told me to get that interview. How do I tell her that I just decided not to do it?" It's a fair question.

We answer in two ways. First, if all the news staff—editors, photographers, and reporters—learn about trauma and work out practical responses to the needs of those caught by the shock waves, editors and reporters or photographers will face fewer such conflicts. But that won't help you today if you and your editor disagree about interviewing or photographing a victim. The burden is on you to justify that decision in the field. This book offers a basis for decisions to leave someone alone as well as to interact sensitively. We are adding another obligation to the many the journalist carries—the obligation to justify to oneself, to the editor, and to others a decision not to intrude in the suffering of others. This decision takes precedence over news value or competition because of a strong moral factor—the choice between preventing harm and causing harm. When the stakes are in the moral realm, personal integrity resides at the center of the decision.

Another matter often comes up when we talk to journalists about these ideas. What we know about trauma comes from psychology, psychiatry, and medical science and is applied in treatments by psychiatrists, other physicians, and therapists trained in psychology. Journalists are not physicians or therapists, they don't know the science that goes along with it, and they are not trained to see or draw out the symptoms of trauma. Journalists ask why they should think about trauma at all.

One doesn't have to attend medical school to be able to respect the suffering of another person. Empathy and sensitivity are human, not medical, traits. In addition, journalists can incorporate information about trauma in their work without invading the specialist's domain of diagnosis and treatment. Indeed, this book is an argument that reporter, victim, and public all will benefit from knowing more about trauma. No reporter would try to cover a World Series game without knowing baseball or try to explain a stock market rally without first studying finance and economics. Every beat in journalism demands special knowledge from the reporter. A crime reporter must be familiar with police, blotters, snitches, arraignments, and plea bargaining. A government and politics reporter learns about caucuses, tax assessments, soft money, and polling. Sports broadcasters know about batting averages, first downs, dunk shots, hat tricks, and aces. Firefighters, police, and military personnel usually are not physicians, yet the application of trauma knowledge has transformed those vocations in recent years. The reporter of a story involving violence can only do better work by learning about trauma.

Finally, we have heard the argument that some events are so cataclysmic, some people so well known, some situations so volatile that the public interest in knowing every detail will override even the best intentions to be sensitive to trauma victims. It may be tempting to invoke the "What a story!" side of journalism, that time when all bets are off, all rules are voided, and anything goes. What about violence against the president, scenes of massive destruction, or moments captured by television and exposed instantly— without regard to individual sensitivities—to huge audiences? Such circumstances do not warrant ignoring the need for humane treatment of those in the story. We think that the public's interest in knowing about the event can generally be served along with due regard for the needs of people who have been harmed. The only certainty in such cases is that media competition will shape the outcome, making it more difficult to respect the needs of people caught in the middle.

We have been asked whether a news organization that committed itself fully to the ideas in this book could expect to stay in business. Cases abound of well-meant, but failed, efforts to challenge the competition by changing the news formula. The difference in this case is that many journalists and their employers already have responded to the trauma crisis. Support, flowing from the public, some in the media, and the mental health professions, encourages such changes. An impressive momentum is behind this new regard for the ethics of covering violence.

Examples of Trauma-Sensitive Reporting

A television station in Orlando, Florida, startled its viewers in 1997 when it downplayed crime stories on its evening news shows. WESH-TV didn't drop crime news; editors merely demoted it to a regular rotation with environment, politics, transportation, and zoning. Viewers slipped away to stations that played bank holdups, animal abuse, and car pileups at the top of their news shows, but over time many returned as regular viewers of the station that did not exploit violent events. Orlando's example was one against hundreds of news channels that did not change, but it set off reviews of news policies at other stations.

In the late 1990s journalists began to talk about trauma and its effects at national writing workshops, at journalism educators' conventions, and at editors' and reporters' meetings. A few news staffs called in trauma experts and therapists after difficult stories. It became routine for news corporations directly affected by the murders and suicides of staff members to offer counseling to employees. Newspapers and journalism schools hosted regional conferences on reporting about violence.

As we prepared this book, we found many examples of excellent reporting of traumatic events and victims. We have incorporated many of them in these chapters and, in particular, in the profiles of five journalists—four who work for newspapers and one for local television news—by Migael Scherer, a Seattle writer who also teaches in the Journalism and Trauma Program at the University of Washington. Her profiles tap the values and experiences of these stellar reporters and photographer—Rick Bragg of the *New York Times*; Lynn Dobson, a freelance photographer formerly with the *Austin American-Statesman*; Jeff Gradney of KING-TV in Seattle; Debra McKinney of the *Anchorage Daily News*; and Scott North of the *Herald* of Everett, Washington. The five journalists illustrate how to translate into news reporting an alertness to trauma issues.

A Final Note

Journalists routinely face and pass trying professional tests—writing a story that will be read, making a photograph in an instant, and interviewing a person who is not prepared for the emotional stress of such contact. Although they make some mistakes, a huge corps of journalists regularly does its work with a high standard of ethical and professional excellence.

We have not written this book out of a sense of despair. Instead, we have written it with the confidence that the best work of skilled reporters, photographers, and editors can guide the efforts of others trying to report about violence. We want to see news that conveys in ethical words and images the experience of the people who suffer harm. We have been moved to write these chapters because so many journalists we know express the same hope.

Scott North

A Witness for the Community

"A murder is an important part of a community's history," says Scott North of the *Herald* in Everett, Washington. "Putting it and the life that was taken into context requires time." North and others on the staff of this daily with a circulation of fifty-five thousand in Snohomish County, north of Seattle, have succeeded in breaking from "get-it-quick, anyway-you-can" journalism. Using a team approach to reporting, they are covering crime with depth, breadth, and an eye for future stories. Most innovative of all, they have invited the community into the process.

North started at the *Herald* in 1987 and is quick to credit then-editor Joann Byrd for establishing an ethic of sensitivity to victims. "She was one

Scott North. PHOTO BY ANDY ROGERS.

of the first in the region to recognize that crime coverage was more than police, courts, and perpetrators," North says. She encouraged *Herald* reporters to seek advice from a local organization, Families and Friends of Victims of Violence, as well as from detectives, and to listen to survivors.

One of North's first stories was the murder of a dope dealer. "There was absolutely nothing sympathetic about the victim," North explains, "but every life has something of value." In this case the "something of value" was the victim's wife. "She needed someone to talk to," he says, "and I would spend time with her, just listening. I'm not a cop, and I'm not a therapist. I couldn't do anything for her, really. So I listened."

Just listening, North learned, led to one story, then another, and another, like nesting dolls, like layers of an onion, like the pages of a photo album turned slowly by the hand of a grieving parent.

"When a parent loses a son or daughter to homicide, they're in a fog," North says. "They hurt so much they can hardly feel, for a while. They're not always ready to talk to me." North is mindful that survivors do not heal on newsroom deadlines. "I tell them that people are going to want to know about their daughter. 'When you're ready,' I say, 'give me a call.'" It may take months. It may take a year. "The fact is," North emphasizes, "a murder case goes on for a long, long time. There's the arrest, the trial, the appeals— there's no need to pressure the family."

How does a reporter like North develop empathy for victims of crime? "I've always been emotional," he says. "I cry, I get angry." His gaze is steady and square. "These sorts of things get me *real* angry." *These sorts of things*: kidnapping, rape, murder—forms that human cruelty can take.

Personality is not enough; even a well-intentioned reporter has to learn the hard way. "You make mistakes," North explains, "and sometimes your mistakes hurt others." He goes on to describe a man whose seventeen-year-old daughter was murdered by a serial killer. "The interview went well, but the story I wrote portrayed the girl as one of a series of victims, not as a *person*." North winces at the memory. "An advocate from Families and Friends let me know her father was hurt by what I had written, and why." Deeply regretful, he called and apologized.

After seven years of covering "crime and nothing but crime," North got a strong taste of secondary trauma in himself. At that time the *Herald*'s handling of high-profile cases put a single reporter in court all day. "You filed the story that evening and were back in court early the next morning, day after day. By the end of the trial you were a husk," he recalls. A series of such cases included the arrest and trial of arsonist Paul Keller (North was the first to interview Keller's parents, who had turned him in) and the execution of rapist and triple murderer Charles Campbell after years of appeals. "I thought I had become detached, but witnessing that execution, watching a human die—I kept asking myself why I was *there*," North says.

The answer that finally made sense led him to realize what was at the core of all his work—he was there as a witness, not for himself or even his newspaper but for the community. And the work had a cost: sleeplessness, flashbacks, numbness. The very detachment he had thought was a sign of strength in a reporter had become corrosive, at home and in the newsroom. "I was a jerk to work with," he admits.

Meanwhile, the *Herald,* under changed editorial leadership, reverted to the "old style." The change backfired when a reporter, responding to directives to be more aggressive, incorporated in his story the name he saw on the mailbox at the crime scene. A practice that is highly questionable when next of kin have not yet been notified was devastating when the father of the young man named learned of his son's murder as he read the newspaper. "It was horrible," North says, "something editors couldn't ignore—a reminder that we shouldn't go back."

The *Herald* badly needed a different approach to crime coverage. The staff was pushing for a reconsideration of newsroom procedures when, in April 1995, seven-year-old Roxanne Doll was abducted, raped, and murdered. Though he had by then pulled away from crime coverage, Scott North was assigned to the story because "I was about the only reporter the police would talk to."

The Western Journalism and Trauma Conference, held in March 1996, was well timed for the *Herald*. This major homicide story was unfolding (pretrial issues alone took a year), and the staff was determined to chart a better course in crime coverage. A month after the conference the paper invited representatives of the University of Washington Journalism and Trauma Program to talk with the entire staff. Faculty affirmed the *Herald'*s need to promote coverage that is sensitive to victims and provided basic information about trauma's effects—primarily on victims but also on caregivers, on police and other emergency responders, and—yes—on reporters.

The resulting changes at the *Herald* creatively incorporate this advice. Reporters formed teams of three to five people who alternate or even share coverage, as well as debrief one another through tough stories. Under this new structure a reporter can come up for air now and then to write about something other than crime and disaster. One of North's "renewal" assignments was a history of intolerance in the community, which allowed him to cover a facet of local life that had improved over the years. Even now his eyes brighten as he describes the piece, and he uses words like *satisfying* and *hopeful*.

As the trial for the person accused of killing Roxanne Doll approached, North, teamed with reporters Dale Steinke and Rebecca Hover, made a conscious decision to take the long view. The story—horrific enough on the surface—had additional complications. The accused was a friend of the father, and, according to testimony, both men were drinking and using drugs together the night of the murder. "We knew we were setting the record now for coverage ten years down the line, when appeals for aggravated murder could still be playing out. We had a huge responsibility to the community to get it right," North says.

To meet this responsibility they made a huge departure from conventional journalism: they requested and formed a panel of community experts and residents for feedback and advice. The panel was diverse, to say the least: a rabbi, a bookseller, an elementary school counselor, a child advocate from the prosecuting attorney's office, a director of a drug and alcohol treatment facility, a former public defender, a funeral director, the president of Mothers Against Violence in America, and a supervisor with the state Department of Corrections.

Every other week reporters and editors sat down with the panel and asked for feedback: How are our stories affecting the community? What effect are they having on Roxanne's schoolmates, friends, and other children her age? On parents and teachers? The staff sought advice on issues normally raised only in the newsroom, such as how to handle the expected graphic testimony of the medical examiner and how the stories should be played.

"We learned a lot," North says, looking back. "For one thing, the panel didn't have our 'beat' instinct; they respected us when we *didn't* follow the pack." Nor did panel members want front-page coverage every day of the trial, reminding reporters to keep the Doll case, as tragic as it was, in perspective; other events were important too. They asked for related stories that would help the community grieve, help parents talk to children about sexual abuse, help everyone feel and be safer. These stories turned out to be especially relevant when, during the course of the trial, another seven-year-old girl was killed in a nearby town.

When the panel disbanded after the trial, all agreed that it had been successful. The community members had learned that those who cover the news are like them, grappling with hard decisions and their own emotions, concerned about the effects of their work. The reporters, shedding their usual observer role, gained a sense of partnership and in doing so became more firmly grounded in the community itself.

As for Scott North: "I got to listen to readers . . . to hear with their ears and see with their eyes as the community reacted to what I was reporting." Still listening as the stories unfold.

Scott North

Slain Mother's Love Manages to Find Daughter

Working closely with the mother and other relatives of murder victim Patti Berry, Scott North developed a six-part series about the investigation of the unsolved crime, giving special attention to Berry's mother and small daughter. The sixth installment told about the two women and the child in ways that emphasize how people come to terms with tragic loss. This installment was published in the Herald, *of Everett, Washington, on July 30, 1999.*

Patti Berry marked her 25th birthday in her mother's kitchen, a celebration that was caught on home video.

She sat at the table, young and blond and tanned even though it was the middle of February. Her family and friends surrounded her with gifts and love and jokes about what it meant to have already lived a quarter-century.

Berry was holding her daughter on her lap. From time to time, she'd plant a kiss on top of the 10-month-old's soft, warm head.

On the videotape, Patti Berry appears happy, vibrant, alive.

But she's been dead since July 31, 1995, almost exactly four years today.

In the summer of her 26th year, Berry ran into a killer as she headed home from her job as a nude dancer at Honey's nightclub south of Everett. The murder is still unsolved.

Berry's daughter is now 6 and already missing a couple of her baby teeth. She has soft brown eyes, loves cats and likes to read books about dinosaurs. She wants to be a ballerina when she grows up.

The child is being raised by her grandmother, Nancy Stensrud, and Patti Berry's close childhood friend, Cherie Gildersleeve of Bryant, the girl's godmother. There's talk of Gildersleeve one day adopting the girl, who already calls her Mom. She was there for the child's birth. Gildersleeve hadn't seen Patti Berry in a long time, but by wonderful coincidence was having dinner with her old friend the night she went into labor.

The child's family doesn't want the girl's name in the newspaper. They worry that other children could be cruel. The girl doesn't remember her birth mother or really understand what happened to her. What she knows about the woman who brought her into this world is based largely on family stories and photographs.

But that doesn't mean Patti Berry is absent from her life.

"My Patti watches down at me," the little girl says, a statement she makes with absolute faith.

The sun will come up tomorrow. My Patti is watching.

The girl keeps a portrait of Patti Berry in her room, displayed in a clear vinyl frame she's decorated with stickers of five tiny horses and a unicorn. If you look close, you can see the marks left by her kisses.

Gildersleeve said the child thinks of Patti Berry not as a mother, but something of a cross between a guardian angel and a playful spirit.

The girl sees Patti Berry in the wind that swirls the soap bubbles she blows in her backyard. When she's playing outside, and a ball gets stuck in a tree, she'll stand underneath, hands upraised, and wait for the branches to move and drop the toy into her arms.

"My Patti did that!" she'll say.

Nancy Stensrud wishes that answers could drop from the sky.

She's been waiting a long time to find out who killed her daughter and is long past frustration. From time to time, the Arlington woman has taken the investigation into her own hands. The trail has taken her inside the club, where her daughter danced on a mirror-backed stage. She's also sat in coffee shops and living rooms, where people who claim to know what happened have spun dark stories about how the murder is linked to everything from killer drug dealers to rogue cops to organized crime.

Most of those same rumors already have been investigated by police who judged them the fantasies of people who see the sinister in every shadow. When they track down the source, the people rarely know any facts that haven't been in the newspaper.

Still, Stensrud has learned things about her daughter she didn't know and never would have guessed.

For example, up until a short time before her death, Patti Berry drove a newer yellow Camaro. She'd told her mother she'd won it in an Oregon bikini contest.

Truth was, the car had been bought for Berry's use by a club owner. When Berry did something that displeased him, he sent repo men to tow the vehicle away.

"I think until Patti died, I lived in a dream world," Stensrud said.

The discoveries also have toughened Patti Berry's mother. She thinks nothing now of knocking on the doors of strangers who she suspects may know something about her daughter's death. She's also not afraid to complain to Snohomish County Sheriff Rick Bart about the seemingly glacial pace of the investigation, or what she views as the stubborn unwillingness of the lead detective to share information.

Stensrud said there's bad chemistry between her and the detective, even though she knows he wants the same thing she does: to bag her daughter's killer.

Sheriff's detective John Padilla said he doesn't take the friction personally. He's committed to catching Patti Berry's killer. Period.

In the years since Patti Berry died, Padilla has investigated hundreds of other violent crimes, more than 60 last year alone. But Berry's unsolved murder is never far from his mind.

He bumps into Patti Berry every day. The detective said he'll be driving down the street, and he'll see a pretty, young, blond woman behind the wheel of a small car, and "I wonder, was that what she was like?"

As the fourth anniversary of her murder nears, Padilla also wonders what is going on in her killer's mind.

He believes Patti's murder was a significant event in the killer's life, significant enough that an anniversary date may trigger changes in behavior.

The detective also believes that sometime since the killing, the person who stabbed Patti Berry to death has shared the dark secret with others.

"Killers talk," he said. "Killers talk and they tell somebody. I believe there is somebody out there who knows."

He hopes that someday his phone will ring and on the other end of the line will be somebody looking to unload that burden.

Nancy Stensrud says she'll try to be ready with answers when Patti Berry's daughter is old enough to ask for the truth about what happened to her birth mother.

She hopes she'll be able to tell the little girl not to worry, the killer is behind bars.

"I want her to see one day that some sort of justice has been done, for her," she said.

Patti Berry is beyond justice now, Stensrud said.

But she's still close enough for a mother's tears.

Chapter 1

Trauma: Assault on an Essential Human System

We all think we have trauma in our lives; indeed, we apply the word loosely to such routine events as being tied up in traffic or arriving at the airport without picture ID. College students say that the final exam was traumatic, whereas their parents think that hearing from the Internal Revenue Service warrants the same term. We've co-opted the word from medical science to signify all those intense, occasional stresses in our lives—"Wasn't the Super Bowl traumatic?"

For those who suffer violence, though, trauma is a specific, devastating, and often long-lasting wound. One dictionary describes trauma this way: "1. a bodily injury or shock. 2. an emotional shock, often having a lasting psychic effect." The definition recognizes two types of trauma—physical wounds that an emergency room might treat after an accident, and emotional wounds. ERs do little for the emotional wounds, yet they may afflict a person long after the broken bone or the internal organs heal. Emotional trauma is not confined to the single shock that comes with an assault. Some people suffer trauma from continuing attacks on their emotional stability. Of course, physical and emotional wounds may be products of the same experience.

Political prisoners and torture victims suffer trauma not from single acts but from months or years of having their sense of safety destroyed. A woman continually abused by a violent spouse and a child repeatedly exploited sexually will be trauma victims as well. The form of trauma that this book addresses is emotional injury, sometimes sudden and unexpected, sometimes taking place during a prolonged assault.

It is important that journalists try to understand the characteristics and differences of the immediate and longer-range trauma responses. Reporters and photographers often are among the first to arrive at an auto accident, house fire, shooting, or other violent event. Someone may be dead. Survivors may be bleeding, unconscious, or in shock. At other times reporters knock on doors weeks, months, or even years after an event. They may be covering a court action or following up on, say, the anniversary of the Oklahoma City bombing or a school shooting. In all those cases the people with whom the reporter speaks may exhibit one or several of the many trauma symptoms.

Natural Versus Human-Caused Trauma

Journalists certainly cover people who have been hurt in accidents and natural disasters such as tornadoes, hurricanes, and floods—the so-called acts of God. People of faith may question whether ascribing divine intention to destructive acts of natural forces is appropriate. Nonetheless, natural disasters do emotionally traumatize even those who survive them without physical injury. An earthquake survivor who watches a building collapse, hears injured people cry, or sees bodies of victims is likely to suffer from emotional trauma.

But what is even more traumatizing to many people is to be injured by a deliberate human act. In an accident or natural disaster victims or their families and friends may find some comfort by telling themselves, "It's nothing personal. It just happened (perhaps to many others, too). It wasn't my fault." A victim of violent crime usually sees it differently: "This was a deliberate attack on me personally—me! I'm angry. I'm bitter. I'm ashamed."

The crash that killed all 229 passengers and crew of Swissair flight 111 in Nova Scotia in 1998 caused heavy grief among surviving relatives and friends. However, they did not suffer some of the pain felt by the loved ones of people aboard Pan Am flight 103 when international terrorists blew the plane up over Lockerbie, Scotland, in 1988, murdering all aboard. The 1995 Oklahoma City bombing generated many of the same kinds of suffering that would have been experienced if the federal building had been destroyed by, say, an accidental natural gas explosion. But the anger and bitterness were multiplied many times over because the bombing was the work of terrorists, and homegrown ones at that.

When Johnny Came Trudging Home

Journalists should not feel guilty if they have failed to recognize and understand many aspects of trauma and victimization. Even psychologists and psychiatrists have only recently come to recognize, name, and devise specific treatments for what now are believed to be the special after-effects of violent crime. Physicians traditionally were not taught to treat crime victims differently than accident victims. So it is not hard to understand why reporters working on deadline may not distinguish such differences or reflect an understanding of them in their interviewing and reporting.

Times are changing. Several recent historic events combined to initiate a recognition of the need to understand victims' suffering and healing, according to Frank M. Ochberg, a psychiatrist who is the former director of the Michigan Department of Mental Health. He says that one factor was the end of the Vietnam War. The terms *shell shock* and *combat fatigue* have long been used to describe the lingering psychological effects of combat experiences. But during and after the ten-year U.S. involvement in the Vietnam War, many more returning veterans seemed to voice such complaints.

Vietnam was a divisive war, and the United States did not win it. Veterans returned home one at a time or in small groups, and they seldom got the public praise and respect accorded the victorious U.S. veterans of earlier wars. Their arrival home by airplane within hours of leaving Vietnam also deprived veterans of the long cruise home that gave veterans of earlier wars time to swap tales and exchange experiences, ways of learning that what they were feeling or had seen or experienced was not unusual, peculiar, or odd. And studies show that just talking about traumatic events relieves the symptoms of trauma, often permanently. Moreover, some Vietnam veterans encountered outright personal hostility against them and their service. Although it may be a myth that many veterans actually were spat on at home, more than a few felt that way psychologically. "Many veterans suffered victimization syndromes," Ochberg says. "They were traumatized, and they felt like losers" (1987:12–13, 41).

For many veterans the lack of respect at home compounded a sense of betrayal at the hands of military leaders and services, according to Jonathan Shay, a Massachusetts psychiatrist who treats veterans' combat trauma. Negligent and irrelevant training, as well as such harmful policies as continually breaking up units, added to the psychological injuries of many veterans (Shay 1994:165–81).

Political terrorism also fostered new studies of trauma effects. Since 1972 international terrorists have demonstrated a continuing fondness for this easy and especially disturbing form of warfare: the bombings of the U.S. Marine barracks in Lebanon, the World Trade Center in New York City, and

Pan Am flight 103 over Scotland; the massacre of Israeli athletes at the Munich Olympics; and the hijacking of the *Achille Lauro* passenger liner in the Mediterranean, to name but a few of the most notorious. The worldwide nature of the terrorism, striking both civilian and military targets, has caused a variety of professions and many nations to collaborate in their efforts to find and stop terrorists and treat their victims.

The Key Contributions of the Women's Movement

Women's experience with and their criticism of the medical establishment have contributed greatly to knowledge about trauma. Concerned and vocal women have forced male-dominated professions to recognize the specific and varied nature of rape trauma, reevaluate father-daughter incest, and to shelter battered women without stigmatizing them as mentally ill. In the early 1970s women moved from raising each other's consciousness through personal disclosures to shaping public and medical response through "speak-outs," research designed and carried out by women, and advocacy. The trauma syndrome their efforts illuminated had striking similarities to that of the combat veterans. The consequences of their efforts were profound. Feminists helped establish a scientific basis for seeing rape as violence, not sex, and showed how it subordinated women through terror, the psychiatrist Judith Lewis Herman writes (1992:30). Studying rape in adults led women to see the unexamined tragedy of sexual abuse in children.

As experts have grasped the causes and effects of trauma, they have seen that it infects populations far beyond war combatants, rape survivors, and abused children. Those vulnerable to emotional trauma include refugees, torture victims, people caught in the devastation of natural disasters, political prisoners, individuals who endure severe poverty, people struck by technological disasters such as the explosion of the Chernobyl nuclear power plant, and those caught up in war and genocide. A litany of such domestic events as school shootings, automobile and plane crashes, and urban riots also belongs on the list. These events are the news media's stock-in-trade, and journalists can convey their meaning more clearly if they understand how trauma will affect those at the center, those first to experience the shock waves.

The Critical Role of Emotions

The journalist who would understand trauma must begin by understanding the powerful role emotions play in our lives. Journalist Daniel Goleman based his popular book, *Emotional Intelligence*, on the science of emotions. "All emotions are, in essence, impulses to act, the instant plans for handling life that evolution has instilled in us," he writes (1995:6). Emotions serve as the radar for both our bodies and the confusing world around us, and they are central to our survival, psychiatrist Sandra Bloom explains (1997:44). Emotions register on our faces and in our body language as we experience fear or pleasure. Emotional communication between baby and parent is critical to its development. Adults and children monitor each other's emotions constantly, even "catching" the hysteria of others or calming other aroused individuals. When we are threatened, our bodies provide an automatic heroic response, what is called the *fight-or-flight* response. Time and again, this system saves our lives.

Our emotional system—complex and resilient as it is—still can lose its balance and spin us out of control. Judith Lewis Herman writes that some experiences "overwhelm the ordinary human adaptations to life." They threaten life or the body. "They confront human beings with the extremities of helplessness and terror, and evoke the responses of catastrophe" (1992:33). Emotions tell us when and how to act, but they sometimes convey the stunning message that we cannot act. We are captive of horrible circumstances, and neither flight nor fighting back is possible. Then the emotional system itself may be torn apart or fragmented.

When the system fails us, we often find respite in such defensive measures as use of drugs or alcohol, surrender of choices to another person, distractions, or dissociation. Dissociation is a mechanism of the brain that we use regularly in everyday circumstances, for example, to plan a project with one part of the brain while another enables us to steer a car through perilous traffic. The mechanism also comes into play in highly stressful situations, enabling us to focus alertly on things going on around us, although we seem not to feel the usual emotional reactions. In cases of prolonged or repeated stress, such as a torture victim might endure, the capacity to dissociate protects us from being overwhelmed. Forgetting, a form of dissociation, enables a person to maneuver through all the potentially upsetting reminders of an earlier traumatic experience without dealing with their full emotional effects. Helpful in times of real stress, dissociation becomes an impediment in calmer times when reminders of the old trauma habitually trigger dissociation.

Trauma injures its victims in several ways. It disables the early warning system—our survival radar. It confuses us because we can no longer keep the details of our lives in order. It not only inhibits the expression of some emotions but it may rob us of the words we need to talk about that loss. The injury may be more severe and costly in early childhood. "For children, every aspect of the self will be distorted and bent in the direction of the traumatic exposure," Bloom says (1997:72). Our ways of remembering change too, planting the traumatic experience deep in our brains. Sometimes effectively suppressed by the brain, those traumatic memories may reach us in horrifying nightmares or intrusive flashbacks to the event, a reliving that we actually "see" but may struggle to translate into words.

Post-Traumatic Stress Disorder and Acute Stress Disorder

The medical profession has, quite logically, approached trauma in its most severe manifestation, the collection of symptoms that persistently troubles a person for a month or longer after a traumatic event. In looking at these long-lasting cases, psychiatrists gave the name post-traumatic stress disorder (PTSD) to the group of symptoms they observed: intrusive recollections, avoidance, and heightened anxiety. Even so, the formal diagnosis called PTSD originated only in 1980. In 1994 the American Psychiatric Association added acute stress disorder (ASD) to the official list of diagnoses, describing effects that last more than two days but not more than four weeks. A diagnosis of ASD is warranted when a trauma survivor has had three PTSD general reactions as well as several abnormal signs of dissociation. PTSD and ASD are closely related conditions, almost indistinguishable to laypeople, except for timing. ASD relates to debilitating recollections, numbing, avoidance, and anxiety for as long as a month after a traumatic event, whereas those symptoms last longer in PTSD.

How the Journalist Encounters Trauma

No reporters we know go about work in the field by sorting the people they meet into categories of ASD, PTSD, or otherwise. In this chapter we describe the PTSD diagnosis in some detail because that is the best way we know to relate what the journalist sees in the immediate aftermath of violence or disaster to an emotional injury that therapists may later try to address.

What the journalist sees and hears needs more commonplace descriptions. Some people will be acting in stunningly inappropriate ways—separating the emotions of an event from other activities, which leads to the often reported anomaly of a "carnival-like atmosphere" at a scene of death or injury. Some observers will be amazingly focused on what happened, ready with the most minute details. Some people may be grieving or hysterical. Others may show no obvious sign of emotion. Police at a scene were "so shocked by what they found that they seemed to pass on [to others] their stress and dread," a reporter told us.

Reporters who reached the city of Lockerbie, Scotland, in the hours after the explosion of Pan Am 103 killed its passengers, crew, and many people on the ground, told writer Joan Deppa and her associates about an amazing range of responses. Right after the crash many people spoke eagerly to reporters; over time more people became reticent and withdrawn. Some stories were incoherent and exaggerated, others tightly controlled. Reporters termed some observers "ghouls," folks who seemed to make an entertainment out of visiting the scene. Other residents were extraordinarily friendly and hospitable, repeatedly offering tea to the reporters. And a reporter found someone who saw the cockpit of the jetliner crash to the ground and bodies strapped in their seats, one still quivering. The young witness, who was "clearly haunted," readily told his story to a reporter whose emotions also were locked away (Deppa et al. 1993:69–99).

Reporters who work on such stories for days after the event may encounter people who display a range of responses, including not only dissociation but self-destructive behaviors such as drinking, feelings of shame and hopelessness, fear of fairly familiar sights and sounds, and impaired relationships, as well the key indicators of long-term traumatic injury. Each person will present a unique array of responses. Reporters cannot make medical diagnoses of each subject, but they can be sensitive about their assumptions. The "ghouls" may be distancing themselves from the pain of the experience; the emotionless folks are not necessarily unaffected, and frenzied reactions often reflect more than excitement.

Finally, reporters are as likely to exhibit this range of responses as the people they encounter. At Lockerbie a reporter frustrated by his inability to get information from a press officer flew into a rage. Later he was able to tie his viewing of bodies on a hillside to his reaction (Deppa et al. 1993:76). In the presence of victims of traumatic injury, we argue, journalists must act in ways that acknowledge and respect the effects on victims— and on them.

In the next section we examine how lasting trauma, characterized in medicine as PTSD, manifests itself in victims. The remainder of this book is our reflection on how journalists can respond to this knowledge.

PTSD

Emotional reactions to trauma are not new, of course; they have always been parts of the human condition. That is why it is remarkable that an in-depth understanding of the emotions is relatively new and still developing. The term *post-traumatic stress disorder*—PTSD—often pops up now as journalists try to report medical explanations of the long-lasting traumatic effects of such events as the Oklahoma City bombing or the string of shootings in middle and high schools. It is important for journalists to understand PTSD so they can alert their audiences to what trauma may be coming, as well as how to cope with what's already there.

The basic PTSD diagnosis—revised by the American Psychiatric Association in 1988 and 1994—has three ingredients. All three reactions in this psychological witches' brew must be present at once and must be caused by an event that terrifies, horrifies, or renders someone helpless. Here's a distillation of the triad of PTSD responses:

- Recurrent and intrusive distressing recollections of an event
- Emotional numbing and constriction of normal activities
- A shift in the fear threshold, affecting sleep, concentration, and sense of security

In other words, the sufferers are so haunted by a terrible event that they cannot forget it. The person isn't mentally ill, even though victims sometimes erroneously think, "I must be going crazy." They aren't, but their lives are crippled.

By definition, a diagnosis of PTSD is not justified unless the three conditions last at least a month. It is understandable if, for example, a bank teller who is robbed at gunpoint feels frightened, angry, and nervous right afterward and for some time to come. It might even be a cause for concern if the teller did *not* seem to feel somewhat shaken for a while. But if three months later he is sleeping well, working normally, and not jumping or cringing at every loud noise, a reporter better not jump to the conclusion that the teller "had PTSD" after the holdup.

Flashbacks

What especially distinguishes PTSD from more temporary effects is the first of the trio of conditions: recurring and unavoidable recollections. That is not just a lasting and unpleasant memory of a bad event but one that hits so often and so hard that the person cannot lead a normal life. Sometimes that recollection is so real that it is called a *flashback*, or a hallucination. The person repeatedly relives the event.

Flashbacks often are associated with combat veterans. A soldier wounded in combat may again see the shell exploding in front of him and hear the screams of a buddy killed at his side. In other types of trauma a woman may feel a rapist grabbing her; a man nearly killed by a drunken driver may "see" the car careening toward him again. In young children, psychiatrists say, the recurrence may take the form of playing out a frightening scene over and over—a boy repeatedly struck by his father may, in turn, pummel his teddy bear.

In some cases the trauma victim may not have such vivid images or perceptions in the daytime, but once the body tries to relax in sleep, the same terrifying dreams of the trauma erupt. On awakening the dreams may not quickly fade away but linger in the conscious memory.

The pain and sorrow someone suffers at the unexpected loss of a spouse or child may not be related to PTSD. As painful as such deaths are, psychiatrists do not put the responses into the PTSD category unless they are accompanied by haunting images of death. (And when death is expected and one can prepare for it, the emotional response usually is grief and not a symptom of trauma.)

All memories related to traumatic injury are not created equal. They also are not all signs of PTSD. A memory of how a loved one died in a drive-by shooting may be very painful but clearly remain just that, a memory, not a terrifying reenactment. Retelling the painful memory under the right conditions can even help reduce and eventually master the pain. Volunteers from the Michigan Victim Alliance tell Michigan State University journalism classes that retelling their stories to sympathetic listeners does help victims to heal. That is an important factor for journalists to remember.

Numbing the Pain

PTSD also is marked by emotional numbing and avoidance. Psychiatrists say it is as if the person's mind decides, "My memories are so terrible that I'm shutting down between them so I won't be overwhelmed." That may give human sufferers some protection but at the cost of robbing them of joy, love, and hope, says psychiatrist Ochberg. He tells of a national PTSD research project in which he interviewed Vietnam War veterans decades after their service. They didn't necessarily look sad or gloomy, "just incapable of delight." Furthermore, Ochberg explains: "They no longer participated in activities that used to be fulfilling. Why bowl or ride horses or climb mountains when the feeling of fun is gone? Some marriages survived, dutiful contracts of cohabitation, but devoid of intimacy and without the shared pride of watching children flourish—even when the children were flourishing" (1996:21).

Avoidance is a symptom of PTSD, although therapists caution that it may not continue for so long that a formal diagnosis of PTSD is warranted. Most survivors of trauma will avoid reminders and change their usual patterns for a while to prevent unpleasant recollections from surfacing. The key phrase is "for a while." Ex-hostages from a notorious train hijacking in The Netherlands avoided all trains for weeks, Ochberg says. Some only avoided the particular train on which they were hijacked. Others took that train but changed to a bus for the few miles near the site of the trauma. Most of these people gradually worked their way out of such mind maneuvers and resumed their former travel habits (Ochberg 1996:21).

Numbing and avoidance, then, can help someone up to a point. The concern in PTSD is that this aspect becomes a serious obstacle to recovery. Journalists interviewing a survivor also can greatly underestimate how much the person still is affected months or years after the violence happened. A man who seems calm, even casual and unconcerned, during an interview about the drive-by shooting death of his son may in fact be numb—and may have lost his wife, friends, and job as a result.

Appearances Aside

William Coté wishes he had understood the numbing aspect of trauma when, as a fledgling police reporter for a small Michigan daily, he covered the preliminary hearing of three youths suspected in the knifing death of another teenager. Two of the youths and some of their family members and those of the victim were agitated, crying, or cursing. One youth and some relatives were so quiet and calm they could have been at a hearing on a mere parking ticket. Cries of joy and, from the victim's family, of disbelief erupted when the judge found insufficient evidence to hold one of the youths over for trial. That young man, the quiet suspect, was released and—with shaking hands—lit up a cigarette out in the hallway. Relatives who had been calm began sobbing with relief. They were not so cool after all. Relatives of the dead teenager variously continued to cry, swear, or look blank.

When the two other youths appeared at trial on murder charges several months later, Coté was a bit perplexed to observe similar behavior in the courtroom; even after a lengthy time, some people on both the victim's and defendants' sides appeared amazingly composed. Others sometimes had to be warned by the judge to quiet down or be expelled from the courtroom. One defendant finally was convicted, the other acquitted. If Coté had understood then what he knows now about trauma and victimization, he would have tried to go beyond the hard news story. How were the family members of the victim and the defendants *really* coping? Were they suffering more than some appeared to be? Was anybody helping them? If so, how?

Ochberg has testified as an expert for the prosecution in several civil suits to explain to juries why certain victims did not seem truly concerned or injured: "The victims were numb or avoidant, or both, and therefore didn't come forward immediately. When they did come forward, they appeared, to untrained observers, indifferent, unconcerned, and unharmed, when, in fact, they were in a state of profound post-traumatic stress" (1996:22).

Detecting such invisible trauma can be even more difficult in a telephone interview than in person. A former *Lansing (Mich.) State Journal* editor recalls assigning a reporter to call the father of a murdered child whose body had just been recovered: "The father seemed fairly calm and willing to answer our questions about his child and the murder. Yet, when the story appeared in the next morning's paper, he called, very angry, and demanded to know where we'd gotten the information and comments. He'd been in such shock the day before that he literally didn't remember even talking to the reporter, much less what was said." The father's immediate reaction would not qualify as PTSD because too little time had elapsed, but reporters do well to expect that either immediate shock or persistent trauma can suppress memories.

Forgetfulness

The numbing aspect of PTSD includes forgetting with a vengeance, as well as memories that cannot be suppressed. Called psychogenic amnesia, this kind of forgetting originates in the mind or in mental or emotional conflict, rather than from physical injury. In this situation the sufferer does not forget the horrible details of the bad experience but cannot remember all of what happened. In fact, the missing pieces lie beneath the protective cloak of forgetfulness, too terrible or painful to be exposed to the daylight of consciousness.

For example, Ochberg knows of an opera singer repeatedly beaten by her husband. When she testified at a divorce settlement hearing, however, she could not recall the most serious beatings. After hypnosis and other counseling she finally remembered that her husband had strangled her. Eventually she even could joke, "He not only threatened my life but my livelihood! No wonder I put that out of my mind" (1996:22). In another case a police officer shot to death a man who threatened her and her partner with a gun. She remembered everything except the sound of the shot. Many years later she finally "heard" the shot, Ochberg told us.

False Alarm

The final PTSD ingredient is a physical, not emotional, condition. It is caused by the mental trauma but takes the form of greatly aroused bodily reactions. This response gives new meaning to the term *jumpy*. The person shudders or jumps at unexpected noises, not necessarily those that are similar to noises that occurred during the original trauma. Apparently, the body's normal alarm mechanism is on a hair trigger, set off by things that really are not dangers. Consider, for instance, a classroom where a professor is lecturing when a student accidentally drops a book on the floor, causing a sharp bang. Most students will check where the sound came from, determine it is a harmless action, and, the instructor hopes, refocus on the lecture. Someone with PTSD, though, may be so shaken by the noise that concentrating or taking notes is impossible. Carried to extremes, that sensitivity can set off so many false alarms that the person cannot concentrate or sleep restfully and is irritable or withdrawn. The ability to enjoy intimacy may fade, making a normal sex life difficult.

One of the scariest variations of the exaggerated startle response is the panic attack. In this case, though, no loud noise or other obvious trigger is evident. The person simply has a sudden, overwhelming feeling of fear or dread. It may feel and look much like a heart attack: dizziness, light-headedness, perhaps a sensation of choking or smothering.

Coté witnessed those signs when he was working with a volunteer group that was serving coffee and donuts to weary travelers at a freeway rest stop during a summertime holiday weekend. A young man approached from a car and asked in a trembling voice whether someone could call an ambulance for him. He was shaking, wobbly on his feet, and said he was cold even though he was sweating. "I think it's a panic attack," he said. "I've had them before, but I'm out of medicine in the car and I feel so terrible." Someone called an ambulance. He was given a blanket and a place to lie down while volunteers comforted him. He returned several hours later, after treatment at a nearby hospital, and continued on his journey.

Actually, the young man did better than many panic sufferers. A comparative few are so afraid of having an attack that they will not even leave their houses, much less set off alone on lengthy highway trips. A larger number avoid supermarkets, church services, and theaters so they will not be embarrassed if they have an attack.

To summarize, post-traumatic stress disorder can show itself in very different and seemingly opposite effects: numbness or hyperactivity, reoccurring bad memories or spot amnesia, extreme irritation or withdrawal. No two people display PTSD exactly the same way. What the sufferers have in common is that a trauma has so distressed their lives that they cannot function well in social, occupational, or other important everyday situations.

People Who Can and Cannot Cope

Some experienced journalists may wonder why one person they interviewed appeared to have obvious trauma symptoms while another victim of the same event did not. In other words, is one person more vulnerable to such trauma than another? Researchers who wondered about such situations framed a definition of coping long before the American Psychiatric Association defined PTSD. Copers, the researchers observed, are people who achieve four goals when they face major life disruptions and transitions. They successfully accomplish necessary tasks, maintain relationships with significant others, preserve their self-esteem, and keep their anxiety within tolerable limits.

The study examined many groups of people for their coping abilities, including students who were adapting to out-of-town colleges, children entering puberty, and soldiers with third-degree (the most serious) burns at an army hospital. Some of those who coped the best were not necessarily those who "faced up" to their problems the most realistically. Instead, they sometimes denied the injury, fantasized, or used their imaginations to focus on other things during the trauma. For instance, soldiers with 50 percent body burns had a better rate of survival when they denied to themselves that they would be disfigured and have a painful recovery than when they recognized grim reality early on. They eventually accepted the seriousness of their injuries, but the delay somehow gave their bodies time to start physical healing.

Similarly, Ochberg cites interviews he had with two employees of the U.S. Information Agency six months after they were released from eighteen months of isolated captivity by Palestinian terrorists near Lebanon. "The one who coped occupied his mind in captivity by visualizing the designs for a house, down to the last detail," Ochberg told us. "And he categorized favorite restaurants, anticipating future menus. He exercised and kept his spirits up. I recall our conversation as pleasant for both of us."

The interview with the second man was very different, Ochberg recalls. "This man spoke guardedly, fearing foreign agents would overhear. He had no sense of humor and smoked nervously. During captivity he counted bricks in his cell and paced. He had no way of occupying his mind." The terrorists treated the two men equally and released them the same week. One celebrated his freedom. The other still felt chained by memories and fears.

Probably neither would have qualified for the diagnosis of PTSD, but clearly one was a coper and the other could not cope. The one who did cope used denial of danger, imagination, and positive thinking to pull him through the ordeal.

Born for PTSD?

Why do some people cope so well with trauma and others do not? Nobody knows. Not for sure, anyway. Most current research shows that the more intense and lasting a traumatic event is, the more likely it is to cause PTSD. That does not seem surprising, but people exposed to the same injury or horror will vary greatly in their response. One speculation from therapists is—to use an old saying—that people should choose their parents and grandparents very carefully. In other words, heredity may play as important a role in traumatic injury as it does in the propensity to many physical diseases.

We know that some children are born shy and some are born with a bolder temperament. Similarly, Ochberg speculates, some people are born with a brain pattern that keeps horror alive, whereas others have a brain pattern that allows them to recover quickly. That is not necessarily a bad thing, Ochberg offers: "As a varied, interdependent human species, we benefit from our differences. Those with daring fight the tigers. Those with PTSD preserve the impact of cruelty for the rest of us" (1996:22).

Continuing studies of trauma are trying to determine why people cope so differently with the same set of circumstances. One idea under study is that coping successfully with minor traumas in childhood protects against major psychological attacks later in life. Other theories about what helps feed or ward off PTSD emphasize the presence or absence of social supports, sustaining religious and spiritual beliefs, use of drugs and alcohol, simultaneous physical and emotional disorders, and the age of the trauma survivor, according to Ochberg.

Children Are Different

The axiom that "children aren't just miniature adults" may be trite, but it is one that journalists must remember when it comes to trauma. For that matter, it is also important simply to remember that children can be traumatized and should not be ignored or trivialized in coverage of events. Consider, for example, the trauma suffered by the schoolmates of students murdered in the spate of school shootings in recent years.

Like adults with PTSD, children may have frightening dreams but without content that is recognizable as related specifically to the cause. Young children may lack the ability to control their emotional response to being threatened. When young children are traumatized, they often regress. A toilet-trained toddler will wet the bed. A child who was chattering nonstop before the trauma may not speak after the shock. Young children also may reenact aspects of the trauma or express them repeatedly in their play. One of the many roles of parents is to provide both protection and nurturing to enable the child to respond to unexpected situations normally. Bloom writes: "Children cannot always soothe themselves and therefore the capacity of adults to soothe frightened, angry, or shamed children is essential to their development" (1997:20).

Even young adults may suffer a heavier toll from trauma than older survivors. That is one factor some researchers cite in considering the relatively high rate of PTSD among veterans of Vietnam, compared with veterans of other wars. The young soldier faced not only the trauma of war but the public disapproval of the conflict at home. He often lost the support of friends in his unit because the brass routinely rotated individuals rather than units. The upshot was that the young veterans had to cope with the demands of adolescence as well as those of war. They had neither the adult experience nor the support of comrades-in-arms to cope with the antiwar protests back home. Psychiatrists do not say that those factors caused PTSD but argue that they made it tougher for the young warriors to cope with their trauma.

Other Responses

In addition to being aware of PTSD and related disorders, journalists should have some knowledge of other emotional conditions that are not listed in the official psychiatric diagnostic manual. We have already touched on one—shame—and it deserves some more attention because of its prominent place in the lives of victims of human cruelty. As we mentioned earlier, trauma survivors often feel shame. At first glance that seems backward. Shouldn't it be the attackers who feel shame? Yes but they rarely do. Instead, the people who have been shot, robbed, or raped often feel ashamed. They may even feel ashamed of feeling ashamed. The shame triggered when people see themselves as helpless, weak, or incapable can itself scramble their thinking abilities, a serious condition that the psychiatrist D. L. Nathanson (1997) calls "cognitive shock."

Survivors' understandable anger at their attackers often quickly turns into blaming themselves. Why didn't I see it coming? Why didn't I defend myself better? Why didn't I stop them somehow? How could I let such a thing happen to me (or to my partner or child)? Such reactions may seem reasonable, but if they are carried too far, long, and deeply, they can eat into a person and cause serious depression.

Another powerful emotion is anger. Again, we easily understand why the victim would be angry, although often the victim's parent or spouse is most angry and after revenge. They can be considered covictims. Take the situation of the Andersons of Michigan. Dan Anderson was shot by a prowler, nearly died, and has since endured more than thirty surgeries. Still, he tells journalism students that he has forgiven his attacker (who never asked for forgiveness during the trial or since then in prison). "I've never ever felt anger toward my attacker; I still don't," he says fourteen years later. Anderson says the shooting "completely turned my life around" by deepening his religious faith and concern for others. He sometimes worries that he might have intended to hit the prowler with a flashlight just before the man shot him. But now listen to Pat Anderson, normally a gentle woman: "Dan's more forgiving than I am. I can't do that, not yet anyway. I'm working on it, but I'm still angry."

Anger can be turned into constructive actions. Many of us know of someone who has started or joined a campaign to wipe out a deadly disease after losing a loved one to the ailment. Perhaps for similar reasons, relatives and friends seek ways to find and punish a perpetrator and, often, to bring to justice other similar attackers.

MADD (Mothers Against Drunk Driving) has led fights in several states to toughen penalties for driving while under the influence of alcohol or drugs. A Massachusetts father whose young son was abducted and murdered hosted a national television series devoted to capturing criminals in unsolved crimes. Family members and friends of four Michigan women murdered by a confessed serial killer formed an organization that worked successfully to find ways to keep him from being paroled. The group also helped get state legislation that bars the early release of inmates for good behavior.

Journalists need to be able to recognize signs of anger or shame because those emotions may greatly color how a victim reacts during an interview, especially in the hours and days after a traumatic event. The interviewee may displace anger from the prime target, the attacker, onto the immediate and convenient target—the reporter or photographer. Similarly, any question or comment that implies that the survivor should have acted differently may turn underlying shame into anger directed very specifically at the journalist.

Having said that, some psychiatrists and psychologists caution that reporters should not necessarily stop an interview because someone is crying or appears to be angry. You might hand the person a tissue or turn off a recorder or camera for awhile; if the person wants to continue, respect that decision and his or her desire to have the story told. Trauma victims often feel hopeless, hostile, withdrawn, threatened, ineffective, or powerless. A thoughtful, accepting interview at the right time may help survivors regain some sense of security, control, balance, and power in their jumbled lives. Letting survivors talk about their experiences is a great prescription, many mental health experts agree—one way journalists can aid trauma sufferers.

The Stockholm Syndrome

Many trauma reactions noted here at least seem plausible. What may, however, be the hardest reaction for many people to understand is the bizarre situation in which the victim expresses friendship, affection, or even love for an attacker or kidnapper. That response is called the *Stockholm syndrome*. The term comes from a robbery in Sweden in 1974 during which the hostage taker and a bank teller fell in love and had sex in the bank vault during the siege.

In the United States the newspaper heiress Patricia Hearst held up a bank with a leftist radical who had sexual relations with her after his group kidnapped her and kept her locked in a closet. Psychiatrists say that people affected by the syndrome deny their assailants are villains and respond to their power in a move to save their lives.

Tincture of Time

Many things can help people recover from trauma, and one of the best medicines often simply is time, experts say. After a natural disaster people begin to feel like their old selves in six to eighteen months, according to Dr. Bruce Hiley-Young of the U.S. Veterans Administration's National Center for Post-Traumatic Stress Disorder in Palo Alto, California. Recovery is likely to take longer, however, when crime is the cause, cautioned Hiley-Young in an interview by the *Daily Oklahoman* (Painter 1995:8); Hiley-Young advised state health officials after the Oklahoma City bombing. The anger, frustration, and loss of the feeling of security that result from deliberate violence often complicate and lengthen the healing process. Many times, Hiley-Young said, survivors benefit from learning what to expect by talking with other victims or trained professionals. Just learning that others have similar reactions can help victims.

Journalists can help in the recovery process by pacing their actions to the expectations of the injured person. That may include carefully explaining your intentions, pausing when the interview terrain gets too rocky, regulating your physical movements and space so the other person is not threatened, and by seeing the story as an element in the recovery process that could be either harmful or helpful.

One Survivor's Responses

Seldom does one person's experience encompass the wide range of trauma reactions we have described. One survivor's story, though, may be helpful because it does reflect several emotional responses common to victims. The person happens to be a journalist. Bruce Shapiro, a contributing editor of the *Nation* magazine, was among seven people stabbed and seriously wounded when a mentally deranged man attacked customers and employees—all strangers to the attacker—in and outside a coffee bar in New Haven, Connecticut. Several years after the 1994 assault, Shapiro vividly recalls what he felt during and after the attack.

The physical pain from the man's two lunges with a hunting knife into Shapiro's back and chest caused pain that "ran over me like an express train," leaving him screaming on a sidewalk (1995:446). Police and emergency medics arrived quickly, summoned by bystanders, but at the time Shapiro thought no one was trying to help him. "I was really aware of just wanting people to help me," he told us. "I was feeling quite frightened. People didn't seem to be there for me. . . . I really perceived these bystanders as not having acted in my behalf."

In an article in the *Nation*, Shapiro explains his response this way: "For weeks I thought obsessively and angrily of those minutes on Audubon Street, when first the nameless woman in the window and then the security guard refused to approach me—as if I, wounded and helpless, were the dangerous one" (1995:449). However, the woman had called police, and a few minutes later the guard helped police chase down the assailant. As Shapiro was loaded into an ambulance, "My heart was going a mile a minute and I was aware I was in a lot of pain. I described to them what I thought had happened. I also was just trying to understand myself what had happened. I kept asking them, 'Just tell me where we're going; what happens next?'" he told us.

Shapiro's reaction to the reporters who interviewed him or tried to in the next few days helps us understand early traumatic reactions of assault victims. On the first day after his life-saving surgery, he felt very weak and turned aside two interview requests from newspaper and television reporters. It was too soon and he did not sense that either reporter truly was concerned about him personally. Two days later he did give an interview to another local reporter he knew. "His first concern was human," he told us. "It made all the difference, especially when he said beforehand that if I decided after the interview that I didn't want any of it to run, it wouldn't."

Details in other interview stories struck him as callous in some cases and careless in others. One that published the names and addresses of the victims "just invited potential burglars to come and steal from their houses while they were hospitalized," he said. He was upset by the coverage of two friends who, sent home to recover, were ambushed by a television crew as they left their physician's office. In common with many victims, he was angered by errors in the stories. Although he was single at the time, a *New York Times* reporter "even invented a wife for me." He told us that "it seemed more humorous later, but I was very irritated at the time."

Over time, Shapiro placed the press coverage in the context of his emotional injuries and ways of coping. The anger he mentions was part and parcel of the trauma he endured. The triggers for some of that anger were provided by journalists through carelessness or ignorance of the likely effects of their work. "Such press coverage inspired in all of us a rage it is impossible to convey," Shapiro writes. "To the victim of violent crime the press may reinforce the perception that the world is an uncomprehending and dangerous place" (1995:450). He also recognizes the frequent correlation of trauma-associated anger and actions calculated to reap revenge—motivations often seized upon by politicians and amplified by press coverage. A better answer, he argues, is to strengthen the social institutions that saved his life and sheltered him from greater injury within moments of the assault.

The Human Family

Journalists may be able to help in some ways, but they should not be expected to act like psychologists, psychiatrists, or social workers. That is not their job, even if they have the necessary training. What journalists can do is learn enough about trauma to understand what normal people may feel when subjected to abnormal circumstances. As more becomes known about the effects of violence, both medical and journalism professionals can use that information to enhance their traditional skills and values.

If journalists treat victims of human cruelty with respect and informed attention, they can ease the effects and channel them into pursuits that are constructive for the victims and everyone the media cover. Recognize that we're all part of the human family and that social support may boost someone's psychological and perhaps even physical recovery from severe stress. In that way we may help victims become something different, as envisioned in the "Survivor's Psalm" by Frank Ochberg:

> I have been victimized.
> I was in a fight that was not a fair fight.
> I did not ask for the fight. I lost.
> There is no shame in losing such fights,
>   only in winning.
> I have reached the state of survivor and
>   am no longer a slave of victim status.
> I look back with sadness rather than hate.
> I look forward with hope rather than despair.
> I may never forget,
>   but I need not constantly remember.
> I was a victim.
> I am a survivor.
>   (1993:782)

Chapter 2

The Journalist's Trauma

Journalists can become trauma victims simply by doing their work—by visiting scenes of destruction, talking to, and photographing people who have been injured or traumatized. Sometimes they feel the effects after seeing dead and injured people and the debris of deadly events. In other cases by hearing tragic stories and by trying to ease the pain of others, journalists join disaster workers and others who experience what therapists call "compassion fatigue," the result of absorbing information about the suffering of others. Not all reporters and photographers are affected by covering traumatic events; the kind of exposure and traits of the person are variables that can mean that some journalists are scarcely affected, if at all, whereas others may need to address trauma symptoms.

Is Reporter Trauma Real?

In fairness, some people in the news industry are skeptical of these ideas. They do not believe that journalists suffer more than momentary effects from doing stories about violence, if they are affected at all. They believe that all but a few journalists—those who are already troubled—manage to cover the most trying assignments with professional polish and immunity to emotional shock. Reporters and photographers sometimes voice these views, and we hear them from editors and company executives. We see these assumptions implied in journalism textbooks that treat violence only as a category of assignment, not as work that might harm the journalist. Because they are common views and because they are often held with deep conviction, we want to examine two arguments against the possibility that trauma affects journalists.

The first argument is that classroom and newsroom education prevents most effects from trauma. Journalists are trained to deal with violence, the first argument says. If the reporter acts as a professional should—concentrates on the job and does not try to play the role of the police officer, rescuer, or medic—the emotional effects will be small. A steady focus on professional conduct at all stages of a reporting assignment protects the journalist.

This argument reflects a belief that the reporter who carefully and deliberately attends to the tasks of reporting, such as taking notes, asking questions, and noticing details, will suffer little. The student learns these skills in the classroom and on the school paper. The novice reporter practices them and sees other reporters doing the same. The skills do not change much; each new assignment tests them in a new way. Thus the capacity to do difficult things on the job grows. Yes, say those who take this view, stress can be too much for a particular reporter. They can remember a colleague or friend who buckled during or after a big story, but they argue that such people will be noticed, supported, and replaced, if necessary. A reporter whose stress becomes apparent will be taken off a beat or an assignment. Someone who does not want to cover a traumatic story will be reassigned. An editor wrote us, "This is done with the simple reasoning that any staff member so affected is unlikely to do a good job on the assignment. These rules are also usually pursued casually and instinctively for humane reasons."

The second argument reflects what some of us think about how our brains work. A good journalist—the argument goes—can compartmentalize, that is, channel raw emotions into one compartment of the mind without interfering with the tasks that have to be carried out in pursuit of the story.

Perhaps doing the task at hand short-circuits the way we'd usually respond to suffering or pain, leaving the journalist mostly unaffected by the experience, no matter how horrible or shocking it might be. Reporters and photographers who have witnessed death describe the effects this way. They talk about detachment, focus, being desensitized, being in control. A few actually use the word *compartmentalize*. They echo the words of a famed World War II correspondent, Marguerite Higgins, who wrote about her visit to the newly liberated German death camp at Buchenwald in 1945. Years later she wrote a memoir in which she talked about feeling no emotion on seeing the dead and dying at the concentration camp. "My condemnation and disgust were of the mind. And I believe that is generally true that a journalist covering a war, a train wreck, a concentration camp, or some other disaster, tends to compartmentalize his emotions and isolate them from professional reactions. He feels no more personal involvement than does a surgeon performing a delicate operation or a regimental commander ordering a comrade into battle" (1955:76). As she ended the memoir, however, Higgins wrote that the death of someone close to her had helped her understand that her efforts at compartmentalization had in fact buried her natural compassion for those she saw.

The first argument—about professionalism—implies that editors and other coworkers will identify and support an affected reporter or photographer. While some newsrooms do enjoy this alert monitoring, in others people are reluctant to act on trauma symptoms even when they are obvious. Our own experience backs up what many reporters write and say: Coworkers and editors do not intervene often enough. Stress is transformed into behaviors, such as drinking, smoking, and arguing, that are often ignored, winked at, or excused as part of the culture of news work.

The second argument—about compartmentalization—may fit some journalists, but it does not describe journalism very well. The argument is attractive nevertheless. Today many journalists strive for professional detachment and believe that the best stance is one that protects them from painful interactions. Compartmentalization, a form of what is often called dissociation, may not be an *ethical* or a *healthy* response. Reporters, one after another, readily affirm the importance of dissociation, which allows them to go about their tasks while keeping their emotions temporarily at bay. Protective in the short term, it can be harmful as a persistent defense against the effects of violence or pain. In part, persistent dissociation exacts a great expenditure of psychic energy to block the body's danger response, a reaction triggered earlier when the journalist witnessed injury, death, fear, or trauma. Some emotion, openly shown, may help a journalist do the story more effectively. A sincere, even emotional, response from a reporter is likely to help a victim. It is not detachment but finding a balance between empathy and the journalistic task that should challenge the journalist. In some cases, we hope, the need for the journalist's skill, strength, or compassion in a time of crisis will completely eclipse news considerations.

Are Journalists Affected by Traumatic Events?

Consider how Peter Maass, a *Washington Post* correspondent who covered the war in Bosnia in the early 1990s, talks about his work in *Love Thy Neighbor*, a book about the war published in 1996. Maass captures powerfully the plight of people he covered: "Refugees who saw friends or family members killed or raped—they exposed their brains to the radiation of tragedy. . . . They would wake up at night screaming and shaking, or they would not wake up at all, because they could not sleep. These people were haunted by a war that was inside of them, lodged somewhere in their brains in a spot that a knife could not get to, nor the soothing words of a best friend" (1996:103–104). And then Maass invoked the argument about the journalist's compartmentalization and promptly contradicted it. "Journalists rarely overdose on tragedy," he declares, before writing that he could not clear his head of his dreams, even on breaks to London or Budapest. "I could spend two weeks in London and still, every night, I would dream of Bosnia. It was inescapable" (104). He was relieved to find that the commander of the first British troops in Bosnia also had such dreams.

Other combat correspondents and photographers tell of such effects. Bob Gassaway, who covered the Vietnam War in the 1960s for the Associated Press, wrote in the late 1980s that the war's effects still pursued him. Still startled by helicopters and car backfires, he resolved to avoid fireworks displays on the Fourth of July: "The bright lights and the loud noises are too real for me" (1989:348)

When an entire newsroom is hit by the shock waves, as was the staff of the *Daily Oklahoman* after the 1995 bombing of the Alfred P. Murrah Federal Building in Oklahoma City, the strain is noticeable. Charlotte Aiken, then a reporter at the newspaper, wrote in 1996: "In the past year, throughout the newsroom, personal relationships have been shaken or ended. Eating disorders and other emotional problems have developed. Use of sick time has skyrocketed" (31). Although the newspaper's management quickly brought in a counselor to help the reporters, only a few women reporters responded. Most of the men, including the editors who "experienced the same fatigue and tension reporters had," stayed away from counseling. Aiken recoiled from the steady need to do stories about the bombing. "I began to dread the endless bombing stories that we wrote every day for an entire year. Enough was enough. Every time I wrote something, I heard that woman screaming for her dead babies" (1996:31). On that staff some reporters still suffer emotional distress when a new facet of the endless story emerges. Too often reporters, photographers, and editors are asked to recall that day and recount their place in its coverage. Invariably, some staff members have intrusive memories and sleep restlessly afterward.

The bombing in Oklahoma City and the war in Bosnia were profoundly troubling events. Virtually every news staff, no matter the size of its community, at some time faces an event that severely taxes its members. A newspaper reporter who had covered crime news for a decade witnessed the fatal shooting of a drug suspect by police officers. "I saw the body moments after he had been shot, the legs dangling there, and I saw the shocked look on the cops' faces," the reporter recalls. His presence at the shooting required his testimony at the inquest. "Somehow you feel responsible. You are this man's last living witness on earth," the reporter says. Within weeks he began to suffer sleeplessness and found himself responding angrily to coworkers and friends. "I became irritable. I began waking up at three or four in the morning for no explicable reason." As he showed signs of depression as he worked his beat at police headquarters, officers commented that the reporter was acting like any officer who had been involved in a shooting. "Why don't you see the police psychologist?" one officer suggested. The newspaper's management had not suggested that the reporter talk to a counselor.

Few reporters actually witness a fatal shooting. Immersion in a drawn-out story about death, though, may cause responses similar to those of the police reporter. Ginger Casey, a Providence, Rhode Island, television anchor and writer, writes about covering a series of child killings in Los Angeles some years ago: "I couldn't understand why I found myself a few weeks later unable to get out of bed, sleeping 12 hours a day. In my dreams, I kept seeing those tiny faces, even though I did the 'professional' thing and showed up for work every day, ready to deliver my reports without a shred of emotion. I didn't want my boss to know these stories were ripping my heart out, lest she think I wasn't up to being a 'real' reporter" (1994:38).

Other reporters who cover crime have described in print their drift from excitement to dull routine. Mark Pinsky, a *Los Angeles Times* reporter, writes that his career as a journalist began with bracing investigations in local courthouses in the southeastern United States. His reward, he says, was rescuing people suffering injustice. Later his preoccupation with trials led to exhausting coverage of murder cases and, in time, a resolve to give it up. A job offer from the *Times* put him back into courtrooms for a long period. "Four days a week I listened to testimony, looked at evidence, and interviewed tearful parents and siblings after the verdicts. On Fridays, sentencing days, I listened as friends and relatives of the slain and maimed told the judge why murderers should be executed or sent to prison forever. Gloom turned to depression. Sleeping became difficult. My home life was affected" (1993:29). Pinsky points to the source of his stress: "If you protect yourself too much by screening out the unpleasantness, you cheat the reader by failing to convey the horror, which is, after all, your job. On the other hand, if you allow yourself to absorb the reality of what you see and hear, you run the risk of destroying yourself emotionally" (29).

Finding the right balance is difficult, as Pinsky says. One of our colleagues left television news reporting in the late 1960s after covering two major murder cases; until recently, she had not linked her urgent request to her employers to transfer her out of news to the experience of being at the scene in both cases. We believe that reporters, like the rest of humanity, risk traumatic wounds from what they see and hear.

What Research Shows

Although journalists' stories about trauma symptoms are numerous, little systematic study of such effects has been done. Mental health scholars have paid little attention to those who are not among those hit by trauma's first shock waves. Police and firefighters are studied more than journalists. The news industry has paid little attention to the problem. However, modest evidence exists that violence leaves news personnel with both short- and long-term symptoms. For example, fifteen journalists who witnessed a gas chamber execution of a murderer in California in 1992 reported short-term anxiety symptoms to researchers (Freinkel, Koopman, and Spiegel 1994). The researchers argue that traumatic effects appear in those who observe violence, such as the journalists, as well as in direct victims of war and violence. Although the execution was an official act, socially sanctioned, the journalists were not immune to its short-term effects and had no special shield against emotional pain. The lesson for journalists is that while they may think that by concentrating on taking the pictures, getting the facts, or interviewing victims they are escaping the shock waves, some of them will be wrong. And if they fail to see and respond to their symptoms, some will risk enduring those symptoms for long periods.

Simpson and Boggs surveyed 130 newspaper reporters, editors, and photographers in several newspapers in Michigan and Washington State in 1996. They included editors because they often have had extensive reporting experience. The group of journalists disclosed a level of symptoms one might find among public safety workers recently engaged in a traumatic event (Simpson and Boggs 1999).

Other important findings emerged from the survey. The longer people had worked as journalists the more likely they were to report trauma symptoms. This was true of intrusion symptoms, such as unwanted recollections, as well as avoidance mechanisms associated with trauma.

One type of assignment was often linked to trauma symptoms. Judging from our experience and that of recent graduates who give us feedback, it is not unusual for cub reporters to be sent to the scene of a fatal highway accident. One graduate said the highlight of his summer internship was going to the scenes of fatal auto crashes on Saturday nights. In the survey those journalists who had gone to crash scenes were likely to report intrusive recollections, in some cases long after the event. Survey respondents offered vivid and detailed accounts of those crashes, some many years and even decades earlier, underlining the power of such events to produce recurring memories over a long period. One reporter said that thirty years later he still sees the image of the dead victims in the car, and another described victims in the road and in the car on a "very cold and windy night" while long lines of cars detoured slowly around the crash. Another remembered the smells of a crash scene. A photographer called his picture of a man who was holding his injured girlfriend in an ambulance "a touching moment, a callous shot." Another recalled "the awesome violence of an auto crash, the blood trails of victims who later died, the scalp left behind by the ambulance crew, the uneaten box of donuts in one car, the half-finished bottle of vodka in the other."

The survey backed our ideas that the shock waves of some events also hit journalists and that they may carry symptoms for long periods. The reporters and photographers had covered many tough assignments, including fatal fires, airplane crashes, and even a deadly charge by a circus elephant, but the auto crash was mentioned most often. Although the fatal auto accident is a common assignment, it is not a benign one for many of the reporters and photographers who witness its results.

We are convinced that news reporters are at some risk of trauma symptoms as early as their first violent assignment. Research suggests that continuing to cover such stories without dealing with the symptoms may affect the reporter adversely. Friends, relatives, and coworkers will find themselves absorbing the fallout. The survey asked reporters in the two states what they observed about the behavior of others in their newsrooms.

The reporters said they notice friends who anger quickly or develop and sustain irritable personalities. Others show sadness, occasional crying, and what coworkers take to be depression. Anxiety and nervousness appear in others. Some reporters see or learn about excessive smoking or drinking and link those behaviors to the stresses of the job.

How do coworkers cope with such stress? Some use drugs, alcohol, or tobacco, while others give in to anger and anxiety. In the answers, though, we found more helpful remedies. Some newspeople isolated themselves until they could work more confidently. Conversations with friends, at lunch or after hours, helped some people. Talking about hard stories was the remedy they mentioned most often. A few others were known to take long walks, listen to music, pray, and share their job stresses with their families.

The symptoms journalists report may be related to the stress of work, but they also may reflect exposure to scenes and images of personal suffering that threaten the emotional stability of the reporter. Symptoms may follow either direct personal experience or indirect exposure. Of course, rarely would the injury be diagnosed medically as a trauma disorder, but a high level of symptoms can nevertheless be damaging to health and productivity.

Journalists interview people about the traumatic losses of family and friends. How do those interviews affect reporters?

Charles Figley, a psychologist, and others have labeled indirect traumatic exposure *compassion fatigue* because it draws on the empathy of a person who works with those who suffer trauma. The journalist absorbs the trauma effect in the same way that a family member shares the emotional upset of a person who has been severely hurt (Figley 1995). Some spouses appear to share a patient's mental illness; a man may exhibit symptoms of pregnancy out of empathy for his wife. Hysteria may sweep through a group, leading to a mass response, presumably conducted by the capacity of each group member to absorb the emotions of others in the group.

The relationship of a traumatized person and a reporter is somewhat like that of a therapist and a client. If the victim's story is compelling and painful to tell, some of the emotional burden will fall on the listening reporter. Some victims want a caring listener, someone who will recognize their pain. Journalists often limit their emotional responses, in part to protect themselves and in part to honor a journalistic value of objectivity and detachment. Other journalists, though, cannot limit their empathy; they care too much about the other person and her story.

A good number of the journalists surveyed in Michigan and Washington State spoke readily about their empathy for victims (Simpson and Boggs 1999). Sixty-eight percent of the journalists said they found some stories emotionally difficult. Stories about children troubled them the most. Several reporters said that interviews with relatives of people who had been killed were most difficult. "The classmates of a teenager who was shot were obviously touched," said one reporter. Another wrote that after interviewing pregnant high school students, she was "drained emotionally." She added, "I kept thinking how hard it was going to be for these young women and they really had no clue." Another person wrote: "The sister of a man who died of AIDS really opened up to me. She was sobbing and I was holding her hands crying with her." Yet another reporter told of going to a swimming pool where a three-year-old boy had drowned. "I ran into the child's parents. They wanted to talk about it but it was emotionally hard on them and I had trouble covering the story because they were portrayed as irresponsible by the police, but they were visibly devastated."

How do these conversations mark the reporter? In part, journalists are like trauma therapists, police, aid workers, and others whose work summons a high degree of emotional intensity. Empathy is the resource everyone brings to such demanding situations, yet showing empathy and sharing with a victim may leave secondary effects with the reporter. The stories may remind him of a similar experience. It is not uncommon for a reporter who has suffered a trauma, such as rape or combat violence, to have traumatic memories during or after an interview. The effects can be particularly strong if the reporter has not worked out the personal trauma. Stories about children, as we have suggested, often arouse deep feelings in the listener, in many cases because they evoke thoughts about one's own children. Psychologists describe an effect called *identification*—a person becomes emotionally involved in the plight of others because of similarities in their circumstances. Some journalists are like firefighters who feel helplessness and guilt about child victims because they identify the victims with their own children. A West Coast reporter who had lost a child drew an assignment to fly to Oklahoma City right after the bombing. Covering that explosion, which killed many children, left emotional wounds that the reporter and his editors had not anticipated.

Several journalists in the survey mentioned guilt feelings that followed covering certain traumatic events (Simpson and Boggs 1999). Guilt may be a potent factor for some journalists because their work usually denies them the chance to help people. Reporters who covered the Oklahoma City bombing in 1995 say that guilt feelings plagued them as they observed rescue efforts but could do little to help. They found their news work wanting, compared with the dogged and sometimes heroic efforts of those at the site.

Editors wisely reminded them that the news media play a key role in keeping the community informed during a stressful time.

What to Do About Trauma

The symptoms of anxiety, intrusive memories, and avoidance of unwanted reminders give the journalist an extra burden to carry through a day's work. But when reporters speak of that burden, they use images that suggest that the burden gets heavier over time. Little attention has been paid in the industry to the sense of helplessness that may increasingly trouble reporters exposed to trauma.

We believe that the stresses of covering violence in some cases will drain a reporter's energy and commitment. We strongly suspect that some journalists who leave the craft do so because of trauma. We also believe that many that stay in the business respond to the stresses in unproductive ways. When Simpson and Boggs (1999) asked the newspaper journalists how they and coworkers dealt with traumatic events, many mentioned excessive smoking and drinking. Coworkers' responses included anger, hostility, excessive talking about the event, loud talk in the newsroom, and cynicism.

Over time the repetition of such behaviors changes the journalist's outlook toward work. Roger Rosenblatt, a *New Republic* and *Time* magazine columnist, described this change after a visit to the troubled African nations of Rwanda and Tanzania in 1994. Journalists respond at first to the suffering around them with shock and "perhaps a twinge of guilty excitement" (16). As they grow accustomed to atrocities, they "get bogged down" in its routine nature. Finally, "embittered, spiteful and inadequate to their work, they curse out their bosses back home for not according them respect; they hate the people on whom they report. Worst of all, they don't allow themselves to enter the third stage, in which everything gets sadder and wiser, worse and strangely better" (16).

Here are our suggestions for dealing with the traumatic symptoms of news work.

- Acknowledge that you may see and hear things for which you are not prepared. One reporter answered the Simpson and Boggs survey by saying that her first assignment would have been less shocking if she had spent a few minutes talking to an editor about what she should expect. Two out of three reporters say they were not prepared for what they saw on their first assignment that involved violence. In some cases the details of that first event—the physical wounds to dead and injured people, for example—prevented reporters from getting information. One reporter confused the order of events. A photographer at the scene of a fatal accident "just went automatic, snapping away like a robot" (15). The first events flood the journalist's senses; the scene may seem like chaos until the organization of the public safety response becomes obvious; the collision of emotions and fact gathering may seem incongruous to some; journalists will not be aware of their dissociation. Although some people are ready for that first event, others need to talk with an editor or another reporter.

- Trying assignments can be brought within the control of the reporter to some degree by concentrating on the tasks at hand: Shoot the photographs, ask the questions, observe the details of the scene, and write your notes. Many reporters speak gratefully of the anchor that those routine tasks gave them during a trying event.

Some reporters and photographers take their time getting used to the scene, circling the site for a while and observing it carefully before trying to talk to or photograph anyone. That advice would fit most assignments if time allows.

When you interview people at the scene or later talk to family members, neighbors, or friends of victims, try to monitor your own reactions. Some reporters become robotic at such times, pumping out the questions without remaining sensitive to the person with whom they are speaking. How can you keep a balance between the task and the emotions of the other person? Our advice is to seek ways to connect with the traumatized person. Put down your notepad and camera from time to time and talk without benefit of those job-defining props. That simple act will enable you to sustain eye contact as the other person speaks. As you maintain eye contact, you will communicate some of your own emotion, empathy, and, surprisingly, calmness. That humane sharing will help both of you. Don't forget that the other person's emotions also are under siege.

- Don't ignore what you have just experienced. After police officers and firefighters endure a traumatic event, they are debriefed about what they have seen and felt. In some cases psychologists debrief officers, but police agencies are increasingly training officers to serve as peer counselors. If your newsroom does not have a therapist or a staff member ready to help, talk to a coworker or friend. There is nothing mysterious about a debriefing. Sometimes the debriefing allows nothing more than a gradual winding down from an intense experience. It may help to write for a few minutes about your thoughts and emotions that are tied to the story. Acknowledge unexpected or unwanted responses.

While even a brief conversation after a traumatic event may be valuable, we believe an effective debriefing has three elements. First, the reporter should speak freely about her or his reactions to the event. Second, the other people in the debriefing should affirm the value of those reactions. There is no benefit if a listener scoffs at the disclosure or laughs and says, "Get on with your work and stop whining." Third, some encouragement toward self-care should be offered. The listener might suggest some ways to reduce stress, point the reporter to others with empathy for his problem, or agree to talk again.

Even without a willing listener, you can care for yourself in ways that will lessen the effects. Take guidance from experienced journalists who realize that they need attention after covering difficult stories. Reporters often talk to spouses or partners, but some say that such conversations have limited value. "I fear I sound like a broken record," one reporter says, "so I don't talk very often." Another says, "It's hard because no one wants to hear the gory details, and often those are the ones you need to express." Some journalists take care of themselves by seeking private time and space, exercising, listening to music, bathing, praying, and crying. We know reporters who ask for time off when their stress is obvious.

- Efforts at self-care may not prevent the onset of trauma symptoms. The insurance and health care programs of many corporations provide counseling as part of employee benefits. We know many journalists who have been helped by a psychiatrist or psychologist. In most cases the journalist decided to seek help. It is a paradox that not far from such newsrooms is a local police department that likely insists that any officer involved in a traumatic event talk to a department psychologist. One respondent to the Simpson and Boggs survey wrote, "There is little recognition of stress in a business that focuses not on what you've done but on what you are doing for tomorrow. My employer makes counseling available as a benefit, but nobody has ever suggested that it be used" (17).

Other barriers prevent journalists from obtaining professional help. In some cases gender may be a factor. When one newspaper's staff faced a traumatic event, the publisher provided a counselor in the newsroom. Most male employees rejected the help. On the other hand, some women have said that job expectations persuaded them not to seek the help of a therapist. A female police reporter comments, "It is still difficult to admit you're having trouble; it's shooting your career in the foot."

Some reporters deal with personal stress by joining a support group of journalists who have similar concerns. After a workshop on trauma and news coverage, a reporter in one part of the state formed an e-mail friendship with a reporter on a newspaper several hundred miles away. E-mail enabled them to tell each other about their experiences and reactions and to offer help to one another.

It isn't our intention to tell anyone how to deal with trauma, whatever clinical form it may take. We are convinced, though, that many journalists who need such attention fear disclosing it or acting on their need. The best working environment is one in which everyone agrees that journalistic work can harm journalists, and each person is alert to signs of distress among coworkers.

- Sometimes many workers in a newsroom are exposed to trauma. A reporter kills himself, stunning and shocking his coworkers. A shooter penetrates a newspaper plant, gunning down employees as they work. The horrors of a plane crash or bombing devastate a city, affecting everyone in the newsroom.

The *Daily Oklahoman* in Oklahoma City is a model for sensitive handling of the newsroom effects of the 1995 bombing of the federal building. The staff's extraordinary commitment to telling the story fully and fairly was matched by the management's efforts to support that mission. A therapist was brought to the newspaper for individual and group meetings and, even after the first troubled weeks, remained on call. Housekeeping rules written to accommodate the newspaper's new building and state-of-the-art technology were changed on the spot. Management sent food to the newsroom for employees who did not leave for days; until the bombing, food was forbidden in the working area. Messages from editors supported the reporters, editors, and the support staff, applauded them for taking on duties they had not prepared for, and tried to address the doubts of those who wondered whether the intensive coverage wasn't "trafficking in the misery of the victims' families."

Other newspapers have responded in thoughtful ways that helped to validate the fears and doubts of journalists. In some cases, though, the traumatic event passes unnoticed within the organization. As symptoms become evident among workers, some news organizations have sought outside help.

Newspapers in both Washington and Michigan have asked our journalism schools to provide workshops on trauma for newsroom staffs. In sessions lasting one to several hours we have invited reporters, photographers, and editors to describe the event, air their responses, and discuss ways to make coverage both sensitive and effective. In one case the staff of the *Wenatchee World,* a daily newspaper in central Washington State, spoke openly about the pressures of a covering an extraordinary series of local events, including murders, forest fires, and accusations of an adult-child sex ring. A few days later Steve Lachowicz, an editor, wrote in his column:

> Reporters and editors are so busy meeting daily deadlines that they have never taken time to recognize that they, too, can suffer from the cumulative emotional strain that comes with tragic stories. Too many come to believe that feeling distant and numb and groaning about their job is a normal state of affairs. In reality, it may be the result of a psychological reaction to the pressures of dealing with death and destruction.
>
> This is not to suggest that we will be able to avoid writing about families who lose their children or about victims of sadistic killers. There will still be those tough morning phone calls to make to the survivors, when the right words are so hard to come by.
>
> But we got a little more education this week in ways we might approach those stories without doing unnecessary harm to the victims or to ourselves.
>
> That shield of invincibility we carry around sometimes protects us. But the weight of it can eventually also drag us into despair.

(1995:2)

Chapter 3

Reporting at the Scene

The reporter and photographer at the scene have unusual power to shape what we remember about searingly violent stories, and what they depict may remain in our minds forever. The stories that we don't remember for very long still help shape our thinking about crime, violence, public preparedness, and our capacity to deal with these things. Thoughtful reporting can prepare readers and viewers to respond intelligently to subsequent events; repeating myths and errors will confuse and undermine individual and community efforts during a crisis.

The journalist at the scene must avoid the traps such events set for the unwary. Reporters and photographers rarely are "ready" for what they face. Journalists may hear themselves voicing the effects—venting—along with the other people there. Clichés about human behavior come too readily in such cases: The people panicked. The victims need everything. Everyone is angry.

Planning Coverage at the Scene

No two scenes are alike. Unfamiliar places challenge the most ingenious journalists. "Parachute" reporters—those sent from distant cities to the site of a crash or natural disaster—and local reporters often have different objectives. But to some extent it won't matter whether the journalist comes from two blocks or two thousand miles away; the disaster or accident will require quick and sensitive action.

Thinking about what might happen ahead of time can equip the reporter or camera crew for what they find. A news staff can plan for local and regional events that could place unusual demands on it. On the Pacific coast earthquakes are familiar events; hurricanes try cities on the Atlantic seaboard and on the Gulf of Mexico, whereas tornadoes are common in the inland South and Midwest. On the coasts and in the Gulf of Mexico boating and shipping accidents are common. Planes crash anywhere. Planning for these events can make a great difference in the quality and accuracy of the reporting. Failing to plan will certainly test the talents of journalists, who may well bumble about as they simultaneously deal with their own emotions and try to make sense of the scene.

Hospitals, police and fire departments, and emergency agencies often hold disaster drills, testing each department and person to see how rapidly and productively each responds. Whereas news media sometimes report the drills, the scenario seldom directly incorporates journalists. News organizations can be crucial to accident and disaster relief; leaving them out of the planning may worsen the situation.

News organizations might benefit from what has been learned in "critical incident" programs, such as that conducted at the University of Virginia. Such programs bring together specialists from various academic disciplines to evaluate and plan responses to devastating occurrences, such as earthquakes, plane crashes, and hazardous materials spills. Journalists could prepare for an event by learning how various agencies would respond, identifying locations where information would be available, and evaluating news coverage of similar events.

But sometimes the only planning time you have is the time it takes to reach the scene, and you can prepare even for that eventuality. First, tell yourself that no amount of planning and little prior experience will fully prepare you for what you are about to see. Expect that some people you will see or meet will be injured physically and suffering psychological shock. Public safety personnel will be under stress that will manifest itself in different ways, ranging from an intense focus on the job at hand to obvious grief or distraction. And prepare yourself for seeing bodies and physical mutilation and for the emotional responses you and others may have. Keep yourself open to the idea that you may need to help people you find. You may reach the scene before rescue workers do; injured or disoriented people may need instant attention. At these times human responses are more helpful than chasing elusive facts.

When a sky bridge in a Kansas City, Missouri, hotel collapsed and killed 111 people during a packed, festive event on a hot night in July 1981, Roger

McCoy, a television reporter, was nearby. He had just come home exhausted from work when his assignment desk called to say the hotel had suffered some sort of structural collapse. He got there ahead of firefighters, ambulance crews, and other aid workers. Near the hotel the first person he saw was an elderly woman who was walking into the street. McCoy led the woman, who was in shock, to people nearby and asked them to watch her.

"Inside, it was utter pandemonium. There were dangling wires, showering sparks, broken water pipes spraying water and all the dust generated by the collapse of the concrete and steel skywalk in the lobby atrium. You could see that some people were dead, with arms and legs hanging out from the rubble. There were pools of blood and cries for help from people trapped under the fallen concrete," says McCoy, now an anchor at a Dayton, Ohio, television station. He told us that the first fire truck arrived a few minutes later, followed by every available ambulance and fire vehicle in the city. The medical examiner set up a makeshift morgue in a hotel conference room. McCoy stayed at the hotel until 3 A.M., doing live reports for his station and occasional feeds to CBS network news.

He told us, "I had an overwhelming sense of chaos and loss and an overwhelming sense of helplessness. That's trapped in my mind, and I've accepted that it's one of those things that will be with me for my life." Of his later reporting, McCoy says, "I did take some comfort in hoping that when I couldn't help physically, I could help bring about the healing process, help them understand the crisis, and maybe give people tools to deal with it all."

One of the most common assignments for newspaper reporters is the auto accident that causes injuries or deaths. First-time reporters are rarely prepared to see the injured and dead victims. Be ready to step back from the scene and think about how to help yourself deal with the experience. Be ready to help if needed, and do not interfere with medical, police, or firefighting efforts. Help with traffic control, if needed. Do not touch or move objects.

Think about the nature of trauma. You may see signs of traumatic stress in nearly everyone around you. Take a few moments to reflect on the possibility that nothing will seem ordinary for a while. Remember that, like the aid workers, witnesses, and survivors, you may get an adrenaline rush just from being there. Your own senses and emotions may seem alien to you. You may find yourself on automatic pilot, working away at a furious pace without taking time to process all that is going on around you. At some point, probably after you leave the scene, your emotions may take charge. Reporters and photographers have no genetic or other immunity against the beating that trauma can deliver to our emotional systems. The event is likely to mark your memory, just as it will become unforgettable to others at the scene. Daniel Goleman, in the book *Emotional Intelligence*, writes that part of the brain primes the body to react to a stunning event, while another part creates an emotional reaction, "stamp[s] the moment in memory with vividness," and stores the memory (1995:20).

Hope Tuttle, a Seattle resident who has worked on Red Cross disaster response teams for many years, told us of an afternoon interview she did with a young radio reporter soon after the Loma Prieta earthquake in northern California in 1989. Three hours later the reporter was on the phone to Tuttle, sobbing and begging for help. She had gone back to work when another of the many aftershocks hit. "I need someone to help me," the reporter told Tuttle. "I can't stand it anymore. It just keeps shaking." The reaction is a common one, but it's safe to say that her training for emergencies did not include the likelihood that her own emotions might get in the way of finishing the story.

Remember that "the scene" will change steadily in the hours and days after an event. The scene may change quickly from the site where shock waves left instant victims and damage to other venues—hospitals, morgues, hotels, briefing rooms, sites of press conferences, courts, and so on. It will be useful for your planning to think in terms of an "immediate scene," the chaotic site where the unexpected has occurred, and the other sites where facets of the story will be revealed over time.

Think about what you are preparing to cover. Is it an accident or a disaster? The character of the event makes a great difference in how you go about covering it. Joseph Scanlon, director of the Emergency Communications Research Unit at Carleton University in Ottawa, says that a *disaster* is something that threatens or actually disrupts a community; the definition does not depend on whether or how many people died. Other experts say that a disaster follows disruptive events that may build over time or occur suddenly. Property may be damaged, people may be injured or killed, and the emergency services of the community may be unable to cope.

By that definition, earthquakes, volcanic eruptions, forest fires, floods, drought, war, and famine are likely to be called *disasters*. In contrast, most air crashes, shipping incidents, fires, and building collapses are *accidents*, even though investigation may eventually show that they were intentional. Some events simply defy inclusion in either of those arbitrary categories.

What about a bombing such as the one that stunned Oklahoma City? The community was able to cope, but people throughout the region felt the effects.

We make the distinction between accidents and disasters here only to point out that you usually can go to the site of an accident, speak to witnesses and public safety people, and gain a fair sense of what happened. You will likely learn what agency or person has vital information about the event, such as the names of those hurt or killed, hometowns, and where they were taken for medical attention. A photographer or camera operator at an accident will have a fair chance of capturing many important facets of the event with relatively little movement.

A disaster, by contrast, does not yield its evidence readily. There often is no central place to obtain information. The effects of a disaster are widespread and not readily known, even to agencies with responsibility, such as federal or state governments. Scanlon comments, "When disaster strikes, there is no site and it may be hours, days, or even weeks before there is a comprehensive picture of the extent of impact. It is unlikely that any agency, no matter how competent, will have a feel for all that has happened" (1998:47).

What to Look for and Do at the Scene

Finding "the scene" may be your first challenge.

When Pan Am flight 103 exploded over Lockerbie, Scotland, in 1988, journalists immediately headed for the town from such nearby cities as Glasgow, Edinburgh, and London. The plane blew up a few minutes after seven on a December evening. As reporters got close to the town in the next few hours, they encountered highways that were closed to all but emergency vehicles. One reporter pulled his car in at the rear of a convoy of ambulances and police vehicles and managed to drive into Lockerbie. Joan Deppa's detailed description of Lockerbie that evening includes the tale of a Glasgow *Daily Record* reporter who arrived at the city in darkness. A man with a flashlight offered to take him to the site of the crash. Deppa writes, "Following his escort through back gardens and streets, the newsman soon found himself near Sherwood Crescent, staring at a huge, burning crater. Nothing in his long career could have prepared him for this or any of the many sights he would see in the hours ahead. It was as if he had arrived in the middle of a war zone" (Deppa et al. 1993:71). Three teenagers escorted another reporter across several fields littered with crash debris until they arrived at the crater.

The image of the crater was burned into the early stories, but reporting in the next few hours took place on city streets, in local pubs, and among the damaged houses. Through the night, as reporting crews continued to arrive, the scene spread over a wide area. By the next day reporters also were focusing attention on the headquarters for search teams and police. And as international news crews reached Lockerbie, authorities restricted access to headquarters buildings and to the areas with crash debris.

A photographer and reporter from the *Daily Oklahoman* were the first journalists to reach the bombed federal building in Oklahoma City in 1995. The photographer had to find places to take the pictures that would effectively tell the multiple stories of damage, injuries and deaths, and rescue efforts. The reporter simply stayed a good distance from the rescue effort, watching the activity and listening to witnesses, survivors, and emergency personnel. News teams sent from distant places found the bombing site under fairly tight control. Reporters who wanted to talk to families of the bombing victims had to go to a church several miles from the federal building where, under the close watch of National Guard troops, they waited for interviews.

Both Lockerbie and Oklahoma City were stages for inevitable meetings of the local reporters and the news teams from national and international media. The two groups often have different goals in mind, and their accounts of the events reflect those differences. Reporters who parachute in would do well to remember the visit of CBS anchor Connie Chung to Oklahoma City a short time after the bombing. Chung not only arrived at the federal building in a limousine but later angered many in Oklahoma City by asking an assistant fire chief whether the city could handle the crisis.

Are there injuries and deaths? How extensive is the damage? You will want to find emergency-response and public safety people who are likely to have credible information later. Determine what other places someone will need to check, such as hospital emergency rooms and field hospitals, temporary morgues, and agency public information offices. Finally, stay out of the way as rescue and relief work goes on, and coordinate your reporting with your city or assignment desk.

As you adjust to the scene, think about what disaster specialists call the phenomenon of *convergence*. In the immediate aftermath of a major event, people may rapidly arrive at the scene by foot, cars, or other vehicles. Convergence also occurs in terms of a storm of communication about the event and a rapid assembly and movement of supplies and equipment. Official movement of personnel, equipment, and information is expected, if not always efficient and coordinated. Journalists and those dealing with the event often do not expect what is called *informal convergence*—the lookie-loos. People come to the scene who are not victims, members of their families, or emergency workers. Sometimes convergence causes additional deaths and injuries. After a tornado struck a school, a child died in the traffic frenzy as parents rushed to the building.

Crowds of observers may make the scene seem more confusing and disorganized than it is. Early broadcast reports that urge people to stay away and to not use telephones may render an important public service. Reporting the precise location soon afterward may draw people to the scene, but it may reassure others that people they know are not affected. Once the word of what happened is out, callers will jam phone lines to learn whether relatives are involved. When a bomb was set off in a park in Atlanta during the 1996 Olympics, people from around the world tried to call Atlanta to learn about casualties. Although an emergency number was created to handle those calls, phone traffic was heavy. Organizers urged athletes to call their families to minimize some of the congestion.

Public Safety Personnel

Police, fire, or other emergency personnel will try to quickly mark the boundaries of the scene to protect relief and investigative activity. Although reporters and photographers have moved among emergency workers at scenes that have not been marked, police expect journalists to stay clear of the boundary markers. Expect a command hierarchy to take shape in the first hours. Police and fire agencies, hazardous materials teams, rescuers, and medical personnel may appear to be working independently, but coordination will eventually be imposed. In many situations a public information person will be designated to handle press questions.

The speed and complexity of public safety control of the situation will vary, of course. State troopers or local police will quickly take charge of an auto accident scene. Similarly, police and fire personnel will promptly take control of a fire scene. A plane crash site may be a large area, some of it inaccessible or difficult to control. Authorities quickly called in the National Guard to enforce boundaries after the Oklahoma City bombing. Sometimes a federal agency, such as the Federal Bureau of Investigation or the Bureau of Alcohol, Tobacco, and Firearms, may be in charge. More often a state or local police agency will oversee all rescue and investigative efforts. You will need to identify key personnel with these agencies and stay in contact with them.

A 1998 story illustrates the way "a scene" becomes the focus of both public safety agencies and the press. Two male students at a middle school in a Jonesboro, Arkansas, killed four female pupils and a woman teacher and wounded nine other students. A study by the Freedom Forum (1998), a foundation that investigates press issues, showed what happened in the first hours after the noontime shooting.

The shooting began moments after 12:30 P.M. when a fire alarm at the school was tripped to send children rushing outside into gunfire from a wooded area nearby. The first call to 911 came in at 12:38, and the sirens of responding ambulances as well as police messages on the newsroom scanners alerted local media. A *Jonesboro Sun* reporter with a camera arrived by 12:50 and immediately photographed students on stretchers, tearful classmates, dazed bystanders, and "teachers and police walking across bloodstained concrete sidewalks" (Freedom Forum 1998:5). By that time sheriff's deputies had found the two boys who later were convicted of the shootings. By 1 P.M. the newspaper reporter, a local television reporter, and the "live truck" supporting him had moved behind police lines. By that time the regional medical center had been on alert to receive shooting victims for fifteen minutes.

In Jonesboro the "immediate scene" of the school was relevant to reporters for a very short time. Within an hour no victims were at the scene, and the boys believed responsible had been taken into custody. The scene was one that the media could exploit for interviews of other children, parents, and teachers. While reporters pursued those interviews, the critical centers for information were becoming the hospital and police offices. Even so, the television reporters who were coming into the city by the dozens stayed close to the school, using it as visual backdrop for their reports. The sheriff allowed the media to stay at the school that day and night, then asked them to move to a nearby school bus yard or to the county jail. Other officials wanted the media moved from the school sooner. In Littleton, Colorado, a year later a high school in which two male students killed several other people and themselves was the center of news interest for hours as police established safety and then slowly reconstructed the murderous trail of the two shooters.

In Jonesboro the school grounds offered local journalists chances to photograph emergency work and to interview witnesses. Yet Curt Hodges, the

Sun reporter who was the first on the scene from his paper, took no pictures of the shooting victims lying outside the school. According to the Freedom Forum report,

> Hodges had a camera with him, and did take a widely distributed photo of one of the victims being rushed from the scene on a gurney. But as he was about to round the corner of the school to where the shootings had taken place, he encountered a police officer who said, "You don't need to be around there."
>
> Hodges said he told the officer he wasn't going to take photographs. "I know it," the officer said, "but it's really bad, and I would really appreciate it if you wouldn't go back there." Hodges obeyed. Did he consider disregarding the officer so he could see, and maybe photograph, the victims and the blood? "No, I didn't. I might have if I worked different, but I never have worked that way."   (1998:5)

The Red Cross

At nearly every accident scene and in the unfolding of a disaster, such as a hurricane or earthquake, you will encounter people from the American Red Cross and its local chapters. The Red Cross has a congressional mandate "to provide prompt services to disaster victims to meet their disaster-caused basic human needs and to assist disaster victims without resources to begin and complete their disaster recovery efforts." Although the language refers to disasters, you will often find the Red Cross helping a family whose home has burned. The organization provides free shelter, food, first aid, mental health assistance, and comfort to victims and disaster workers. When recovery begins, the Red Cross can provide the means to buy food, clothing, shelter, furnishings, medical services, funeral services, and some supplies needed for work. Such support may continue for months.

After TWA flight 800 exploded near New York City in 1996, the Red Cross agreed to coordinate some services previously managed by airlines and other corporations involved in such crashes. Since the TWA 800 accident, the Red Cross has coordinated mental health and public affairs efforts at accident scenes, in addition to its relief and recovery efforts.

As the event unfolds, you are increasingly likely to be working with a volunteer who works on the Red Cross rapid response public affairs teams. After the first day reporters covering the Oklahoma City bombing talked with family members of victims through Red Cross team members. The Red Cross asked family members to volunteer for the press interviews; as reporters in small groups talked with the family members, Red Cross personnel stood by to assist. Beforehand, they had coached the families on the voluntary nature of the interviews and reminded them that they could end the sessions if they felt the need to do so. Unlike many accident scenes, National Guard troops limited the movement of the reporters, keeping them together near a church where family members were gathered. After TWA flight 800 exploded, family members stayed in a hotel where their privacy was guarded. When family members were willing to talk to the media, Red Cross volunteers assisted them.

The public affairs teams generally get high marks from journalists. Members are experienced professional people working both inside and outside the Red Cross. When they are on alert, they have their bags packed so they can be on a plane to the scene within four hours of a call. They often are the principal intermediaries between the press and those most affected. They are not sources of official information about an accident or disaster, but they often provide invaluable support to journalists. When a network television crew needed to have a live story about floods near Houston, Texas, on the air at 7 A.M. in the East, the Red Cross found high school students who wanted to help and a homeowner who literally needed mud shoveled out of his house. All were in place by 4:30 A.M. for the 6 A.M. transmission.

Informal Controls

As police, military, and other agencies gradually bring the chaotic nature of information about what happened under control, reporters and photographers may encounter unofficial but important efforts to limit access. After a school shooting in Springfield, Oregon, in 1998 students and the high school staff created a buffer zone for their grieving. Media personnel were told to respect that claim of privacy. The action was similar to that taken in Dunblane, Scotland, after the killing of several students at a school there. After an initial frenzy of reporting from Dunblane, the community acted to separate its children from the media. After a seven-hour siege at a Melbourne, Australia, preschool in 1989, four wounded children were taken to the nearby Royal Children's Hospital. To meet reporters' demands for details about injuries and treatment, the hospital staff convened a press conference the next morning. The staff gave reporters information about the injuries and educated them about trauma and the recovery process for children, including how the children might react to the many strange experiences they were confronting. Challenged by hospital personnel to choose between staying away from the children and their families and increasing the likelihood of trauma, all media representatives chose to stay away and adhered to that decision even through later legal proceedings.

When deaths occur, funeral homes and family representatives may seek to limit the media presence. Although these actions often keep the press at a distance from funeral ceremonies, family gatherings, and grieving, we know of many print and broadcast reporters who, against the wishes of survivors, gained access to morgues, funerals and burials, and family gatherings. There is no simple answer to this. We think the best approach for the news media is to plan coverage of funerals and memorial ceremonies with the survivors and their representatives. No good will follow a reporter's intrusion into a private viewing of a body or electronic eavesdropping on a grieving family. Funerals, on the other hand, are often intended for the community as well as the family and offer opportunities for collective recognition of the people who died and of the value of their lives. After the shootings in Jonesboro, the local newspaper, the *Jonesboro Sun,* devoted long stories to the funerals of the girls killed at the school, including the minister's remarks and photos of mourners. When eight thousand residents attended the Service for Hope and Healing several days after the shootings, the newspaper reported on the music, the tributes, the videotaped comments of President Clinton, and details about the mourners. The Freedom Forum report added, "The stories are written in ways that reflect the power and emotion of the evening while avoiding maudlin language" (1998:20). Camera and sound technology allow photographers and television cameras to work some distance from the people gathered at a funeral or a gravesite. Even so, it is easy to underestimate the sense of intrusion funeral participants may feel when they see a swarm of media people with their equipment.

People Affected by the Event and the Media

Chapter 4 addresses ways to interview people at the scene who have been directly affected by the event. Here we urge you to remember that the people you are likely to encounter at the scene are responding both physically and emotionally to a startling event. Some will be on a kind of high alert that may enable some to act heroically and others to persevere at horrifying work. If you could give them physical tests, you might find a rapid pulse and an increased blood volume in the heart. If you asked questions moments after an event, you might find some details reported with crystal clarity while others were greatly distorted. As time passes, both victims and rescue workers begin to adapt to the prolonged anxiety they must endure. They become accustomed to the increased flow of adrenaline and think more critically about what they heretofore grasped automatically. At this time you may also see acts of heroism and sacrifice. People readily help each other, managing to balance hope and exhilaration with their fear and grief. To some degree this description will fit you and other journalists at the scene.

Such conditions are often present in tumultuous situations that have come to be called media feeding frenzies. Reporters drive for every fact, face, and facet of the scene, unaware that they manifest some of the same psychological signs as those they are trying to photograph or interview. As the numbers of reporters and cameras multiply, a common occurrence at violent events, the frenzy grows—those in it feed off the emotional highs of others. Each reporter wants a unique piece of the story. Consider what children and parents encountered at the school the evening of the day of the shootings in Jonesboro. Satellite vans for the television reporters lined nearby streets. "When a child and a family would get out of the car to come to the gymnasium (for counseling), there'd be cameramen and people . . . shoving [microphones] in their faces," a social worker told the Freedom Forum (1998:35). Helicopters hired by television stations from Memphis and Little Rock were circling the school grounds. While some television reporters refrained from sticking a camera in the faces of children, others did not. Parents and children approached reporters, ready to tell their version of events.

At 10 P.M. on the day of the shooting, a counselor leaving the school noticed that the press had separated parents from children and one reporter was plying a little boy with questions. "I understand that that's their job, and he [the reporter] was doing what he needed to do, but he wasn't taking into account that this child had no parents there. The little boy was very scared and didn't know what was going on. They were asking him his phone number and where he lived" (Freedom Forum 1998:8). At a nearby candlelight prayer vigil for the victims, television camera operators stood in the middle of the prayer circle photographing the faces of those present, including children. Whether such zeal reflects competitive tenacity, an emotional rush, or insensitivity to others is not clear. In any case the action intrudes on those who are attempting to recover from the event.

While those most affected by the event and bystanders are often receptive to being interviewed or photographed soon afterward, you must balance what you gain against the harm that you may do. Find the details and information that help you tell the story and place it in context. Suffering is an arresting facet of such scenes, but it does not tell the full story. Jane Harrigan, a former editor and AP reporter who now teaches at the University of New Hampshire, happened to be in Kobe, Japan, when the earth shook on January 17, 1995. She later wrote,

> Journalists who cover disasters need to remember one crucial fact: The survivors aren't thinking straight. They ricochet constantly from hysterical elation at being alive to abject fear of imminent doom. These mood swings don't leave a lot of brain cells free for remembering the basic tenets of journalism. So treat disaster survivors gently. Inquire after their well being. Listen to their responses. Explain what you're doing and what you hope they can contribute. Ask specific questions, and give them time to organize their jumbled thoughts. You may be rewarded with a quote that, unlike most of what's reported from disaster scenes, is actually worth printing or broadcasting. And if you get a quote, quote it correctly. (1997:46)

Avoiding Damaging Clichés

People who work in accident and disaster relief have been heard to say that some reporters they have met could have informed their audiences just as poorly if they had remained in their newsroom. Their sarcasm about journalists and their reports from the scene is real. Consider some of the examples they offer.

After the 1989 Loma Prieta earthquake a news report carried a northern California shelter manager's response to a question about what was in short supply. "We're always running out of disposable diapers," he said, not mentioning that the diaper supply was replenished every morning. Within twenty-four hours trucks filled with diapers began to arrive at the shelter, occupying space, requiring attention, and frustrating relief efforts. Although the shelter manager might have been more careful, the reporter who passed on the comment should have understood that requests for specific items often have devastating results.

Hope Tuttle, the Red Cross Disaster Response Team member, offers a compelling example of a reporter's bad judgment:

> In Hurricane Andrew, CNN flew a reporter and satellite broadcasting equipment by helicopter to Homestead, Florida, the hardest hit town, right after the storm passed. The reporter interviewed people who had broken into a school for shelter. They had no food. The media presence fed the emotions of the people being interviewed. Their angry accusation that their plight was being ignored was shown across the country.

The reporter didn't explain that the people had been ordered to evacuate before the hurricane hit. They had broken the law by staying there. Shelters were not set up in Homestead because of the potential for significant damage. Because of the likelihood of damage from hurricanes, Florida residents are advised to have three days' supply of food and water. This group did not.

No matter. The story inspired thousands of people to try to take food, clothing, blankets, and jugs of water to the victims at Homestead. Because of the traffic jams, emergency response feeding vans that provide hot meals could not get into the area. The Red Cross could only send in military MREs (meals ready to eat) by military helicopter.

Media across the country want to be helpful, so they collect things. They then pay to have the goods transported to the scene. They don't think that the same thing is being done in thousands of cities across the country. You can't imagine this until you've seen a football field ten feet deep with unneeded and unwanted items being bulldozed under in southern Florida. There had been no storage available, it had rained, and then the heat had rotted the supplies.

Outside the prime area of impact, most stores and businesses were open and needing business. Most supplies could be bought locally. Yet people paid a lot of money to transport unneeded things across the country. As the trucks arrived, they completely overwhelmed the recovery system. Items had to be sorted, sized, and often cleaned, but relief agencies were too busy providing essential services. Many items were ludicrously inappropriate. Thousands of heavy wool blankets arrived in southern Florida.

Tuttle's story suggests one of the frequent misleading clichés of "at the scene" reporting. Reporters easily find people who are angry, grief stricken, or appear to be in shock—all signs of the emotional turmoil wrought by the event. Without context, quick visual impressions of such people can create a compelling but false sense of the mood and resilience of those being interviewed. In Seattle an apartment manager angrily complained to the media that undeserving people had crashed food lines after a five-alarm fire had displaced several hundred people from her building. Viewers' blood might have boiled at the callous insensitivity of those people. In that case a reporter did some checking before the story was broadcast; the so-called line crashers were people who had been ordered to evacuate homes threatened by the apartment blaze. The station did not use the interview, and the apartment manager later apologized for her remarks, Tuttle told us. Angry people sometimes capture the essence of a scene, but just as often their emotion needs to be checked and explained. Grieving people also trigger emotional responses in viewers and readers, yet sometimes such examples eclipse stories of aid and relief. People who appear too stunned to even speak may help a reporter show that everybody at the scene is "in shock." Some of those people "in shock" recover from their weariness moments later and return to their duties. The shock cliché occurs often in news reports. Yet relief workers and disaster researchers say that those stunned survivors, far from being incapacitated, generally get the relief and cleanup efforts going well before relief agencies actually arrive.

Such clichés as the shocked survivor are part of what disaster specialists have come to call disaster mythology. Henry W. Fischer III, a sociologist, offers this version of the mythology based on numerous studies in sociology, anthropology, psychology, and other fields:

> Most of us assume that individuals cease to act in a predictable, orderly fashion. . . . They are expected to flee in panic, suffer from psychological dependency and disaster shock. It is often believed that evacuation of these people must not be called too soon for fear of causing massive flight behavior. It is believed that shelters overflow beyond capacity with organizers unable to deal with the mob mentality. Both survivors and those converging to the scene are believed to be driven by base, depraved instincts. These individuals are commonly perceived as likely to loot property, price gouge one another, and generally behave in other selfish ways—most of which are imagined to spread from individual to individual in a contagious fashion. (1994:11–12)

These behaviors are myths precisely because actual experience contradicts them. Reporters at the scene can avoid perpetuating the myths by describing and carefully considering only what they see. Scanlon's critique of journalism textbooks notes the frequent exhortations to budding reporters to look for examples of panic at the scene. Scanlon comments, "In fact, panic is so rare it is almost impossible to study. During the crowd rush at Hillsborough soccer stadium [in Liverpool, England, 1989], those who died did so while helping others over the fence that stopped spectators from going onto the field. Similarly, at the Beverly Hills Supper Club fire in Kentucky [1977], many victims helped each other even at the cost of their own lives" (1998:49). Studies of other high-fatality fires have recognized that those who died had tried but failed to find an escape route. Rather than being irrational and panicked, the victims' last efforts were logical and focused, if desperate and finally futile.

Other parts of the disaster mythology similarly fall apart when subjected to close scrutiny. Fischer's study of media coverage of Hurricane Gilbert, which struck the south Texas gulf coast in September 1988, showed this in detail. He and an associate studied both broadcast and print media in the region, interviewed journalists and local officials, and observed behavior during the hurricane (1994:38–71). The study credited the media with accuracy in reporting rational preparation for the storm while perpetuating such myths as looting, price gouging, and panic. Reporters exaggerated evacuation rates and shelter populations. The researchers noted greater accuracy in the local broadcast media than in network television. After interviewing a number of reporters for both print and electronic media, Fischer speculated that some exaggeration was the result of the journalists' own belief in the elements of disaster mythology (1994:69).

E. L. Quarantelli, a student of the reporting of accidents and disasters, offers these conclusions based on numerous published studies of the behavior of people under extreme stress:

> They seldom engage in antisocial or criminal behavior such as looting. Similarly, on the whole victims neither go "crazy" nor psychologically break down, nor do they manifest severe mental health problems as a result of disasters. Those officials and others with community responsibilities do not abandon their work roles to favor their family roles. In the aftermath of the disaster impact, survivors do not passively wait for outside assistance, but actively initiate the first search-and-rescue efforts, taking the injured to medical care and doing whatever can be done in the crisis. Mass shelters are avoided. Those forced out of their homes go overwhelmingly to places offered by relatives and friends. (1989:6)

Although victims are often unfairly reported as irrational, Quarantelli notes that the relief agencies are generally portrayed—equally unfairly—as more rational and better organized than they are (1989:7). Journalists seem eager to show that emergency agencies have accomplished a good deal; the weight of research suggests that the convergence of relief and emergency agencies at the scene may complicate, rather than ease, the suffering. In the 1995 Kobe, Japan, earthquake, authorities failed to restrict highways to official use, leading to delay in the arrival of police and fire vehicles. Officials also were slow to ask for support from the armed forces. Similar complaints arose in regard to the official response in Turkey after the first devastating earthquake in 1999. A reporter ought to be looking in a fair but critical way at the overall management of the scene rather than seeking to convince the audience that whatever agencies responded have matters firmly in hand.

Invoking the myths of accidents and disasters will weaken your reporting. An equally serious problem in reporting on events that are not natural disasters is the pressure you will experience from editors and other media to find an explanation. James Carey, a commentator on the character of American journalism, writes: "How and why are the most problematic aspects of American journalism: the dark continent and invisible landscape. Why and how are what we most want to get out of a news story and are least likely to receive or what we must in most cases supply ourselves" (1987:149). Carey says that journalists faced with an unexplained event will try to attribute it to some rational motive: "If journalists cannot find a rational motive, they have to bring in psychiatrists, psychologists, sociologists, and other experts on national character and the behavior of strange people to provide an irrational one" (188–89).

Carey's analysis was exemplified by a series of shootings in schools in several states in the winter and spring of 1998 and in 1999. When boys killed other students, reporters vied for such instant explanations as racism or gender difference. Some reporters focused on troubles between the shooter and his parents, while others tried to show that a "gun culture" led to their actions. Other media, eschewing a ready cause, made their stories fit the "believe it or not" formula—the shootings happened in small towns where such things just do not happen.

After the Jonesboro shootings in 1998, all three national newsmagazines—*Time, Newsweek* and *U.S. News & World Report*—emphasized the gun-culture explanation. *Time* and *Newsweek* ran cover photographs of one of the suspects holding a firearm. Although some accounts disavowed the explanation or noted the anger of Jonesboro residents about repetition of the theme, network coverage reinforced the idea. A CNN correspondent, speaking about the funerals, speculated that mourners were wondering whether the familiarity of youngsters with guns "may have had something to do with this" (Freedom Forum 1998:25). While some details about the boys' use and knowledge of guns were relevant, these quickly became the single answer or explanation that eclipsed other possibilities. A year later, in Littleton, Colorado, the media looked for the "why" in evidence of enmity between athletes and other students.

What Is Missing

When authorities predict a natural disaster is about to occur, the reporter's most urgent responsibility is to accurately report the warnings that may help people protect themselves or move to safer locations. Yet one study of residents of Galveston, Texas, a city on the gulf coast that frequently suffers hurricanes, found that only 10 percent of the population always flees the area when a hurricane is announced, while twice as many prepare to stay through the storm. The remaining residents monitor the news and listen to what other people are saying as they decide what to do. As John Ledingham and Lynne Masel Walters have observed, "If they [official warnings] prompt evacuation and a storm does not materialize, the impact of those warnings may be lessened when a new threat arises. Conversely, failure to unite in a call for evacuation may leave residents confused as to appropriate response, which could result in many injuries and fatalities if the storm actually hits" (1989:44). Their research is a reminder that warnings, whether crystal clear or ambiguous, are taken into account by people who also listen to friends, relatives, and coworkers and who apply their own experience with hurricanes when they make their final decision. The simplistic lead that says that "residents are fleeing" or "residents are staying" does not do justice to most situations.

When you cover an accident, you may not be around survivors and those directly affected long enough to notice changes in their emotional responses. If you stay at the scene of a disaster, you may notice what one experienced disaster worker calls the "heroic," "honeymoon," "disillusionment," and "reconstruction" phases. Hope Tuttle says that in the heroic phase people come together to help each other. Responders may be victims, but they are all pulling together. The heroic phase lasts through the immediate response, rescues, aid, and cleanup. "Reality has not set in," Tuttle says. Often, within a week the honeymoon phase begins as people take care of basic needs for food, shelter, and safety. It is a honeymoon, she says, because people have unrealistic expectations about how long recovery may take and how difficult it will be: "They see progress and assume it will continue quickly. Victims deny that they have emotional needs as well as physical needs."

In the disillusionment phase, which may last a year or longer, survivors discover the frustration of dealing with recovery agencies and the government, get irritated at how slowly repair and rebuilding actually occur, and become weary of the long recovery process. "Anger is common, and whoever is standing there is likely to be the target of that anger," Tuttle told us. In the reconstruction phase, long after the event, survivors can see their progress and find comfort in a return to conditions as they knew them before the disaster. And even as life becomes more comfortable and predictable, symptoms of the initial traumatic experience may appear.

Tuttle's observations are packed with relevance for journalists. Continue to monitor as many parts of the affected region as possible. You can contribute to the recovery of those affected by seeing the story as an evolving one, continually changing to reflect new efforts and new consequences for those affected by the event. People at the center of disasters often direct their anger at the media for abandoning their story of recovery. Floods and heavy rains devastated western Washington State in December 1996 and January 1997. The floods, mud slides, and building collapses were, of course, widely reported in the media. A month later, though, a major bridge remained closed, people throughout the region were struggling to get homes and businesses back to normal, and recovery workers still were meeting with affected families. Aside from occasional brief updates, the local media were no longer paying attention to the story; recovery was not news.

On your own and in your newsroom plan how to cover major accidents and disasters. Know what to do—and not do—in the first minutes and hours after you hear the sirens or calls on the police scanner. Remember that the sooner you reach the scene, the more options you will have for taking photographs and talking to injured and startled people. You can decide in advance not to photograph injured people and the bodies of victims. Although you may find people at the scene willing to talk to you and to be photographed, the "scene" of the story will rapidly shift to other locations, places where critical information may be available. Excess attention to victims and bystanders may detract from accurate and thorough coverage of the event. In disasters—events that threaten to destroy a community's capacity to continue—numerous scenes need coverage; you will need to inform the assignment editors of what and where these venues are, so they can send reporters or redirect your efforts. Finally, remember that those most affected by the event, including rescuers, public safety workers, and relief volunteers, will encounter a period when their energy wanes, when they become disillusioned about their efforts. We believe that continuing to report through all the stages of a disaster will provide an important service to that community.

Rick Bragg:

Uncovering What's Already There

"I can do just one thing well," says Rick Bragg, a Miami-based reporter on the national staff of the *New York Times*. "I can write about people who are hurting." That's about the only praise this Pulitzer Prize–winning reporter will allow himself. He is more comfortable talking up someone else, like another reporter's "remarkable work" or the "gracious, thoughtful" woman whose husband was killed in the Oklahoma City bombing.

Bragg is known for his gripping leads—many in the business can recite one or more from memory—and for the way in which he covers traumatic events. Instead of sensationalizing, he focuses on the small and ordinary, and in describing the details of normal life he somehow makes the horror

Rick Bragg. PHOTO BY JEFFREY CANTRELL.

more immediate and real. Bragg deflects these compliments in the plainest terms: "I would love to pretend I know what I'm doing. The truth is, I'm scared to death every time I do one of these stories."

Despite his fear (or perhaps because of it), Bragg arrives at the scene of a tragedy attuned to seemingly extraneous details: notices pinned on bulletin boards, the names of restaurants and stores, signs announcing local events. He does not so much enter the scene as circle it. According to Bragg, this is no studied journalistic technique. "I usually get lost," he says. But in getting found he keeps his eyes open to what surrounds a neighborhood, a town, a city—what ultimately gives him a sense of its spirit and place.

This departure from pack journalism results in stories that connect readers with the community he writes about rather than distancing them from it. When, for example, many reporters jumped on the "gun culture" to explain the Jonesboro, Arkansas, school shootings in which four children and a teacher were killed by two boys, Bragg described the town as it was *before* the event. To reduce an entire community with the gun culture label was, in his opinion, "a slap—these people were *suffering*. I tried *not* to write the easy story."

Bragg acknowledges that his "old-fashioned" southern politeness probably helps him get close to people. But talking to victims is always difficult: "Never—not one time—have I not dreaded the contact." When approaching someone after a traumatic incident, "I just start apologizing. I introduce myself and then I say, 'I'm sorry for your loss.' You say this because you are, you better be, or you don't belong there. And then I ask, 'Is there anything you can tell me about the person you lost? I want to put a human face on this tragedy—can you help me?'" Some people back away, his cue to step back himself. "I've never chased anyone with a microphone," he says. "I never call a second time."

In interviewing, Bragg tries not to cause more pain. "People are generally unhappy with our presence," he says of reporters. What reassures him, in part, is the knowledge that he is not really asking anyone to talk about something that is not on their mind already. And just as he circles around the scene of the tragedy, so he circles back with the survivor, to a time when the dead person was alive, the injured life whole. Predictably, the friend or relative describes the loved one in positive ways—"Death brushes away the burrs," Bragg notes. But humans are not saints, and he draws out the humanity by asking about quirks as well as accomplishments and joys. The person fills out and becomes real.

Bragg began his reporting life by covering sports, where he learned to use details to make stories come alive. But he did not, he concedes, show his empathy for victims that early. "We always wrote about [stock car races] the same way, those stories," Bragg explains in his memoir, *All Over but the Shoutin'*. "In the third or fourth paragraph would be, 'The race was overshadowed by the death of (insert name here).' I didn't know any better. I should have done better. I should have written, in the first paragraph: 'A man died here today, and a race was won'" (1997:139). It was in the first story he wrote as a news reporter, about deer hunters killing each other by accident, that he experienced that "odd mixed emotion, of pride in the work . . . and of that terrible sadness that the words contained" (140).

This ability to acknowledge the reality of emotion in news coverage is something Bragg attributes to his childhood, growing up "poor as dirt" in rural Alabama, with two brothers, a violent alcoholic father, and a mother who, despite repeated humiliations and suffering, never gave up on her children. To this day she is the hero of his life. "Because of her, I could understand the pain and the sadness of the people I wrote about, and could make others feel it," he wrote in his memoir (318).

Bragg is reluctant to advise others. Instead, he offers his own mistakes. The tone that wasn't "right" in his piece on the killing of a black man in Jasper, Texas, how he "failed miserably" to get any real insights. His difficulty in general with writing about accused killers: "Everyone wants to know *why*, but we really don't know—or maybe I'm just not smart enough." How he was duped by the young woman who had killed her children in Union, South Carolina, when he should have questioned her story about a carjacker as even his own mother did: "I dropped the ball. I was dumb." And probably his biggest regret—talking "coldheartedly" over dinner with other reporters in Oklahoma City while covering the bombing, within earshot of a woman who had lost her baby in the blast. He apologized to her.

"You can make incredible mistakes by clumsiness," he says, "but every now and then we help a little. The nicest thing is when you do the story and the person calls and says thank you." Yet even in this he won't take the credit. "In writing about sad things, it's only natural to write with feeling." Reporters are just outside observers, Bragg wrote: "All you do is uncover the dignity, the feeling, that is already there" (182).

Rick Bragg

Piedmont Journal: Tried by Deadly Tornado, An Anchor of Faith Holds

This feature about people who lost friends and family members in a tornado in north-eastern Alabama shows Bragg's ability to find in survivors the strength that was there before the trauma. In his memoir, All Over but the Shoutin', he describes serving as rewrite in New York City when the first account of deadly tornadoes that swept across the Southeast came in from the Associated Press. He knew the place and the people, and the next day he flew to Atlanta, rented a car, and drove into Alabama. He explains, "I wrote the story over two days. It was important to me that it be good, I guess because I wanted people there to think well of me, but also because it was my responsibility. I was one of them. Nothing that had ever happened, over all the years I had been away, had changed that" (1997:246). The story was published in the New York Times on Sunday, April 3, 1994.

PIEDMONT, Ala., April 2—This is a place where grandmothers hold babies on their laps under the stars and whisper in their ears that the lights in the sky are holes in the floor of heaven. This is a place where the song "Jesus Loves Me" has rocked generations to sleep, and heaven is not a concept, but a destination.

Yet in this place where many things, even storms, are viewed as God's will, people strong in their faith and their children have died in, of all places, a church.

"We are trained from birth not to question God," said 23-year-old Robyn Tucker King of Piedmont, where 20 people, including six children, were killed when a tornado tore through the Goshen United Methodist Church on Palm Sunday.

"But why?" she said. "Why a church? Why those little children? Why? Why? Why?"

The destruction of this little country church and the deaths, including the pastor's vivacious 4-year-old daughter, have shaken the faith of many people who live in this deeply religious corner of Alabama, about 80 miles northeast of Birmingham.

It is not that it has turned them against God. But it has hurt them in a place usually safe from hurt, like a bruise on the soul.

They saw friends and family crushed in what they believed to be the safest place on earth, then carried away on makeshift stretchers of splintered church pews. They saw two other nearby churches destroyed, those congregations somehow spared while funerals for Goshen went on all week and the obituaries filled an entire page in the local paper.

But more troubling than anything, said the people who lost friends and family in the Goshen church, were the tiny patent-leather children's shoes scattered in the ruin. They were new Easter shoes, bought especially for church.

"If that don't shake your faith," said Michael Spears, who works at Lively's Food Market in downtown Piedmont, "nothing will."

The minister of the Goshen church, the Rev. Kelly Clem, her face covered with bruises from the fallen roof, buried her daughter Hannah on Wednesday. Of all people, she understands how hurtful it is to have the walls of the church broken down.

"This might shake people's faith for a long time," said Mrs. Clem, who led a congregation of 140 on the day of the storm. "I think that is normal. But having your faith shaken is not the same as losing it."

Ministers here believe that the churches will be more crowded than usual on Easter Sunday. Some will come for blessings, but others expect an answer.

Mrs. Clem and her husband, Dale, who is also a minister, do not believe God sent the storm that killed their daughter and 40 other people across the Southeast in a few short hours that day. The Clems make a distinction between God's laws and the laws of nature, something theologians have debated for years: what does God control, and not control?

The people here know only that they have always trusted in the kindness and mercy of God and that their neighbors died in His house while praising His name. It only strengthens the faith in some people, who believe that those who die inside any church will find the gates of heaven wide open.

Others are confused. Beyond the sadness and pain is a feeling of something lost, maybe forever.

"It was church," said Jerri Kernes, delivering flowers to a funeral home where the dead and their families filled every room.

"It isn't supposed to happen in church."

The blooming dogwood trees stand out like lace in the dark pine barrens in the hills around Piedmont. The landscape is pastoral, mountain ridges and rolling hills divided by pastures of fat cows and red-clay fields that will soon be high cotton and sweet corn.

The people, the children of farmers, mill workers, carpenters and steelworkers, now make tires at the Goodyear plant in Gadsden, spin yarn at the cotton mill and process poultry for Tyson Foods Inc., which is known here as just the chicken plant.

Yet, Piedmont, population 5,200, depending on who is home, exists in the failed economic promise of the New South. The roof on the empty brickyard has rusted through, and the pretty little train station on the Selma, Rome & Dalton line is just for show. The cotton mill just had a new round of layoffs.

As economic uncertainty grows, the people go to the altar for hope, said Vera Stewart, Piedmont's 70-year-old Mayor. Piedmont, after all, has two doctors' offices but 20 churches.

"As long as we have our faith, we are as strong as our faith," Mrs. Stewart said. "Because no matter how dark it is, if I have faith, I have a song in the night."

But in the long days since last Sunday, when the sky opened, she, too, has felt that belief tremble.

What all the troubles of the everyday failed to do, one sudden, violent moment did.

Tornadoes snapped 200-year-old trees and ruined houses and lives in five states. Goshen was the centerpiece of an agony shared by Spring Garden, Rock Run, Possum Trot, Bennefield's Gap, Knighten's Crossroad and Webster's Chapel. At Mount Gilead Church, about 10 miles from Goshen, the wind pulled tombstones from the earth and smashed them.

People here are accustomed to the damage that the winds do, but what happened at the Goshen church last Sunday was off the scale of their experience. Rescue workers found neighbors limp and broken on the ground, and strong men sobbed like babies in the arms of other men when the last of the living and dead had been dug from the rubble.

In a makeshift morgue in the National Guard Armory, one volunteer wiped the faces of the dead children before zipping up the body bags. The bags were too long, and had to be rolled up from the bottom.

But in the days after, the shock started to wear off, and the pride took hold again. So, when the truckloads of donated food and clothes arrived, some of the needy refused aid because they did not earn it with their own sweat.

Sam Goss runs a filling station, and believes in heaven the same way he believes that walking in the Coosa River will get him wet.

Mr. Goss, 49, stood in a line 50 yards long to pay respects to the dead at the town's largest funeral home. He smoked a cigarette, cried and talked of going to Glory.

He was a friend of Derek Watson, who died with his wife, Glenda Kay, and their 18-year-old daughter, Jessica. Mr. Goss said Derek, who worked at the Super Valu, had not planned to go to church that day but changed his mind.

"Maybe that's what people mean when they say God works in mysterious ways," Mr. Goss said. "I know the boy. He could not have lived if his wife and child were gone."

It is the same reason, he said, that God took Ruth Peek, 64, and Cicero Peek, 72.

"It's hard not to question God in this," he said. "But they say there ain't no tears in heaven. We're the ones left to hurt. You see, God took them because he knew they were ready to go. He's just giving all the rest of us a second chance."

The first step toward healing might have been in a funeral processional for a child.

In life, 4-year-old Hannah Clem had been a dancer and painter and singer.

In death she has become a focus of the question why.

For three days Kelly and Dale Clem worked for their friends and parishioners and swallowed their own pain, gracious and strong. They did not shake their fist at heaven, but told Vice President Al Gore that a better storm warning might have saved lives.

It was wind and not God, they said, that killed their daughter.

"My God is a God of hope," Mr. Clem said. "It is never his will for anyone to die."

It is a departure from the Christian mainstream belief that God controls all. But then so is Mrs. Clem herself, a female minister with a growing congregation in a small town in the Deep South.

On Wednesday, she followed Hannah's tiny white and pink casket up the aisle at the First United Methodist Church in Anniston, 20 miles from Goshen. Members of her congregation and old friends filled the church.

"People have asked, why did it happen in a church," said the Rev. Bobby Green, in his service. "There is no reason. Our faith is not determined by reason. Our faith is undergirded by belief, when there is no reason."

In the Bible, Palm Sunday is a day of destruction, not hope, he said. Hope comes later, on Easter Sunday.

The 400 mourners stood and said the Lord's Prayer. Then, Hannah's coffin was moved slowly back down the aisle to the hearse. The organist played "Jesus Loves Me."

Chapter 4

The Interview: Assault or Catharsis?

We read newspaper interviews with people caught up in traumatic events and watch them tell their stories on television. The interview is an old fixture in news, used for at least 150 years. In the beginning the interview offered a way for leading figures of the day—politicians, church leaders, and explorers—to offer their stories. Horace Greeley's two-hour interview with Mormon leader Brigham Young in 1859 was among the first journalistic interviews conducted outside a prison and beyond the influence of a jailer or other public official. The novelty of direct access to celebrated people helped establish the interview as a newspaper staple. The interview evolved from the other innovation fostered by the penny press of the early nineteenth century—the reporter became a seeker of stories rather than a stenographer for speeches, sermons, and legislative debate.

By the end of the century the interview—once branded "a thing of ill savor in all decent nostrils"—was passing from a device as likely to be fraudulent as real to an essential tool of the journalist, a ready complement to the reporter's eyewitness account. In that transition common people joined celebrities as subjects of interviews, particularly if they were swept into suffering or loss by events such as fires, floods, earthquakes, and sensational crimes. The reporter could descend on any scene, ready both to observe its details and to question anyone in sight with a shred of information about what had happened. When Marguerite Higgins, then a correspondent for the *New York Herald-Tribune,* entered the newly liberated German concentration camp at Buchenwald in 1945, she was staggered by the sights of death and suffering but remembered some of the false atrocity stories blamed on

Germany in World War I. "So at the concentration camp I questioned and cross-questioned the miserable inmates with a relentless insistence on detail that must have seemed morbid," she later wrote (1955:74–75).

Today many news interviews are brief encounters with people who have no interest in the spotlight; they were simply in a bad place at a bad time. Some of these brief interviews provoke angry public reaction, whereas others simply feed our fascination with extraordinary experiences. Some people say they appreciated a reporter's questions at a time of crisis; others remain angry about such interviews long afterward.

The reporter's dilemma comes from this practical capacity to see and to ask questions and to incorporate both the images and the words into the final report. How do you strike the right balance between trusting your senses to help you describe accurately what is going on and calling on the words of others close at hand? When does it make sense to interview someone caught in the shock waves of a violent event, and when is it best to leave the person alone? Deciding whether any person will contribute substantially to the final report is not easy in the frenzy of a reporting assignment. In some cases an interview will cause further harm. If you cannot easily figure out whether an interview would cause harm—and that often is the case— the decision to interview ought to rest on a judgment the journalist can make: Is the person fully able to consent to an interview? If a thoughtful answer to that question is no, don't do the interview. The least defensible stand is that anyone at the scene is fair game for the journalist. This chapter discusses questions a journalist ought to ask before doing an interview. How you answer these questions will have a lot to do with your ability to meet a person affected by trauma, do a good interview, and report it so the public will benefit and the interviewee will not be hurt. Now is a better time to examine these questions and to make your decisions than that dicey moment when the city editor or the assignment editor points toward the door and tells you to get moving.

Is it necessary to immediately interview those who have suffered a traumatic event? What is the value of intruding on people when they are grieving, disoriented, shocked, and frightened? What should you discuss with someone before that person consents to an interview?

Few practices seem as contradictory as interviews of people in a crisis situation. On one hand, people carefully read the stories built on such interviews; on television, interviews with victims command audience attention.

People close to those involved are deeply affected by the event and follow any news about it closely. Strangers also eagerly consume reports about the victims and the violence. In the *Nation* Bruce Shapiro describes being stabbed while he was in a New Haven, Connecticut, coffee shop. Friends, neighbors, and strangers told him that they were shaken by what had happened. "The reaction of most was a combination of decent horrified empathy and a clear sense that their own presumption of safety was undermined," Shapiro writes (1995:448).

We believe the interview with a person caught in a violent event is a staple of news because it puts us in touch with the voice, face, and emotions of a person who is suffering. Life sometimes offers an unsettling array of threats and opportunities. The threats alarm us, but we gain some information about them from the mishaps of others. We learn about the risks in our lives from hearing about the misfortunes of others. In some cases we are curious in a healthy way about that victim—perhaps we have had a similar experience and can appreciate and understand what the other person is enduring. Our curiosity may come from a life sheltered from such grief or shock. In that case we hope to learn something about human experience. We want to know how likely we are to face personal threats, when and where they are most likely to occur, and what we should do if we are threatened. Our reasons for reading and watching are diverse and not so simple as a desire to be entertained by another person's misery.

Journalists and those in the audience understand that every story needs a "who," a person who will humanize the event, and stories about violence and victims of crime and disaster are no different. Violence stories let us read about and see relatively unknown people, people whose stories are not shaped by predictable formal roles such as business executive, politician, or expert. Herbert Gans, a sociologist, has shown that well-known people (politicians and celebrities, for example) outnumber "unknowns," such as victims in news stories, by a ratio of 4 to 1. One could argue that violence news is journalism's way of linking the public with ordinary people.

Why, then, are viewers and readers often upset by such interviews? Perhaps some of us fear that we are being voyeurs, inappropriately fascinated by witnessing another person in pain. Others worry that watching the pain of a person we do not know excuses us from any obligation or responsibility. We are at the center of a planet full of human beings, but usually only those closest to us make moral claims on us—family, friends, coworkers, and lovers. The suffering of those who are not in that inner circle reminds us that other moral obligations exist, yet those duties may not lead us to truly care about what we see on the evening news. Michael Ignatieff, a historian of moral ideas, writes that the brief unconnected television glimpses of victims in other lands "militate against the minimum moral requirements of engagement with another person's suffering: that one spends time with them, time to learn, to suffer with, to pierce the carapace of self-absorption and estrangement that separates us from the moral worlds of others" (1985:73).

Ignatieff had in mind the viewer and the victim, bound by images but separated by technology. The moral relationship of the victim and the reporter is quite different. They are connected by intimate communication—intimate because the reporter enters the victim's life at a moment of extraordinary stress. The reporter's duty to the public may well coincide with the needs of the victim, but the reporter cannot use that duty to excuse exploitation of victims for other reasons, such as better ratings or awards.

Let's look more closely at what reporter and victim bring to the interview—assumptions about the other person, her or his needs, and the skills that doing an effective interview requires. In the hours after a violent event a victim, survivor, or witness may want to help apprehend a violent person, stop a pattern of violence in a community, or simply give voice to the emotions aroused by the devastating fire, flood, or earthquake. Family members of victims may be eager to help police identify and arrest a perpetrator or get help for a relative left homeless by a natural disaster. And some people, because of their heightened awareness, will be ready to speak to anyone who is interested. You may find a willing interviewee who won't know whether talking to a reporter will be helpful or unsettling. A reporter's presence alone may persuade some victims and witnesses that they should ignore their discomfort in order to help the reporter. Others will act as though they have a duty to speak to the press.

As time passes, victims of violence may want to keep public attention focused on the crime, the search for suspects, pending legislation, or the needs of others. Some survivors will eagerly take on the role of public advocate, even seeking out journalists to give quotes or suggest story ideas. In contrast, some who have experienced physical or psychological wounds will react to stressful case developments, such as arrests, arraignments, trials, executions, or paroles, by avoiding contact with the media. Journalists should never view that other person in a simplistic or stereotypical way; his or her reactions to media attention will depend on many factors and may change frequently.

The journalist carries a heavy ethical burden into an interview. The press, the columnist Walter Lippmann wrote in the 1920s, "is like the beam of a searchlight that moves restlessly about, bringing one episode and then another out of darkness into vision." Lippmann argued that a moment of exposure to bright light is too little to inform us about our world. Seventy years later the news media still place the violent event in the spotlight briefly, usually with interviews of survivors and bystanders. Such news may offer a rich and complex idea of how an event affects a community: aid services; public safety responses; the workings of the criminal justice system; relief and recovery for victims, families, and friends; and how individuals cope with harm and violence. Often, though, the event is only a brief reminder of perils, and the interview yields too little about the person, the context of the event, or information about how we can deal with the perils.

Interviews also serve the need of the television station or the newspaper to attract and hold an audience. Mayhem not only leads but also often dominates the first several minutes of television news shows. A 1993 study of local news programs in California found that violence was the single most frequent story topic. Frequently, crime news takes up half or more of the time available for local news. Television audiences appear to be more likely to watch news programs that emphasize violence, an echo of what newspaper circulation managers learned back in the days when most newspapers were sold on the street—stories and photographs of crime scenes and survivors of violence draw an audience (Dorfman et al. 1997). Although crime rates have been declining in urban centers for some years, a number of studies of local television news affirm the industry's consistent penchant for news of crime and violence. In some months, the notorious "sweeps periods" (those in which audience ratings are used to set advertising rates), news teams search for the most bizarre and emotional subjects.

Newspaper reporters, working in the same web of public attention and curiosity as television reporters, cover the same stories and seek interviews with the same people. The visual elements of a violent event, such as a victim's physical response, a witness's story, and such objects as a charred building, a wrecked car, or a body bag, attract television news. In turn, newspaper reporters are certain to cover stories that people will remember from television. Crime and violence stories may make up a quarter or more of the locally generated stories in a newspaper.

However, the willingness of suffering people to talk to the news media does not give reporters a license to interview anyone right after a traumatic event. Reporters should not hesitate to decide that it is not a good time to interview a victim of violence, a child witness or friend, or a family member. We know effective reporters who observe the scene but stay away from those affected by the event. We know others who introduce themselves, perhaps offer a business card, and ask for a chance to talk sometime in the near future. Bruce Shapiro, the journalist who was a stabbing victim, thinks fondly of the newspaper reporter who arrived at the coffee shop just minutes after Shapiro and others were attacked. "Instead of trying to interview anyone, he saw that the incident was causing instant gridlock on the nearby streets and began directing traffic," Shapiro told us.

Each interview needs a deliberate judgment about the capacity of the other person to understand what an interview entails, including potential ramifications for the interviewee, family members, and friends. It is not enough that a person agrees to an interview. The ethical burden is not on the interview subject but on the journalist. We argue that doing the interview is not ethical unless the reporter has received what some journalists call "informed consent," a phrase they picked up from medicine.

A few journalism ethicists have argued that difficult interviews require that consent be based on detailed disclosure by the journalist. "Journalists have an obligation to disclose to their sources, at a minimum, the implications, advantages, and risks involved in agreeing to an interview," Sandra Borden writes (1993:222). Neal Shine, former publisher of the *Detroit Free Press*, proposes that victims be "read their rights," something like the Miranda warning police give suspects, and told that they don't have to do everything reporters ask. Frank Ochberg, the Michigan psychiatrist, suggests bringing up some of the harmful effects of doing the interview, something like: "Remembering, however, may be painful for you. And your name will be used. You might have some unwanted recollections after we talk and after the story appears. In the long run, telling your story to me should be a positive thing. Any questions before we begin?" Ochberg adds, "From an ethical point of view, you should afford your interviewee as much control as possible and as much foreknowledge as possible. You can do this by explaining your journalistic objective. For example, you might begin, 'I'm really interested in the facts of the robbery. I know this may be upsetting right after it happened, but I won't be reporting on how he made you feel'" (1996:24–25).

Some journalists oppose these suggestions. In their thinking the reporter ought to control the interview. Reporters have learned by trial and error how to get information from reluctant sources; they fear compromising an opportunity to elicit as much information as possible by using this form of negotiation with the victim or witness. In some interviews the information at stake is so important that it should not be compromised away by the reporter's good intentions. Some sources have eyewitness details to reveal or may turn out to be a suspect. We do not believe that gaining informed consent detracts in any way from what the reporter might pick up in the interview. It does, however, offer the journalist's subject useful knowledge about what an interview may entail.

Find out all you can—by careful listening—about the other person's readiness to talk to you. Does this person understand that revealing certain details in an interview may later be cause for regret? With an assailant at large does the person realize that comments offered in a moment of excitement may place people's lives at risk? Will revisiting a trauma reopen emotional wounds for the person or for others? Remember that in the course of an interview a person at first eager to talk may grow uncomfortable and frightened by what you discuss.

What should the interviewer think about before beginning an interview? What questions are helpful, and what questions are harmful?

A familiar definition of empathy is that it is the capacity to walk in someone else's shoes, to appreciate what the other person is enduring. An empathetic reporter need not have suffered in the same way as the person being interviewed. We define empathy as a way of thinking that enables us to get a better understanding of the feelings and experiences of another person. The more empathetic the journalist, we believe, the better the resulting story will be and the less likely it is to result in harm to another person. We believe that empathy is revealed in the work of journalists who encourage people to tell the story their way, who balance expert voices with the voices of those who were hurt, and who listen carefully when another person speaks honestly about what she or he has experienced.

The first step to an empathetic interview is preparation—as much as time will allow. In the few minutes it takes to reach your destination, you can prepare yourself in several important ways. Expect that many of the police, firefighters, and other trained emergency workers are savvy about interviews. Remind yourself, though, that many victims, witnesses, friends, and family members will not have the same degree of self-control, awareness of surroundings, knowledge of how a reporter works, and capacity to deal with new information. In the few moments he has before an interview, Seattle television reporter Jeff Gradney, whose profile follows this chapter, goes through a mental process that "puts me in the other person's shoes." The result, viewers and coworkers attest, often is an unusually respectful interview. The pages that follow are interspersed with guidelines for reporters who are interviewing people whose lives have been disrupted by a traumatic event.

In most types of stories the reporter's gender does not—or should not—matter much in terms of the openness of communication between reporter and subject. There usually is no reason a reporter cannot do a professional, ethical job in gathering information and writing stories, regardless of the gender of the source or writer.

But when the news scene turns to more personalized and traumatic stories, gender sometimes can be important. There usually is no time to consider gender when reporting breaking news about violence. If a serial rapist strikes again, the police reporter—man or woman—probably will do the story. If the reporter is male, however, he should be very wary of trying to directly approach a rape survivor.

Reporters—male or female—do not, thankfully, routinely knock on rape victims' doors. An interview may be appropriate occasionally, though, in special circumstances such as when police are seeking a serial rapist and a woman wants to encourage other victims to come forward. Another interview situation might be months or years after a rape when, for example, a victim talks about coping and recovery programs available in a community. Whatever the timing, think about how the survivor may react to a reporter.

"In the first few days afterward, I was very squirrelly around any men," says Memyo Lyons, a Michigan radio reporter and rape survivor. "That's unfair, but there it is." It would be better to have a woman interview a female rape survivor when what happened is "very fresh," says Lyons, now a television news assignment editor. For that matter, she believes it is wrong for a reporter, male or female, to approach a recent rape survivor without first telephoning. "If someone, anyone, had knocked at my door for an interview a day or two afterward, I'd have lost my mind. The phone is a critical link then." After months or years, Lyons says, whether the reporter is a man or woman does not really matter "as long as they're respectful."

Even when years have passed, some stories about sexual crimes may be difficult for men to cover. The three women in the "Malignant Memories" account of childhood incest (see the excerpt that follows chapter 7) say they would not have talked freely if the reporter and photographer had been men. Many details in the prize-winning story by Debra McKinney came from observing what the women were doing or saying while McKinney and photographer Fran Durner accompanied them to discussions and on trips.

Even so, time, patience, and mutual respect can bridge many gender-sensitive situations.

Respect the other person's efforts to regain balance after a horrible experience.

The man, woman, or child you face in an interview will someday be an expert on surviving a violent, devastating experience but probably does not yet know how to communicate that knowledge. It may be hard to appreciate what the victim is enduring or to understand exactly what he wants to say. Sometimes he won't be able to find the words he wants. You may be too busy asking questions to notice that he is having trouble answering. You may be persuaded that a coherent response means less than a response that shows confusion, anger, or grief. Your needs will command your energy, and you may overlook the other person's confusion and desire for privacy or support.

Offer as much support to the interviewee as conditions will allow. Suggesting that the interviewee ask a friend, neighbor, or relative to be present may reassure her and may help the two of you talk more usefully. This will be especially important if there are barriers to communication, such as different language skills, ages, genders, classes, and cultures. Give some thought to where you do the interview. Don't make her look at damaged vehicles, covered or uncovered bodies, and tense rescue workers while you talk. Find a place away from the activity of the scene and give her and her companion a chance to sit. Sit so that you can maintain eye contact as you talk; do not stand if the other person is sitting.

Watch what you say.

At this stage your words carry a lot of weight. They can lead the victim to seek promises from you, to exaggerate what you will be able to do, and to assume that you are willing to be a friend as well as a reporter. This is a difficult balancing act. You will be speaking to a person who needs support. In the case of notorious "death knock" interviews—the reporter knocks on the door of a survivor's house minutes after someone's death—the interview may be over before a person fully comprehends that a loved one has died. (We do not endorse such interviews, although they are commonplace in both print and electronic journalism.) By listening carefully, by keeping your line of questions close to what the person truly knows, and by not looking for past history or theories about why something happened, you will maintain trust without opening the way to unrealistic expectations. People who have suffered violence sometimes speak about reporters whose sincerity, body language, and obvious concern suggested empathy. Yet when they saw the videotape or read about themselves in condensed and tightly edited stories, they found avoidable errors in the facts, or failed to find their comments at all, and felt betrayed.

People at the scene will not be ready for what some reporters call their "con." Reporters quickly learn how to act fascinated with someone's story and how to build rapport through eye contact, facial expression, and body language. Some people they interview do not appreciate the extent to which the reporter's manner may be a professional pose. Unwary people also easily fall prey to reporters' tricks, such as knocking on the front door with a request to use a bathroom as a ploy to observe what is in the house or to cadge an interview with someone inside.

As soon as possible, let the other person know who you are, not just your name but that you are a reporter and the name of the publication or station you work for. You may have to repeat this information, but that is far easier than having to explain later how someone's confidences wound up in a newspaper article. A Michigan newspaper reporter said she had identified herself clearly to a man whose murdered child had been found. The next day, after her story was published, the man complained bitterly about some of the information; he did not remember that he had talked to the reporter. Forgetting such details goes with trauma, but the reporter could have mentioned her profession a second or even a third time.

Your manner and your first words will tell the other person whether he should trust you and how sincere you are. Those first impressions may decide whether you are ever again able to interview that person. If you are talking to someone who has just lost someone close to him, say you are sorry. Martin Symonds, a former deputy commissioner of the New York City Police Department who later became a therapist, says that at least one of three comments always will be appropriate: " 'I'm sorry this happened to you.' 'I'm glad you weren't killed.' 'It's not your fault'" (Ochberg 1987:12–13, 41).

The words "I'm sorry," spoken sincerely, can be reassuring and calming. The same words tossed off casually so that the reporter can start asking questions will leave a lasting negative impression. Do not try to announce your empathy by saying you know how the other person feels or by telling of one of your own ordeals. We often are tempted to bring up our own terrible experiences because we have just been reminded powerfully of them. We may want to share our hard-earned wisdom about the length and difficulty of recovery. By all means, keep those insights to yourself.

Respect the other person's need to focus on his circumstances. And avoid the question that drives some victims and survivors to distrust reporters: "How do you feel?" Marc Klaas, the father of Polly Klaas, who was kidnapped and murdered in California in 1993, says reporters never stopped asking the question from the time of the kidnapping through the trial of the murderer. " 'How do you feel?' Don't ask. I felt like shit. We feel awful and we'll probably always feel awful. Don't ask how we feel. Ask us what we need," he told a group of reporters and editors at a conference in Oklahoma. The question is used so often it is a painful cliché in newscasts. Reporters will swear they never use it until a close look at their tapes or stories shows that they have. On rare occasions, though, a thoughtful question about someone's feelings may open the way to a story that readers or viewers will understand and that will help the one who tells it.

Prepare yourself for the time when you will be the first person to announce a death to a survivor. Reporters often have run into a family member near an accident scene or appeared at a home for a "death knock" interview, only to find that family members have not been informed. An Ypsilanti, Michigan, reporter called the widow of a man killed in a traffic accident for facts about his life. "I want to express my sympathy," the reporter said. "About what?" the woman asked. The reporter, startled, awkwardly suggested the woman call the police. After that, the newspaper made it a policy to call the home of an accident victim only after the police had notified the family. A call to the local police (or another agency that handles notification of next of kin) would have helped another reporter, who invented a story on the spot when he learned that the woman he was interviewing was unaware of her husband's death. He told her that he was seeking details for a story about an award. Compare his relief at not having to bear the bad tidings with the hurt the woman must have felt when she read in the newspaper the details she had volunteered. And if your intent is not to reveal a victim's identity until police have notified the family, pay attention to details. A Seattle television reporter planted himself in front of an accident victim's highly visible law office sign to report his death and to say, evidently quite sincerely, that the name was being withheld until the family was notified. The lawyer's wife, who did not know that her husband had died, was watching the news.

Reporters may not anticipate that interview subjects sometimes view them as a source of information. People know that police may have given a reporter facts of which the victim is unaware and that a journalist sees or hears things that the interviewee is unaware of. In tense emotional situations an interview may turn into bargaining over information. What you say may have unintended consequences.

If an act of violence is involved, your story may well include information about how someone was killed or injured, about what might have led to the violent act, about the possibility of a pattern of such attacks, and so on. Questions about these matters should be directed to the police; such details may only harm the survivor if you bring them up during the interview. Avoid speculation about what caused someone's death. Family members often say they are plagued by mental images in which they try to imagine the moments before their loved one died. News stories that include such details often are troubling to survivors, and mentioning such details in an interview soon after a death can also cause them to suffer unwanted and unexpected images of the death scene.

Our advice is to give out any information that might help the person you are interviewing to get in touch with friends or family members and agencies such as the police and fire departments, American Red Cross, or medics. Think carefully about giving out details that have come to you secondhand. Generally, one or more public safety officers at the scene will provide essential information; that is rarely a reporter's role.

Set the stage for the interview.

Your first questions will provide you with two kinds of information. The first kind—details of the other person's knowledge of the situation—will help you begin to grasp what has happened. Ask a "when" question: When did you hear the news? When did the police arrive? When did you arrive? In a few seconds you may learn the sequence of events that involved the other person. Ask what other people have asked for information.

As you talk, you will be learning about the other person's capacity, or willingness, to talk to you. A question about an earlier interview may help a reporter determine whether and how to proceed with an interview. If the person has spoken with a public safety officer, you might simply ask, "How did that conversation go for you?"

Explain the ground rules.

This is the time to gain informed consent by identifying risks to the interview subject. It is also the time to help your source understand what you intend to do. The other person knows you are a reporter but has no idea what information you need, how you will use it, or how your story may affect her. The start of the interview is the best time to explain the ground rules. Explain why you are there, what kind of story you are expected to write or report, when it is likely to run, and why it is important for her to speak to you. Do not promise something you cannot guarantee; the comments you are about to write down or tape may never make it into print or on the air.

Share control with the interviewee.

Most seasoned reporters appear to be models of efficiency as they hurry among the police, emergency workers, and bystanders. They have a mission, know how to carry it out, and generally stay out of the way of others with urgent tasks. The person in trauma, on the other hand, has just lost control of his world. He doesn't fully understand what has happened, is subject to the orders and directions of others, and can do little to gain personal control over the chaotic situation.

Ask short open-ended questions. What have you learned? Who has spoken to you so far? How long have you been here? What happened? These questions carry no judgments and give the other person a chance to orient himself and the reporter to the event.

A person jolted by an event may need, and will certainly appreciate, a chance to decide some of the conditions of the interview. Would he like to sit or stand? Does he want to remain here or go somewhere away from the turmoil of the scene? Is there someone he would like to have present during the interview? Some reporters will insist that they cannot do an effective interview with a friend or relative of the victim looking on. But the interviewee will benefit by having a trusted person at hand and may give more thoughtful comments. In addition, he will be more likely to speak to you at another time because you offered such support in your first interview.

Anticipate emotional responses.

Frank Ochberg, the psychiatrist, offers this useful advice about dealing with emotional responses soon after a traumatic event:

As an interviewer, you can either elicit or avoid emotion. Most reporters would prefer to have their interviewees describe rather than display strong emotions (TV talk-show hosts excepted). So would I, in initial interviews with trauma survivors. It is not uncommon for tears to flow during the telling of an emotional event. Therapists offer tissues. Reporters should bring tissues if a tearful interview is anticipated. . . .

When survivors cry during interviews, they are not necessarily reluctant to continue. They may have difficulty communicating, but they often want to tell their stories. Interrupting them may be experienced as patronizing and denying an opportunity to testify. Remember, if you terminate an interview unilaterally, because you find it upsetting, or you incorrectly assume that your subject wants to stop, you may be re-victimizing the victim. (1996:24, 25)

Listen.

In reporting, as in most other activities, we are not well trained to listen to the other person. We hear what we want or need to hear and often screen out signals that we do not expect or do not understand. Good listening requires hearing not only the words that are spoken and making sense of them but also noticing gestures, facial expressions, emotions, and body language. Take the other person fully into account, then remember and make sense of what that person heard and saw. Ken Metzler, a journalism teacher who is an authority on journalistic listening, compares the best listeners and the worst listeners. The best, he says, use the time to think about what is being said, anticipate what will be said next, and listen "between the lines for ideas and attitudes hinted at but not expressed directly." The worst listeners, he says, wait for facts, try to memorize them, are easily distracted or bored, and may jump on a single emotion-laden word (1989:87).

Think of conversation as a series of ideas (words) that are loosely linked in the structure of a sentence. When we write and edit carefully, those ideas are tightly packed, logical, and coherent. In conversations we space out our ideas, leaving unsaid much of what we might want to say. The interview with someone who has suffered a violent act is a good example of this. That person's account will hold conspicuous spaces. Damage to the emotions may make some thoughts unspeakable. A good interviewer will listen for those spaces and seek to understand what is missing and why.

Review with the interviewee what you have learned.

You may see the close of the interview as the end of a routine task, but the person with whom you have been talking may see the closing quite differently. In a state of heightened awareness she has confided in someone who has appeared to be genuinely interested in the story. In those few moments another person has worked with you to reconstruct an event that has left her on terribly shaky ground. This is the time to go back over the facts, to read back statements that you may want to quote, and to arrange to obtain photographs, continue the interview, or check back for other information. It is also the time to be frank about what the interview may yield in terms of a printed or broadcast story. When will the story be published? Is it likely the interview will be a major part of it? Finally, once again identify your publication or station. Leave a business card or telephone number. (We have described a one-on-one interview when time permits such care. Obviously, chaotic disaster scenes and imminent deadlines will limit your options. And we are not advocating that you read your story back to each person you interviewed. We think that the practices outlined here will prevent many postpublication complaints from people interviewed at the scene.)

Think through what you have heard and seen.

The interview you have just completed was not a routine one. Think about what made it different. The person with whom you talked was enduring one of the most trying experiences in life. Such an interview can alter many of the assumptions journalists make about the people they talk to. Issues of trust, harm, and responsibility to others emerge from such meetings to a degree unmatched in most news interviewing. This is a time for a few moments of reflection about what you have just heard and seen.

Finally, give some attention to yourself. Whenever you are near a scene of violence, or are talking to a trauma victim, you may have an emotional response. Monitor how you feel and are responding to reminders of the event you have witnessed. Some reporters seek solitude and become almost fanatical about their privacy after doing difficult stories. Recognize your own response to the interview, talk about it with others, or give yourself a chance to reflect on it.

How do follow-up interviews differ from those done right after an event? Is there ever a good time to interview someone in trauma? What happens when a reporter becomes emotionally involved in the victim's story?

Disasters and tragic stories invariably become subjects of news stories on their anniversaries. Anniversaries of such events as the TWA flight 800 explosion in 1996 and the bombing of the Oklahoma City federal building

in 1995 still are marked with widespread news coverage. Shorter anniversaries—one month, six months—are excuses for revisiting the event and the
people it affected. Editors love anniversary stories, which may serve as useful reminders of safety, criminal justice, or other issues. The good of such
stories, though, is often exceeded by the harm done to trauma survivors
when they are asked to again relive the event, either in an interview, or by
when your story is broadcast or printed. We cannot repeat too often that
such details may be painful to survivors and in some cases may set back their
recovery from the initial trauma.

But an anniversary interview that emphasizes how a victim is recovering
from loss and trauma can be helpful to the survivor and informative to the
public. In chapter 5 we call these Act I and Act II stories: Act I is the breaking story; Act II is the follow-up that examines how all those affected are
seeking ways to cope with the recurring trauma and its setbacks as well as
the progress they have made.

During the follow-up interview you should observe all the guidelines for
the interview at the scene. Let the other person decide when and where the
interview will occur, whether a companion will be present for support,
whether and how long a tape recorder will run. Do not assume—as many
producers, editors, and reporters do—that the person wants to be interviewed at home. A television reporter asked a rape survivor for an interview
in her home; the woman agreed to the interview only if it were conducted in
the reporter's home. When the survivor arrived, she was greeted by an
exhausted reporter who had risen early and worked much of the morning to
make her living room presentable for the television interview. "Now you
know what it's like to be asked for interviews at your home," the survivor said.

The story also makes a good point about the timing of interviews. A
morning interview might seem right for a reporter who likes to write in the
afternoon. But a victim may find mornings difficult because of trauma-
related illnesses or recovery from physical injuries. Our advice is to ask what
time of the day the person would prefer to do an interview. Television
reporters often are assigned to do live interviews for early evening news programs. Because that period often is reserved for meals or family gatherings,
an interview can be disruptive.

The person you are interviewing may appear much more composed and
in control of his thoughts and emotions than when he was interviewed at
the scene of the violent event. You will be more relaxed, familiar with the
original story, and (if you have prepared for the interview) aware of much

that has happened to this person since. It will be easy to expect that this interview will be a routine one. That is a dangerous assumption.

A university student proposed to do a story for the student newspaper on a young woman killed in a fatal accident whose corneas were donated for transplant. The woman's mother readily agreed to interviews, thinking the story would credit her daughter and encourage others to become organ donors. Yet as the interview progressed, the mother became more anxious and uncomfortable. Neither she nor the reporter had anticipated that the interview would revive painful memories and questions about her daughter's death. Although the reporter did not expect the woman to be troubled by the interview, she might have taken the early signs of anxiety as an opportunity to offer the mother the chance to end or postpone the interview. (In contrast, if the reporter suddenly decided to end the conversation, the mother might be troubled, reminded once again of how little control she has over traumatic symptoms.)

It is essential that reporters anticipate these effects on survivors and family members. Focus on recovery, rather than the cause of the trauma, but even then you run the risk of evoking memories that will cause the other person pain. If your intention is to revisit the traumatic event, you have an obligation to explain that in advance and to be certain that the other person is willing to face those memories. Be explicit: say that the interview may cause the person unexpected stress, including sleeplessness, unwanted memories, and heightened anxiety. You have to remember that the trauma survivor may be vulnerable to troublesome memories, dreams, and fears even several years after an event. Think about the characteristic symptoms of post-traumatic stress disorder—unwanted memories, numbing, and heightened anxiety. Even six months later an interview is likely to be stressful.

It is helpful to say that you wish to focus on recovery and the aftermath of the event, rather than on the details of the event. The survivor knows a great deal about recovery, after all, and is likely to value an opportunity to reflect on his capacity to regain old interests, revive old friendships, and to make decisions that reconnect him with the world. Your interest in that process will be more welcome than a proposal to retell the details of an old and troubling story.

As you ask a survivor to tell how he began to recover, keep these values in mind. Do not blame or judge the victim. Respect the courage of someone who tells such a private story. Do not ask questions that force the other person to revisit the traumatic experience.

Consider these words of E. K. Rynearson, a Seattle psychiatrist, about how the survivor uses a story over a long period to mend his injuries:

Rather than a brief chronicle, the narrative of someone traumatized will be intertwined with narrative identities from the past and will become a narrative theme of future identity as well. . . . To understand how and why this trauma happened to us or someone in our family begins a long inventory of actions and values. Are we responsible? How could we have avoided this? How could something so awful happen? How can I trust that anyone cares? Why should I risk caring for anyone else? Since there are no answers to this paradox-filled inquest, the tone of this long-term narrative is one of contrast and ambiguity. Unlike the reporter's story, this one has no answer and no ending. (n.d.:6)

Although those who suffered violent events sometimes want and need to tell their stories as a way of understanding what has happened to them, those stories are not necessarily going to provide the answers that reporters seek. In cases that are most troubling to survivors, reporters substitute a different story for the one the survivor told; all that the interviewee really contributes may be a fact or two or some quotable comments. The survivor saw the interview as an important event, even a step in the recovery process. Yet when the paper arrived or the news show came on, little from the interview survived.

Most traumatic events bring reporters and survivors together only once and then only for a brief time. In some cases a reporter may need to talk to the survivor again because of legal developments or because of an anniversary story. In a very small number of cases reporters develop a continuing interest in, and a relationship with, a survivor.

The Oklahoma City bombing is typical of events that bring reporters and survivors together repeatedly over a long period of time. Reporters in Oklahoma City revisited survivors and family members of those who died, saw them at memorials and other community events, and in some cases talked to them during ensuing trials. Reporters learned to walk a delicate line between their feelings for other members of their community and keeping some professional distance. Reporters noticed that some survivors used their experience to speak out whenever possible on victim issues. Reporters who recognized that they were being lobbied to promote the survivors' ideas quickly became sensitive to conflicts between their responsibilities and the demands of what some called "professional victims."

In other cases reporters and survivors have developed close emotional relationships. A television reporter helped prepare special reports about a seven-year-old girl who disappeared after she set out for school one morning. Then the reporter's station aired a special report that the girl had been murdered—before authorities had notified the family. After that the reporter became obsessed with solving the homicide. The reporter provided a steady flow of information to the distraught family, and the desperate family members grew increasingly dependent on the reporter.

The reporter and the girl's mother made themselves into an unofficial investigative team, demanding leads from detectives. They repeatedly viewed the videotape of the death scene, identified its location, and then visited it. They tried to imagine the murder, their thoughts embellished by a specialist in extrasensory perception. As months passed and the murder remained unsolved, the mother grew increasingly depressed and suicidal. She became enraged at the reporter who had invested so much in trying to respond to her needs and accused the reporter of being incompetent and uncaring.

The psychiatrist who worked for many months to help the mother escape the obsession with finding the murderer showed how the reporter's fascination with various scenarios for the murder had caused extraordinary distress for the mother. Each new version of the murder dragged the mother again into the painful experience of "seeing" her daughter die. The reporter's logical, news-oriented questions were devastating to the woman: Was there a sexual assault? Was the murder done by a serial killer? Why didn't the school district do more to protect the child? Did the little girl take a risk that led to her death? The mother had repeatedly showed signs of trauma, signs that the reporter did not or would not recognize.

Some reporters eagerly identify with those who survive violence because of a personal history of abuse, sexual assault, or other traumas. That identification may be so strong that the reporter ignores professional boundaries in order to become a confidante and even advocate. A skilled reporter needs to concentrate on understanding and reporting events accurately; deep emotional connections to people in those stories can undermine those goals. Yet we would agree with those who say a reporter sometimes can be very helpful to a victim or family member. But we believe that the best result for everyone occurs when the reporter understands his own needs and is sensitive to signs of trauma and growing distress in others.

Constructive interviews result from self-awareness and knowledge of trauma's effects on others. Trauma stories need to be told if we are to support its victims as they travel the long road toward recovery.

Jeff Gradney

Focusing on the Humanity

The deadlines are extreme and the competition fierce. From assignment to air can be as little as half an hour. Violence always leads. Yet TV reporter Jeff Gradney consistently brings humanity to his stories.

" 'How does it feel?' is the most ignorant, idiotic question you can ask," Gradney says, wincing with disgust. The question is bad not only because it pokes at the fresh wounds of survivors—the father of a missing child, the sister of a murdered brother—but also because how someone feels is not news. "We already *know* how they feel. It's obvious," Gradney says. Instead,

Jeff Gradney. PHOTO BY MIGAEL SCHERER.

he coaxes the survivor around the raw emotion by asking questions that reflect on, rather than exploit, human pain: What is running through your mind right now? What would you like others to know about what is happening to you, your family, your community?

Despite the time pressures, Gradney leaves the camera behind when he approaches survivors. "To hell with taping that first moment of intense emotion," he says. "This story will air for a couple of minutes at most; if we do it right, it'll replay for a day or two. But the family lives with it for a lifetime." In his view people have the right to respond to his expression of sorrow for their loss in private, to compose themselves, to refuse to talk to him, although they rarely do; usually, the person is more than willing. In fact, says Gradney, they are hungry for what *he* knows: "We can be a source of information to *them*." Reporting goes both ways, and whether they talk to him or not, he invites them to call him for further developments. "It's a matter of trust."

Gradney finds that he can make people comfortable most quickly by explaining why he is there and how he and the photographer work as a news team. "I let them know they can stop during the interview or start over." Pushing is not necessary—"Sometimes I just leave the family alone"—but often the simple lack of pressure puts people at ease, and they agree to be interviewed.

This knack for connecting with people is bone deep. Gradney has seen violence from the perspective of law enforcement and the military; a competitive power lifter in college, he worked as a bouncer, a sheriff's deputy jailer, and eventually as a U.S. Marine Corps grunt. He understands the anguish of a death notification and can identify with many of the people he now reports on.

Two experiences stand out in his life as a journalist. One, the Oklahoma City bombing, occurred when he was working for station KJRH–Channel 2 in Tulsa. The first body found was that of his ex-wife's sister. "She was family to me," he says, his voice tight with emotion he does not try to hide. The station let him do a story on her—an "ode," he calls it—that tapped a depth he can still feel. That whole period gave him a sensitivity to loss he believes he would not have otherwise.

The second critical period for Gradney was in Bosnia. The Tulsa station sent him and a camera operator there to answer one question for Oklahoma viewers: Why are U.S. troops there? "We showed them," Gradney says proudly. "When our troops were there, the bombings *stopped*." Yes, children were living and playing in bombed-out buildings, but it was better than being under constant attack. "We didn't bring permanent peace to the region—who does?—but we saved lives." This knowledge, that people can make a difference for the good, infuses his reporting.

Gradney's heroes are Edward R. Murrow, Walter Cronkite, and especially Charles Kuralt, broadcast journalists from an era when ratings didn't depend on the slight attention of channel surfers. Nonetheless, he insists that the "vein of humanity" so evident in their coverage should remain. Kuralt's *On the Road* style inspired one of Gradney's early stories about a methamphetamine bust in a small Texas town. While other stations covered it as a police story, he covered it as the town's story. The news wasn't the crime and the arrest—"Bad things can happen anywhere"—but rather how the townspeople pulled together to help law enforcement. More recently, for KING–Channel 5 in Seattle, he covered a suspected arson in a suburb by focusing not on the investigation or even the awfulness of the fire but on the twenty-two-year-old "paperboy" who saved the couple sleeping in the house. At a time when TV news often makes people more fearful and isolated, Gradney's heartening approach emphasizes positive action that ordinary people can take when violence occurs.

Consistent with his distaste for non-news, Gradney avoids stand-ups that imply the backdrop is important when it usually is not. Whenever he can, he walks through and explains why the place is important or finds the place that is. As for images of draped bodies being wheeled away on gurneys, "it's not automatic. But there are times when it's the best way to show the reality of what's happened, without gore—which I hate." He appreciates KING's "limited use if at all" policy regarding such shots.

Gradney knows stories of violence rarely have happy endings and tries to include that awareness in his broadcasts. Some closure may occur after a successful prosecution and sentencing, but these processes themselves are difficult; at most, he feels, they are "a start." The effort to make this complex understanding instantly clear for viewers can make his reporting overly simplistic, something he regrets.

"Sensitivity is an integral part of me," he acknowledges. "To be just human—in the end it gets *me* through." As for the competition—"It's not the drive to get ahead that keeps me going. It's feeling good about the stories I tell."

By Jeff Gradney

The Deep, Familiar Pain

For the first of these two stories, Jeff Gradney interviewed Pearl Buckner, a woman whose son had been murdered that morning, shot to death like his father years earlier. He captured her undeniable shock and grief with dignity. The "deep, familiar pain" she describes seems a reflection of the entire community's pain. The segment was broadcast on September 20, 1996. In the second segment, broadcast on August 8, 1996, Gradney recognized the contributions to community life of a woman killed in a traffic accident.

GRADNEY: *Police say they're still trying to learn more about what led to the shooting death of a thirty-one-year-old man here this morning.*

PEARL BUCKNER: *I just think it's horrible. This was a young man, thirty-one years old. Three children. He never hurt anybody. He always had a smile for everybody.*

GRADNEY: *Pearl Buckner will never see her oldest son's smile again. Someone shot Alonzo Buckner to death here early this morning. Police say it may have started when he was outside talking to three men.*

POLICE: *At some point, one of the males and our victim walked inside the house and that's where the shooting occurred, we believe. In addition to that, apparently two additional suspects came into the house and ultimately all fled.*

GRADNEY: *Buckner's wife and children were in the house when it happened. His wife woke up to hear her husband screaming he'd been shot. Police aren't talking about what may have led to this yet.*

POLICE: *Right now, we don't have any suspects. But we have detained one male who has been interviewed. And hopefully, something good will come from that.*

GRADNEY: *But here they know nothing good will come from this.*

PEARL BUCKNER: *It's just a loss. The world has lost someone here today.*

GRADNEY: *And now Pearl Buckner feels a deep, familiar pain—because she lost her husband, Alonzo Buckner's father, the same way—in a shooting—years ago. Much has changed here since then, she says. But one thing remains the same.*

PEARL BUCKNER: *It hurt so many people. Not only is he gone. It hurt his brother, his sister, his children—everybody who loved him. Their lives will never be the same again—they'll never be the same again.*

GRADNEY: *Police are still not referring to the man they have in custody as a suspect in this shooting. This is Jeff Gradney, in Federal Way for King 5 News.*

GRADNEY: *Today these children remembered someone very special by placing flowers on her car.*

CHILD: *She took me places when my mom couldn't. She bought me things when my mom couldn't.*

GRADNEY: *She did the same and more for dozens of other children in this Federal Way community. Her name was Jill Kalning. But they called her a guardian angel.*

    Today their angel is gone. Kalning was pushing a stroller with a two-year-old girl in it when a truck came speeding around a corner and hit her and the stroller. The man police say was driving the truck drove off, then came back and turned himself in. The two-year-old in the stroller is alright—but Kalning died hours after they were hit.

FRIEND: *It's not just Jill's personal family who's suffering. It's the whole community. It's the children.*

GRADNEY (AT COMMUNITY CENTER): *Here, they say Jill Kalning spent countless hours, at this church, and in the local community center, calling on kids, trying to make a positive difference in their lives. They take some solace in the fact that some of her last few hours were spent doing what she loved. And that was taking care of these kids.*

FRIEND: *I mean it's like she's a heroine and that she'll live on in the memories of these children. I don't think they'll ever forget what they saw here.*

GRADNEY: *Not just the accident but the kindness Kalning showed the children long before she died. In Federal Way, Jeff Gradney—King 5 News.*

Chapter 5

Writing the Story

Writing the trauma story can be as challenging as the interviewing because these stories are always different. Both green writers and pros acknowledge that their fingers hesitate over the keyboard on trauma stories, and they sweat out exact words and word pictures that might do justice to the person and topic.

One helpful starting point is remembering that a victim's story really is a story. That is, it is not simply a news "story," but a true account about a particular, real human being and the traumatic events in that life.

Like any well-told story, it has a beginning (lead), middle, and end. Unlike novels and fairytales, it probably does not have a happily-ever-after ending; it may have a "kicker" in more than the usual journalistic sense of a news story climax with a twist or jolt. After all, it is a real person's story, with all the potential for toil and trouble, trauma and tragedy, and drama and inspiration that a real life can bring.

Another useful reference point is that the story is the victim's story— or should be. Trauma may leave a person feeling violated, angry, powerless. Psychiatrist Frank M. Ochberg tells reporters at journalism conferences and workshops that many trauma victims he counsels feel their suffering has had some purpose if their story is told at the right time and in the right way. It can be a catharsis that releases some pain and gives their lives new dignity. That is a step in the process of progressing from victim to survivor.

Accuracy Counts

Many things in the way a story is written may upset a person, but what that person finds to be upsetting sometimes is not what journalists would expect. Soon after the Victims and the Media Program began at Michigan State University, William Coté sat down with leaders of the Michigan Victim Alliance, people who had been raped or shot or were parents of murdered children. Asked what had bothered them most about print or broadcast reports about their experiences, they did not cite brutish interviewers or sensationalistic stories. Several of these survivors replied, almost in unison, "The mistakes! The mistakes!"

They complained about stories with misspelled names, incorrect ages and addresses, wrong job descriptions, or a mangled chronology of events and dates. To be sure, they went on to list other serious and hurtful things, but the factual errors sprang first to their minds.

It is too often true that sources complain about mistakes in news reports. (Just ask friends who have been quoted in print or on the air.) The officers of the Victim Alliance, though, felt the stings of inaccuracies more keenly. Perhaps they could not say exactly why, but the complaints seemed to be prompted by a feeling that "if you don't get even the simplest things such as my age and occupation right, I feel you don't really care about me; you're just doing a job."

That perception seems to fit the reactions of Bruce Shapiro, the contributing editor of the *Nation* magazine who survived a knife assault by a deranged man in a New Haven, Connecticut, coffee shop in 1994. As we noted in chapter 1, one of Shapiro's several complaints about media coverage was that a reporter "invented a wife for me," even though he was unmarried at the time. However that happened, Shapiro says the mistake rankled greatly at the time. "The obligation that journalists have to get the facts straight applies doubly and triply at times like this," he told us. "Making a mistake like that or other errors somehow implies to the victim a lack of attention and true concern for the person."

Psychiatrist Ochberg understands that reaction from survivors and explains that it is part of their need to assemble their stories for themselves and others. Most survivors of trauma want their story told, and told accurately, because they desperately want to "re-enter" their community, and they see the story as a potential passport. "Their dignity and the sense of community inclusion that's so very important was shaken," he explains.

"There was a breach of the social contract. Their society was supposed to protect them but didn't. For a moment an individual is singled out and harmed. They feel shame and a feeling of being excluded from their own community."

You, the journalist, will be in the role of a giver of help—you will help an injured person tell a story. Of course, journalists are not trained therapists. A journalist's primary job is to inform, not heal, but you can earn another person's trust. Mistakes in those all-important stories can shatter the trust and confidence the survivor craves.

Stories can further shatter the trust and confidence of survivors when errors or omissions leave the impression that people are partly responsible for the violence against them. A story noting that a raped woman was wearing a miniskirt when she was attacked might give the impression that she was "asking for it." A television tape showing a bar where a bystander was shot to death in the crossfire of a gun battle might be taken to imply, "Well, if he hadn't been in a place like that . . ."

Whether such impressions are intended or not, victims and their families and friends will be especially sensitive to every word, description, and fact. Try to think how the story, photo, or tape will look or sound from the perspective of those most affected by what happened. It is true that you cannot edit solely to please them. Your audience is much bigger than that, and survivors and families may be so upset or defensive that they do not realize when expecting something to be used or not used is unreasonable. You, the reporter or editor, have to decide that. Nonetheless, you can consider whether certain details and facts form a tone or impression that you do not intend or are extraneous to the story.

When Dan Anderson was shot and nearly killed by a prowler in his yard, he was too sick for days to worry about how it was being reported. (His wife, Pat, had to cope with those earliest stories by herself, as we will see later.) As he recovered, though, and began reading the stories, the Lansing, Michigan, resident saw in one newspaper's first account that he was shot when he "went outside to investigate a prowler." That, he felt, made him appear to be stupid or reckless.

Actually, Anderson explains, he called the police about a prowler and the dispatcher asked him whether he could get a description of the man. Anderson then went outside to look—and was shot—only because he thought he was following the dispatcher's directions. Just a relatively minor difference? Not to Dan Anderson and his self-esteem.

It is true that mistakes that sources complain about sometimes do not originate with reporters. Mistakes can abound on the initial incident forms filled out by harried police officers. Witnesses and suspects often give conflicting and confusing statements at crime scenes. Other information a reporter gets often is second- or thirdhand, filtered through intermediaries such as police desk sergeants and public relations people. But who is likely to be blamed for any mistakes in print or on the air? The reporter, of course.

You can do a lot to avoid these pitfalls by double-checking every fact, no matter how basic. If something is not certain or relevant, leave it out of the story. Should you include in the story a casual comment from a police officer that the driver in a fatal accident "may" have been drinking if you don't know the result of blood alcohol tests or, indeed, whether any were taken? If mentioning alcohol seems necessary, it is often better simply to say something like, "Under routine procedures, police will conduct blood tests to determine whether alcohol could have played any role in the accident."

Mistakes also can creep, or jump, into stories by implication or association when the writer lumps too many people into one category without careful distinctions. Sometimes that happens as much by what the writer does not say as by what the story does say. A combination of coverage that said too much and not enough prompted a friend of a woman killed by a serial murderer in the Seattle area in the 1980s, to write a letter to the *Seattle Times* to protest how the story had characterized her friend. Because several of the victims had been identified as prostitutes, coverage regularly used that identification. The letter reflects the hurt in such cases:

> She had three children and a man who loved her very much. She lived in a normal neighborhood, in a normal house with hardwood floors located on Crown Hill. She had training in Montessory school teaching and her hobbies were designing children's toys and studying religion. She was not and never had been a prostitute. . . .
>
> What the media did to that family was nearly as tragic as the circumstance of her death. . . . Some referred to her as a "Street Person," some said nothing at all about who or what she was, all they talked about was prostitution, one station even made the mistake of calling her a prostitute. The kids were returning home from school each day in tears. . . . I am sick to death of these being written off as "Justifiable Homicides." . . . Listen, folks, it's time that we all get real about this thing, and address the REAL problem, which is MURDER!!! NOT PROSTITUTION!!! (Guillen 1990:95–6)

In all, accuracy is the first step in discharging the professional journalist's duty in writing a story. It is not the journalist's job to heal, but it certainly is the journalist's obligation to do no harm.

The Devil—and Pain—in Details

Even accurate facts that might appear to be harmless sometimes can wound someone who is already suffering. Hugh Leach, a veteran reporter and copy editor at the *Lansing (Michigan) State Journal,* learned that painfully. He has covered many violent events in his career, but he tells journalism students that he did not fully appreciate all the potential ramifications of what he and others reported until he found himself on the other side of the journalistic fence.

Leach's seventy-year-old mother was savagely beaten and left to bleed to death by two robbers who broke into her Arizona retirement home. Leach traveled to Arizona to help handle the funeral arrangements and to deal with media inquiries. He thought many of the newspaper and television reports in Arizona and Michigan about the murder were accurate and sensitive. He found, though, that three little words in one paragraph of an Arizona paper's feature profiling his mother offended him keenly: the description within the lead noted she "weighed 90 pounds, loved to smoke, took in stray cats and was sweet to her neighbors." It was the "loved to smoke" that offended him.

"It's true that she smoked cigarettes," Leach told us. "That was accurate, but why did they have to mention it in the story? Her smoking didn't have anything to do with someone breaking into her house and killing her. I was surprised it bothered me so much, but it did. I know they were just trying to do a personality profile of her. I understand that type of story. But is that one of the things to remember about her? It hurt. It hurt." Again, details that seem to add dimension to a story about someone's life might be received differently by sensitized readers.

Journalists would do well to remember what a reporter character in a movie said when intimate aspects of her own life were about to be published: "Yes, it's accurate—but is it true?"

Sometimes, sadly, it is impossible not to report critical details of a crime without adding to the grief of families and friends. Journalists often must be the bearers of bad news, like it or not. When the head but not the body of an abducted child is found, reporting that information is going to hurt the parents, but reporters cannot omit such basic facts. How could the discovery be reported otherwise?

Similarly, a California newspaper ran a powerful package of stories about murdered teenagers in the city, reporting how one youth was killed when he drove with friends into a high-crime neighborhood to buy drugs. Family members, suffering deeply, protested that mentioning why the young men were in the neighborhood was not necessary. Most of the paper's readers, though, probably would have guessed that drugs were involved or would have imagined even worse reasons. The reason he was there was an unavoidable link in the chain of events that led to the killing.

On the other hand, some details that unnecessarily provoke horror or repulsion do not have to be reported. By all means tell everything that is necessary to make sense of what happened, but consider how many and what details to use. If a truck runs over a man, saying he "suffered severe internal injuries" usually is sufficient; reporting that "the body was squashed flat" serves no one. That might seem to be a matter of ordinary taste and common sense, but reporters too often include such details in their stories.

Some facts that have to be reported need not be repeated in subsequent stories. That's a frequent complaint from upset families that do not need to be reminded of details of their loved ones' deaths, especially not years after the crimes. For a look at how families feel on that point, consider, for example, the aftermath of the *Challenger* shuttle explosion. For hours, days, and weeks television stations replayed repeatedly the critical moments of the accident—sometimes in slow motion.

The hurt to families can be even worse when reporters repeatedly describe the cruelty responsible for the deaths. That was highlighted in a letter to *Time* magazine from the sister of a 1975 victim of the serial killer Theodore Bundy. From the time her body was discovered to the time of his execution in 1989, stories mentioned where her body was found. "We, her family, did not need to hear, see and read the same fact for 14 years," the sister wrote.

Picture This

Photographs are a particular source of agony for victims and families. Chapter 6 covers issues of importance of to video- and photojournalists, but for now we simply urge editors to recognize the importance of pictures. Readers sometimes complain about a story when the quarrel really is with the photo that went with it. Many a trauma story, however, has been enhanced by a touching or inspiring picture that draws praise from a victim's family and friends.

It should be standard procedure for the writer to work with photographers and editors to help ensure the right look for the whole package, text *and* photos.

Just as the reactions of victims tend to depend on how long ago the trauma happened—hours, months, or years—the best way to write a trauma story can hinge greatly on the time factor. One approach is appropriate when a man is still fighting for his life in a hospital burn unit after someone firebombed his apartment building. You, as the reporter, want to tell readers when and where it happened, whether police have suspects, the condition of all survivors, and how the police investigation is proceeding.

A different approach is appropriate for an anniversary feature about how a particular man copes with his crippling and disfiguring injuries, as the *Austin American-Statesman* did in an inspiring word and photo feature. The two-part series by reporter Michele Stanush and photographer Lynne Dobson details the struggles of thirty-seven-year-old Emmett Jackson to deal with his devastating injuries and the death of his wife, Diathia, and child at the hands of an arsonist who was seeking revenge against someone in the building.

Stories right after the firebombing understandably focused on the crime and the attacker, but the *American-Statesman* two years later unsentimentally and vividly treated the lengthy and painful process of Jackson's recovery, with little and big successes and setbacks. Even two years can be a short period in a trauma story. *Anchorage Daily News* reporter Debra McKinney and photographer Fran Durner documented the spirited growth of three women who had been haunted by incest they suffered as little girls more than three decades earlier.

One way to examine the two different types of stories and their timing and approach is to consider them as acts in a real-life play or drama. That idea surfaced in Seattle at the University of Washington's Western Journalism and Trauma Conference in 1996. A breakfast conversation between Frank Ochberg, the psychiatrist, and Bruce Shapiro, the magazine editor and stabbing victim, led them to suggest at the conference that the different types of trauma and reporting situations be called Act I and Act II.

Act I includes the reporting right after an event, telling readers, listeners, or viewers the traditional "5Ws"—who, what, when, where, and why.

Act II, by contrast, portrays the longer-term effects of trauma, profiling the victims months or years later and describing how they cope in the continuing recovery process.

Reporters usually are much more geared by instinct, tradition, the routines of their work, and competitive pressure to do Act I stories swiftly after a traumatic event. One of the hallmark criteria of "news," after all, is that we are reporting for the first time something that has happened very recently or has just been uncovered. Otherwise, it is old news or not news at all. On top of that is the hurry-hurry that comes from deadlines and the desire (if you want to keep your job) of beating the competition.

It definitely was an Act I situation, for example, when Dan Anderson was shot by the intruder in his yard. Hours after the shooting he was on a respirator and unable to communicate when a reporter tried to enter his intensive care room to interview him. Intercepted and removed by nurses, the reporter then tried to find Pat Anderson. She was in a nearby lounge but turned down the request. This was a situation in which no interview was appropriate.

"If the reporter had called me later at home, or even asked in advance to talk with me in a lounge at the hospital, I'd probably have done it," she recalls, "but I sure didn't want to talk right then and there and especially not after what he tried to do. His timing was terrible."

Now, more than twenty-three years and about thirty surgeries later for Dan, the Andersons tell their experiences to Michigan State journalism students, who are assigned to craft Act II stories that explore how trauma affects victims and their families. "I'm glad to talk about it and proud if maybe it helps these young people," Dan says after one classroom interview.

Profiles

Personality profiles are virtually indispensable in writing about particular people who have suffered trauma, so it is useful to review what this type of human-interest writing usually includes and how best to apply it in the context of trauma. As with any profile, the aim is to make the reader know the person vividly through the skillful blending of details, observations, word pictures, and creative writing.

Tell what the person looks, sounds, and acts like. Note the subject's age, hobbies, family, occupation, favorite foods, pets—in short, anything and everything that makes the person real for readers or viewers. Then think carefully about whether any one thing or incident seems to capture the person's essence in a dramatic capsule. Lead with that, or set up the things that lead to it smoothly, quickly, and irresistibly.

Melvin Mencher, in *News Reporting and Writing*, says a profile consists of

- The person's background (birth, upbringing, education, occupation).
- Anecdotes and incidents involving the subject.
- Quotes by the individual relevant to his or her newsworthiness.
- The reporter's observations.
- Comments of those who know the interviewee.
- A news peg, whenever possible. (1997:330)

That excellent outline can apply to many types of profiles, but writing about victims has important variations. The main character is not always alive, and the news peg may be all too obvious or painfully well known. Comments from people who know or knew the subject become doubly important. It is also especially necessary—and effective—to try to put the reader in the other person's shoes.

Some of the best profilers in journalism say they consciously use techniques traditionally attributed to good fiction writers: rich, colorful details and vivid narration that immediately drop the reader into the middle of the scene (action) and compel further reading.

The Curtain Raiser

As with any story, the lead is your lure, hook, and showcase, your only opportunity to grab readers or viewers and make the story so enticing that they will not turn away until they have savored the last word. Leads are particularly challenging in stories about violence. Both Act I and Act II situations offer great opportunities to write dramatic, prize-winning stories or scripts. They also offer many opportunities to sensationalize and titillate the audience or to demean and injure victims and their families and friends. The difference between one and the other often can seem subtle—except to those who like or detest a tone, approach, or phrase in a story. Let's look at some leads.

The first in the two-part series "The Test of Fire" in the *Austin American-Statesman* begins with this lead by Michele Stanush:

> April 1993—Emmett Jackson sits rod-straight in the front row of a federal courtroom, a Dallas Cowboys cap guarding his scarred scalp and a black patch covering his left eye.
>
> Metal claws have replaced Emmett's fingers. There are bare nasal cavities where he once had a nose and holes where there once were ears. His lips were rebuilt by doctors. (1994:G1)

Stanush goes on to relate that Jackson is in the courtroom to hear what will become of the arsonist who killed his wife and little girl and left him so disfigured. The lead does not draw a pretty picture, but the word image it conjures is so vivid and compelling that readers cannot resist the rest of the story.

Ralph De La Cruz powerfully presents similarly stark drama in his lead for "Path of a Bullet," from the Long Beach, California, *Press-Telegram:*

> Three hours short of his 17th birthday, Martine Perry is lying naked on a stainless steel hospital table, life seeping out of his body.
>
> A baby wails in a distant corner of the emergency room. An elderly woman pleads with a nurse to hold off putting a tube down her throat. And Martine lies silent, motionless, blood oozing from his head, as eight people work frantically to revive him. (1996:K1)

Again, the lead is dramatic and plunges the reader instantly into the middle of the action, blending background facts (name and age) and the sights and sounds of the hospital emergency room.

Leads about trauma, however, do not always have to immediately focus on gore or physical descriptions. Sometimes a lead can set the scene for horrific narratives to come, using suspenseful wording to encourage the reader to read on and on. That is the approach chosen by Debra McKinney for "Malignant Memories" from the *Anchorage Daily News,* describing how three women dared to face their haunting recollections of childhood incest:

> SEATTLE—Twenty-five years have come and gone since Margie last visited the old man's farm. She's not sure she can even find the place. She's not sure she even wants to.
>
> The 51-year-old Anchorage travel agent has made a lot of progress lately confronting her fears. But she still has trouble talking about what happened in the barn. (1993:A1)

The writer was physically right there with the people she described. Often accompanying people as they relive traumatic scenes is not possible, but when it is, the effort is well worth it. For that to happen the writer and photographer must have the trust and confidence of the people involved. People who have been suffering post-traumatic stress for months or for decades are not going to open themselves up to journalists who seemingly might not give them respect and dignity. They have been hurt enough. Why should they give reporters a chance to wound them more?

Only when the writer has proved in initial interviews and contacts that the survivor will be the focus and not the target of the story is the subject likely to say to the journalist, "Okay, come along with me."

Mine the Details

Once you have the basic facts and your lead, the three most important things in writing a compelling story about trauma are details, details, and details—the appropriate ones, that is. Boring and tedious details will impel a reader to move on. Inaccurate or unnecessary details, as we've seen, may disgust or upset the audience. Illuminating, flowing, and dramatic details make the story come, and stay, alive until the last word. Take, for example, this background detail in Stanush's story about burn victim Jackson: "In his old life, Emmett Jackson was an easy-going supermarket baker who loved the feel of raw dough between his fingers. *Texture is the key,* he'd say."

That's a poignant observation about a man who now has no fingers or hands. Stanush also broke a journalistic custom by using italics in that quote and in others, such as *"Why am I not dead?"* spotted strategically throughout the story. Newspapers seldom use italics in news stories because, among other reasons, they can be distracting and overwrought, but she did it deliberately—and effectively—to show readers when she was conveying something Jackson was thinking. How did she know that? One way, of course, was to interview him about what he was thinking at key points. She also loaned him a tape recorder so that he could relate his private thoughts when he was alone.

In addition, Stanush interviewed Jackson's family and friends, doctors, counselors, therapists, paramedics, and coworkers over a fifteen-month period. She told of his triumphs, such as getting a driver's license again and climbing a steep hill outside his rehabilitation center, inspiring therapists to name the mound Jackson Hill. Many quotes and observations tell of his love for his lost wife and baby, his regularly attending church services, and his hope of becoming a public speaker, talking to people about fire and crime.

The Jackson stories were unsentimental and frank. In addition to relating many inspiring and ennobling facets of Jackson's life, the accounts also note that he had served nearly three years in prison for forgery and burglary, and before he met Diathia, he "padded his pockets with big bills, drove a Lincoln Continental and hung out with fast-living women." Today, the stories reveal, he indulges in smoking, some drinking, and night clubbing. "In the rehab hospital, he jokes to nurses: '*When I get outta here, all I want is a bottle of Bud and a babe.*'"

A key factor here is that Jackson was willing to have such events and thoughts revealed. To him the reporting of his past and current lifestyles—

good and not-so-good—was an important step in helping him feel he was rejoining the human race and his community. He wasn't nominating himself for sainthood. He simply wanted people to understand something of what he had been through and to know that he was trying to be a better person but still Emmett, still human. Such details, for better or worse, counted.

Descriptions of people, places, and things are among the details that keep the audience moving along. Debra McKinney combined those three elements, along with quotes, in this passage as the three women searched for the house where one of them had been abused decades earlier:

> Slowly the car headed down the gravel drive. At the bottom, Vivian stopped in front of a little yellow farm house, the kind you'd expect to have an apple pie cooling in the windowsill.
>
> "Amazing," Margie said.
>
> The place was just the way she remembered it. There was the chicken coop. And the old chopping block. And the big pear tree the guinea hens used to roost in. And there, behind the little house, beyond the gate with the "Keep Out" sign, was the barn.
>
> "I don't want to get out," Margie said.
>
> Vivian put an arm around her and hugged her. Ezzie gently rubbed her back.
>
> They all got out of the car. (1993:A8)

Don't you want to read what they find and how Margie reacts? Thousands of readers did want to know and kept reading as the story unfolded. A lot of it wasn't pretty, but it was compelling and, ultimately, inspiring.

Just as inspiring and riveting was the story of a sixteen-year-old Florida boy who was abducted one hot July morning and stuffed into the trunk of his father's car. He was dumped out and left for dead after being driven for five hours around the city while the heat of the day was magnified to 130 degrees in the tight, dark trunk. Reporter Craig Dezern's story, "The Miracle of Philip Chandler," in the *Orlando Sentinel* used powerful writing and moving narrative to tell what editor John Haile rightly labels "a gripping tale of terror, survival and hope." Again, telling details were woven into the vivid story and photos after the teenager's parents gave Dezern and photographer Angela Peterson access to Philip's hospital room, home, church, and school at each stage in his recovery.

Among the grabbing details of the story is a section in which Philip's adoptive parents keep watch at his hospital bed as he tries to overcome the severe brain damage caused by heat stroke. The parents are no longer planning his funeral, but doctors warn them that Philip may never come out of his deep coma. After one day's vigil his parents are about to say good night to their son:

> Eve leans in, and one more time she asks, "Philip, can you give me a hug?"
>
> Slow and shaky, but with a purpose, Philip lifts his arms from the bed and drops them around his mother's neck.
>
> It is eerie, like being hugged by a dead man. Philip's face is still emotionless, his eyes fixed at something far away.
>
> "Jim did you see that?"
>
> "Do it again."
>
> Eve asks for another hug. Philip responds the same.
>
> She is ecstatic, laughing and crying. This is the miracle she prayed for, but didn't dare hope for. (1993:7)

Anyone who contends that "a respectful story is a dull story" should reconsider after reading these stories. All the stories cited here focus on victims, all pretty ordinary people who had extraordinary things happen to them. Extraordinary bad things. The details of how they sought to cope and recover from the blows furnished the stuff of exciting journalism, illuminating not so much the evil visited on them but how courage, faith, love, and simple endurance often match and overcome evil.

The Kicker

Reviewers of novels are harsh on writers who do not have an exciting denouement or at least wrap things up nicely and leave the reader with a sigh, gasp, or laugh. Readers of news stories and features should be just as demanding, yet many a promising story seems to end with hardly a whimper or fails to leave a feeling of any kind. That especially should not happen with stories about people who suffer trauma. By their very nature such chronicles are ready made for a concluding kicker. The problem may be deciding which of several tacks to take in ending the piece.

A hard news, Act I story right after an event may almost write its own ending, and you may need time and space only to make sure no questions or facts are left dangling. Act II stories give the writer more opportunity to tell the whole story and then end it with something that focuses on the person, whether a quote, observation, or fact. The point is to leave the reader with a certain impression, a certain feeling that will help sear the total message of the story into memory for a long time to come. It could be a near-perfect kicker if it magically manages to combine a sense of both what the person has lost and is now regaining in recovery.

Craig Dezern perhaps comes close to such a kicker in "The Miracle of Philip Chandler." The sixteen-year-old finally is home after four months in the hospital but still struggling to overcome the crippling physical and mental effects of the brain injury. The closing scene is in his den, where he is watching the movie *Aladdin* on television. Dezern asks Philip if, like Aladdin, he had three wishes, what would he ask for?

> Philip imagines this for a minute, one eyebrow cocked in speculation. He holds out one long finger to begin counting off his wishes.
> "To be normal again."
> He holds out two fingers and thinks some more, longer this time. Then he closes his hand.
> "That's really all I can think of." (1993:16)

It is impossible to fully appreciate a kicker without reading the whole story, but even in isolation the power and imagery of that writing shines through. Built on the crafted foundation of a skillful lead, smooth flow, and telling details, such an ending brings the reader and another person together for at least this one close look into the survivor's world.

Act III?

While the concept of the two acts seems valuable, some trauma and media specialists have had a nagging feeling that something still is missing in describing and encouraging even longer-range and broader news coverage. That became a topic when two Australians visited East Lansing in late 1997. What is needed is Act III, suggested Gary Embelton, a psychologist, and Cratis Hippocrates, then the chair of the Queensland University of Technology journalism school.

Act III, they propose, can refer to coverage that places specific traumatic events within broader sociological, historical, or even economic contexts. Such coverage is sorely lacking in explaining events. If well done, the Australians believe, it could even help newspapers regain lost numbers of readers by providing something rarely available in other media. Most important, a benefit to society might be that citizens, acting in their roles as voters and taxpayers, might gain a deeper and stronger knowledge base for making critical decisions about how to cope with violence in their communities, nation, and the world. For a concrete and imaginative example of some aspects of Act III journalism, consider again the story from the *Press-Telegram* of Long Beach, California, "Path of a Bullet." It leads readers through the aftermath of the gang shooting death of a seventeen-year-old, as starkly noted in the lead that describes Martine Perry on an emergency room gurney. The 22-cent handgun bullet that killed Perry caused devastating physical and emotional costs, but the report also traces the economic costs—$1.2 million for hospital expenses, police investigations, court proceedings against his killer, and dozens of other things.

"Path of a Bullet" (with the secondary head "We All Pay the Price") actually was not one story but a package. The central narrative by Ralph De La Cruz tells of Perry's death, life, and funeral. Other stories, photos, and charts explore such aspects as tracking down suspects, how tracing gun ownership often fails to produce suspects, the costs of prosecution, why youth kill, and ending gangs.

The *Press-Telegram*'s special report is graphic, so much so that Jim Crutchfield, then the executive editor, cautioned readers in a plain cover wrapped around the package that the contents might be too harsh for children. That, of course, could entice readers to look inside, but it is also a responsible way to give parents some control over what their youngsters see.

"Path" may not include every aspect of a comprehensive Act III approach, but the sociological and economic perspectives, and the attempt to put everything into one framework, make the report a fine example of this genre.

It might seem daunting for publications without the journalistic and financial resources of the *New York Times* or *Newsweek* to tackle such comprehensive ventures. The *Press-Telegram* demonstrates, however, that the midsized and smaller papers that serve most U.S. readers can marshal their staffs for worthy Act III stories. One key is to focus on what a paper knows best: its own community. Then choose a topic that deeply affects that community, whether gangs, domestic abuse, illegal drugs, or another subject that directly or indirectly victimizes many residents.

The products of such teamwork also generally are skillful combinations of intense reporting on individuals and illuminating data that put the personal stories into an overall community perspective. That means a paper needs to have one or more researchers with expertise in computer-assisted journalism. Increasing numbers of papers have such specialists on staff. When they do not, an area university or private company often can supply a consultant to design a computer program to analyze the data. For example, a project on drug-related crimes in a city might profile a number of individual victims while data analysis could provide a picture of the geographic, economic, and racial backgrounds of the victims.

Most journalists, especially early in their careers, will encounter opportunities to write Act I and II stories about violence much more often than Act III stories. Still, all three parts of the drama entail the same ingredients basic to all types of reporting and especially for covering violence: Get the facts, get them straight, tell the story well, and remember it is for and about real people. Make the writing as dramatic and engrossing as the facts as you know them permit. Let the reader see, hear, and feel in words and images the victim's tragedies and triumphs. But don't lure readers at the cost of unnecessarily wounding people who are already suffering.

Chapter 6

Pictures and Sounds of Trauma

The loudest cries of rage and hurt come when pictures and sounds collide with viewers' and listeners' sensibilities. Visual and audio media make an instant impression on the eye or ear, in contrast to the newspaper reader's more deliberate choice to read or keep reading printed text word for word. By the time we decide we do not want to see the image or hear the details, it is too late; the real or the mental picture is in our brain for better or worse.

We make no apologies for the presence of photographic and electronic media at the scene of violent newsworthy incidents and disasters. They, like print media, have a right and duty to be there as a proxy for the public. Our discussion will be about how and exactly when those responsibilities are carried out. This chapter combines radio and television reports with newspaper and magazine photography because so many of the problems—and opportunities—are similar or interrelated.

Nearly everyone has seen a similar scenario: A terrible accident, murder, or other horrible event has occurred. Someone shoves a microphone and camera in the face of the stunned or bleeding victim or bereaved relative. Then comes the question: "So how do you feel?" (Now that your child has been killed, or your home has been leveled in a tornado, how do you feel?) The resulting mumble, usually accompanied by tears and sobs, shows up on the evening news or in a close-up in the next morning's paper.

"Flashbulb Memories"

Can you remember offhand precisely where you were and what you were doing on November 22 just last year? Probably not. Yet nearly everyone who was older than a toddler on November 22, 1963, can remember exactly where they were and what they were doing when they heard the shocking news that John F. Kennedy had been assassinated. Similarly, millions of people can recall the moment and their surroundings on December 7, 1941, when they heard on the radio that Japanese planes had attacked Pearl Harbor, forcing the United States into World War II. Powerful and lasting memories of nearly equal force seize many people who can recall when men first walked on the moon in 1969 and when the *Challenger* space shuttle exploded on takeoff in 1986.

All are vivid examples of what some psychiatrists and psychologists call *flashbulb memories*, historic events that are burned into the minds of individuals, communities, or whole nations. Photography and radio gave us powerful sights and sounds and then continued to help unite the nation as we grieved or celebrated. The value then and now of such sights and sounds is enormous and growing.

The Kennedy shooting scene itself, as replayed for nearly forty years on the Zapruder tape (now available for $19.98), is horrifying . . . terrible . . . yet fascinating. Exactly why and how we are drawn to watch such moments of history, good and bad, again and again, has not been fully established, but these images are locked into our individual and collective consciousness for better or worse. The goal of photographers and camera operators is visual journalism that captures the "better" rather than the "worse." Either way, the power of pictures is enormous.

"If It Bleeds, It Leads"

The local evening newscast spotlights how television wields that power. Nearly every viewer probably can predict exactly when during the newscast that heart-wrenching or bloody story of a violent event will air. *After* a report about the opening of a new school or the community's need for more fire trucks? Not likely, you'll say, and you will nearly always be right. Many stations have the practice, if not policy, that "if it bleeds, it leads." Few television viewers or newspaper readers have not seen and reacted viscerally to such images as rescuers pulling a limp body from a river, grieving mothers writhing on an airport floor, or the blood-splattered interior of a wrecked car.

The blood is one reason for frequent complaints, but even that is often overshadowed by furor and fury about news teams that run after survivors of a disaster or make callous attempts to gain information and get an interview. Many viewers were outraged by the coverage of the bombing of Pan Am flight 103 over Lockerbie, Scotland, on December 21, 1988. Scores of reporters traveled first to New York's John F. Kennedy International Airport, where the Pan Am flight had been scheduled to arrive, to question stunned family members and friends, many of whom were just then learning the fate of the passengers. Journalists then hit Syracuse University, the intended destination of thirty-five students killed in the blast.

In subsequent days print and broadcast journalists overran the upstate New York campus looking to interview friends, relatives, and professors of the dead students. They rarely took "no comment" or "leave us alone" for an answer. Critics (the professionals as well as ordinary viewers) chastised television reporters, in particular, for what the audience repeatedly tagged the "stupid question" that sought the feelings of survivors without seeming to care about them.

The depth and persistence of the outraged reaction to the Pan Am 103 coverage did not soon fade, either. Interviews by scholars several years after the bombing uncovered a strong undercurrent of persistent bitterness among relatives against all the media and especially television.

Probably the ultimate in accusations of harm resulting from media harassment by photographers came after Princess Diana's death in 1997. The paparazzi that pursued her everywhere to snap candid shots were accused not just of bothering her but perhaps of causing her death and that of her friend, Dodi Al Fayed. Critics contended the high-speed crash in the Paris tunnel would not have occurred if her driver had not been trying to elude the superaggressive photographers who perpetually hounded Diana and whomever she was with. That feeling remained strong even after French authorities determined that her driver had been drinking heavily and taking prescription drugs before the fatal drive. The princess was not the usual type of victim. She sometimes manipulated the media, sometimes to publicize charitable causes and sometimes as part of her power struggle with the royal family. However mixed the intentions of all involved, Diana's family members and others charged that the media frenzy led to her death and made victims of her royal sons and other surviving relatives.

Why?

If survivors and the public decry broadcast and photo coverage of people's reactions to violence, why does it persist? One reason, to put it bluntly, is that it sells. Much of the public wants and watches emotion-laden newscasts and picks up newspapers and magazines with graphic photos. David Bartlett, former national president of the Radio-TV News Directors Association (RTNDA), does not defend the tabloid branch of broadcast journalism, but he does point out that no one forces viewers to watch such fare on their television news. They can, he points out, watch another channel or none at all. Indeed, if tabloid newscasts were not profitable (drawing the large numbers of viewers that in turn lure many advertising dollars), they would not proliferate, Bartlett told us.

That comment may be self-serving, but Bartlett is, no doubt, sadly correct that the public's taste for violence is considerable, protests or not. That view, however, does not consider the competitive pressure to churn out such reports or the effect on children who may see violence on the news. Walter Jacobson of WFLD-TV in Chicago and Howard Kurtz, media critic for the *Washington Post*, made another point at an Alfred I. du Pont–Columbia Forum on the demise of broadcast television standards. They argued that the growth in tabloid-style journalism on television and the decline of standards trace to the belief that "junk journalism" is easier, quicker, and cheaper to air than stories of more weight. Besides, they noted, "dull news" often lacks exciting video.

Equipment Tyranny

One reason that electronic journalists face so much internal and external criticism is the nature of the mechanical beast—the equipment. The very pieces of hardware that make it possible to hear and see so much also can intrude and frighten. Microphones and television cameras, complete with their bright lights, are necessary tools for broadcast reporters, but they can intimidate people. Even in happy situations more than a few normally talkative people suddenly are struck dumb when the mike or lens turns to them. When someone already is disturbed or grieving, the presence of in-your-face equipment can exacerbate the trauma.

In addition to criticizing the emotional distress such techniques cause, many citizens have complained when crushes of television and radio people blocked driveways and streets with vans and equipment, trampled and littered their yards, or knocked over furniture inside their houses while taking pictures or "awaiting developments." In June 1986 a battery from a television photographer's camera dropped twenty-five hundred feet from a helicopter through the roof and bedroom ceiling of a house in Bergen County, New Jersey. Fortunately, nobody was hurt, but the incident prompted organizations of news photographers to alert colleagues to the increasing likelihood and dangers of similar aerial bombardments. Again, the result of such mishaps can be anger and alienation from news consumers who already view the media with suspicion and disdain.

Little Things Matter

Common sense, experience, and some deliberate experiments do show that broadcast and print photographers and sound technicians can use their equipment sensitively and still get dynamite interviews. So often the trivial things are what can either upset or soothe someone. That became apparent in the taping of scenarios for instructional videotapes in the Victims and the Media Program of the Michigan State University School of Journalism. The tapes feature working reporters and editors who interview actors playing the parts of victims and relatives.

In the many critiques that followed the tapings, the actors, real victims, and their advocates often talked about the equipment. One frequent complaint was that a male television photographer and sound technician should not have placed a lapel microphone on a woman "rape victim" for the interview, even though he told her what he was about to do.

Another complaint was that the television reporter and camera operator had promised the rape survivor that they would hide her face so well that nobody could identify her, but viewers sometimes could make out her face. That should not happen in these days of electronic masking, which can blank out faces on tape. If masking is not available or desirable, the photographer can position the camera from the rear so showing the person's face is simply impossible.

Reporting teams can avoid or diminish some objections about radio and photo coverage with a little forethought and by using specialized equipment. "Gun" mikes can pick up voices from far enough away that shoving a mike in someone's face is simply inexcusable. Thankfully for those exposed to the popping little explosions of light for newspaper and magazine cameras, the days of flashbulbs are over; a person caught at a moment of grief or terror endured them only painfully. Modern strobe lights operate so briefly that, according to studies, subjects do not experience lingering physical effects.

Television floodlights are another matter. A battery of those powerful lights from the cameras of several stations at a scene still can heat up, literally and figuratively, already uncomfortable victims and families. Short deadlines and competitive pressure often make it tough to avoid that lighting excess. When possible, one option is for one station at a time to photograph the person, reducing the number of mounted camera lights and perhaps allowing for more careful indirect lighting. One station could provide the lighting while everyone else makes photographs.

Sometimes, though, the best step a photojournalist can take is to turn the camera off—or not turn it on in the first place. That may not earn praise from the boss, or even guarantee gratitude from the victim, but if a photographer or broadcast reporter really does not want to do harm, it may be necessary.

Radio interviews introduce another kind of "reality" issue. Trauma sufferers, especially witnesses to crime, often do not want their real voices on the air. An answer to that—if using a sound bite of a source is absolutely necessary—is to use electronic scramblers that distort voices enough to ensure identification is impossible. (Some scramblers even can make a female voice sound male and vice versa.) As with cameras, sometimes the best move in taping a radio interview when a victim is upset is to turn off the recorder. Sobs may make for "great" sound bites, but they also cause pain for concerned listeners. Interviewees who are given the opportunity to compose themselves when the recorder is off may be more able, and more inclined, to keep talking later.

Biology and Pictorial Horror

So *why* do blood and guts sell? We suspect that a basic attraction to violence and horror is rooted somewhere deep in the human condition. Psychologists and psychiatrists who study children's behavior find many cross-cultural examples of attractions to gory details in fairytales. Just think of some of the murderous and savage scenes in "Little Red Riding Hood" (a wolf devours a grandmother and in due course is killed by a wood chopper) and "Hansel and Gretel" (children abandoned by their parents end up shoving a witch in an oven).

"There is an undeniable interest when one is very, very young in horror and terror," the psychiatrist Frank Ochberg told us in an interview. "My take on all this is we do need to have certain images in our minds, and certain pathways in our brains, that allow us to incorporate scenes of violence, of horrible human cruelty and destruction. The way we digest them is to coat these scenes with humor, with mystery, with detachment, with kinds of pleasant shock and relief. This is the way we swallow the pill." That "pill" may be necessary, he contends, because we are not born with every image in our minds that we fear—or should fear.

"If we put all this together," Ochberg continued, "we can see there is a biological attraction to images of horror and terror, and an emotional response to it, whether it's television news or television fiction, or movie fiction or books or whatever. Our usual response is curiosity, interest, and even a certain amount of pleasure. That doesn't mean we're callous or corrupt or sadistic. It just means we're participating in a biological reality. Eventually, with enough experience and book learning, you come to know some of these things in your head are to be greatly feared, and you develop good ideas of what should be avoided."

Ochberg, however, has counseled hundreds of victims of traumatic stress and emphasizes that he is not advocating bigger and more frightening "doses" of horror and terror on television and in photos. "There are times when a dose of violence imagery is important," he says. "Does that mean we shouldn't have self-censorship? No; there are times when the dosage is excessive and not an 'inoculation.'"

History

The doctor may be on to something, if the history of visual journalism in the United States is a good indicator. Long before radio and television—or even published photography—newspaper and magazine readers were fascinated by illustrations of mayhem and disaster. In the mid-1800s newspapers and weekly magazines such as *Leslie's Illustrated Newspaper* (launched in 1855) and *Harper's Weekly* (founded in 1857) printed illustrations from woodcuts, drawings laboriously engraved by hand on wooden blocks. Sometimes the drawings were subjects such as sports, the latest fashionable clothing for ladies and gentlemen, or the likenesses of prominent officials and public figures. Other times, the illustrations featured crimes and disasters, and these usually boosted street sales.

The Civil War, though, saw the most intense use of illustrations in newspapers and magazines and the introduction—although not in publications—of photography. Combat artists watched the fighting and drew battle scenes and military leaders that were transferred to woodcuts by engravers at the newspapers and magazines. Eager readers in Richmond, Virginia, New York City, and many other communities of the North and South snapped up papers that might depict the scenes where their men in blue or gray were fighting and dying in huge numbers for four years.

Photography Develops

Public fascination with illustrated gore jumped during the Civil War, although it would be 1880 before a practical photoengraving process allowed U.S. newspapers and magazines to begin printing photographs. That did not stop the pioneering war photographer Mathew B. Brady from becoming a familiar sight around battlegrounds. Union soldiers, in fact, came to dread seeing Brady's little black wagon coming into camp because they knew it meant fighting was about to begin. He and his assistants took pictures of living and dead soldiers and horses, destroyed buildings, and devastated landscapes.

Photographers' primitive equipment could not capture live action, but for the first time it caught the aftermath, death and destruction, in real images. Just as worried and curious people lined up to read the latest battle casualty lists outside newspaper offices, they also thronged to studios to see photographs from recent battlefields. Part of the attraction undoubtedly was that many civilians desperately wanted to see something that might make them feel closer to their men in uniform, even if the scenes often were of death and destruction. Another aspect, though, apparently was that people felt drawn to the drama and violence of the war, even when their loved ones were not directly involved (Sloan and Startt 1996:208–10).

Of course, visual depictions of violence have long been attractive in and of themselves, just as their written counterparts have drawn readers for centuries. The newer technologies of movies, radio, and television certainly brought the sounds and images home in ways unimagined in the 1800s, but the public appetite for blood and gore seems impossible to sate.

Tabloid Photography

One of the hallmarks of tabloid journalism always has been the use of sensational photographs and illustrations, often related to crime and violence. Along with screaming headlines, comic strips, and stories of sex and crime, tabloid photography sought to catch the reader's eye at any cost. An infamous example is a New York *Daily News* extra (special) edition of 1928. It featured a photo of the death in the electric chair of Ruth Snyder, who had been convicted with her lover of murdering her husband. Photographer Tom Howard sneaked a camera strapped to his leg into Sing Sing to get the picture, which shows her body stiffening as the current surges through her. Many people protested the photo, but the *Daily News* could afford to withstand the complaints after selling an estimated half-million copies more than its usual daily circulation.

Before you say, "Well, that was the 1920s," consider that the term *tabloid journalism* seems to be having a rebirth today in reference to Princess Diana and the media feeding frenzy that accompanied the O. J. Simpson criminal trial.

Many of the most sensationalized pictures (and stories) are in the "super-market tabloids" that form a gauntlet at many stores' checkout counters, but does the public carefully distinguish between such publications and the mainstream press? Are, say, the *Washington Post* and *Los Angeles Times* lumped together with the *National Enquirer* and the *Globe* in many people's minds? Or, for example, are the network evening news shows blurred together with *Hard Copy* and *Extra!?* It often appears that they are, justifiably or not.

One reason for a fuzzy public perception of the differences may be that mainstream media are increasingly taking on the trappings of supermarket tabloids. At least, more "regular" media outlets seem to wait for the other type of publications to report some sensational tidbit and then use that as an excuse also to print or air the matter. In the case of television another reason may be that the networks often follow a nonsensational regular local news broadcast with a syndicated sensational tabloid show. Typical viewers might be forgiven for having a hard time distinguishing among the sources and formats that tumble one after the other on the same channel.

Frontline Shooters

News photographers and videographers often take the first battery of complaints about outrageous coverage of victims because these "shooters" (as they are often called within the trade) may be the first media people on the scene of a calamity and are working under intense deadline pressures. Because they often are the first to arrive, even before rescue personnel, the photographers may become participants in the very news they are covering.

All those factors were part of the mix in Anniston, Alabama, in 1983 when a small television station's camera crew (no reporters were immediately available) taped a man setting himself on fire. The thirty-seven-year-old jobless roofer had telephoned the station earlier and asked it to cover the self-immolation, which he said was to be a protest against unemployment.

The two television videographers (one experienced and the other an intern) notified police, then went to the park. Police found the site and left before both the man and the television crew arrived. As the videographers approached, the man doused himself with lighter fluid and tried to ignite it. The first match went out after fifteen seconds. He lit a second match. This time the flames spread swiftly over his body. After the man was engulfed in flames, one of the camera operators did try to put out the fire with his notebook. The man survived after he rushed across the park and a volunteer firefighter put out the flames with an extinguisher. Interestingly, it was the eighteen-year-old college intern who tried to put out the fire, while his experienced colleague kept the camera rolling.

Agonizing questions arose afterward: Why didn't the television crew immediately try to stop the man from lighting that first match, much less the second? For that matter, if the videographers had not shown up in the first place, might the fire not have occurred?

The shooters' bosses defended their actions and inactions, pointing out that the two did try to stop the man, but he warned them off several times before he lit the matches. Also, the station did not broadcast any of the tape showing the man ablaze, only the aftermath. The networks, though, picked up copies of the full tape and aired heavily edited scenes of the torching within a week. The case has been used to support an argument that journalists are too callous, as well as a contrary assertion that the photographers fully expected the police to stop the man and were doing their duty—concentrating on recording the event.

Not as much debate surfaced over another point: The victim *asked* for the coverage. That is why he called the station. Journalists have to consider whether their response may affect the plans of somebody who is seriously agitated.

Harrisburg Horror

But R. Budd Dwyer, the Pennsylvania state treasurer who killed himself before reporters and photographers at a news conference in the state capitol in Harrisburg, gave no advance warning of his intentions. Dwyer was facing prison after convictions for bribery, mail fraud, and racketeering. He presumably was going to make a statement about the matter and, many reporters thought, resign. Nobody but Dwyer apparently knew what he really intended. Cameras were rolling and clicking when he pulled a .357-caliber Magnum out of an envelope, put the long-barreled pistol in his mouth, and pulled the trigger.

The 1987 news conference was not being televised live, but all the journalists there and their bosses had to make quick decisions. This was not a scene involving an unknown private citizen in a quiet park but a well-known public official in a public building before at least eight television crews and five still photographers and reporters.

Could any of them have stopped him in time? Almost all later said no. Many said they thought the gun probably was just a prop and that Dwyer did not intend to shoot himself. Others worried briefly that perhaps he would turn the weapon on them. At any rate, Dwyer, his back to a wall, had put a blockade of desks and chairs around himself, and only fifteen seconds elapsed from the time he produced the gun until he fired.

The question after the shooting became how much to show on air and in print. Many editors and news directors in Pennsylvania and across the nation agonized over how much of Dwyer's press conference they should show. Several television stations had taped the whole sequence and had to decide how much of it to air. The Associated Press moved a series of photos that included the gun in Dwyer's mouth and another at the moment of death. *News Photographer* magazine later ran a special twenty-page report analyzing how print photos and television tapes were used in the Harrisburg case.

Taken together, who used what often depended on how close a station or paper was to the event, the *News Photographer* found. In general, the farther from Harrisburg, the more likely it was that a station or paper would show the most graphic photos. The *Patriot*, Harrisburg's hometown daily, used a large front-page photo showing Dwyer with the gun in one hand and warding off the observers with his other hand. Hundreds of miles away, the *New York Daily News* ran four large photos on inside pages, showing Dwyer warding off observers, the gun in Dwyer's mouth, the instant of death, and Dwyer's bloody body slumped on the floor. The *Washington Post* used the stand-back photo on its front page and the gun-in-mouth and moment-of-death pictures inside.

There was little sign in the Dwyer case that editors and news directors asked the print and video photographers what they thought about which pictures their papers and stations should use. Photojournalists in this and other situations have complained that too often they are treated merely as mechanical tools that help take the picture, rather than flesh-and-blood professionals whose opinions and sensibilities ought to be considered. Indeed, editors and directors have to make the ultimate decisions on video and photo use. What they see on their computer monitors, however, can be quite detached from the intimate view the photographers had as they peered through their lenses at their subjects.

Among the many complaints about media coverage of Dwyer's suicide, one was less concerned with the initial televising than with repeated showings. If it is deemed necessary to show a gory scene once to inform people (and/or keep up with competition), does it follow that it serves a useful purpose to multiply the broadcasts? A broadcast fact of life, of course, is that a station or network cannot predict when or how often a particular viewer or listener will hear or see something. Still, hour after hour, day after day, of showing the same tape can reasonably be called overkill.

The Harrisburg suicide, bizarre as it was, simply may be an extreme example of situations in which a photo or tape is considered too gruesome to be shown in the hometown newspaper or on a station near the event but is deemed acceptable for audiences hundreds or thousands of miles away in order to satisfy the interest or morbid curiosity of strangers.

The Proximity Factor

Television news directors and newspaper editors who were stung by criticism about their visual choices in the Dwyer case sometimes noted this phenomenon: The same evening that the networks declined to run the Dwyer tapes, they showed soldiers shooting down demonstrators in the Philippines. Similarly, the next day several prominent papers that withheld the Harrisburg photos ran gory photos, often on the front page and in color, of the dead or wounded Filipinos.

The editors and news directors described a situation that has bothered many journalists for years. Every journalism student is told that proximity is one factor that can make something newsworthy. The folks in Peoria are more likely to be interested in—and directly affected by ("impact")—a broken gas main in their own downtown than a murder in Los Angeles. But what if a suspect in that murder case happens to be someone named O. J. Simpson? The Simpson story triggered other newsworthy elements— prominence (a widely known sports and entertainment figure) and conflict (crime, the murder of two people).

Add to that brew another news element, novelty, and the recipe seems irresistible to many papers and magazines. That appeared to be the situation in 1963, when U.S. newspapers everywhere ran photos of a Buddhist monk in South Vietnam as he set himself on fire to protest government actions, and later when photos showed a six-year-old naked, screaming Vietnamese girl running toward the camera after being burned by American napalm bombs. The Associated Press won a Pulitzer Prize for Eddie Adams's 1968 photo of a suspected Vietcong agent the instant he was shot in the head at point-blank range by a South Vietnamese national police commander before a group of journalists on a Saigon street. NBC broadcast film of the execution. Would the photo or television film have run if it had been an American being shot?

Heavy public criticism and internal journalism debate did erupt in 1980 over use of photos showing the burned bodies of American commandos killed in an aborted attempt to rescue U.S. embassy hostages in Iran. Still greater outcries later followed when television broadcast tape (and newspapers published photos) of a dead American soldier dragged through a street by gleeful Somalis during the U.S. humanitarian intervention in that African land's civil strife.

In all, editors long have known it is more acceptable to run photos of dead people who are not local, that a body bag probably is less offensive than showing the body itself, and that even showing a body may be acceptable if the face is not visible.

What is changing is that more readers and viewers seem to be taking offense at those practices as well as gorier instances. Is there, finally, an overload setting in among the public? The continuing popularity of the supermarket tabloids and their television equivalents seems to challenge that notion, but it would not be the first time that society's opposition to a certain behavior grows alongside its popularity until a critical mass of hostility is reached. (Consider the antismoking movement, for example.) The resulting explosion can be painful or fatal to the targeted group. The print and electronic news media probably have enough survival and growth obstacles to deal with these days without fostering further erosion of trust.

Live—Death Before Your Eyes!

One of the obvious and powerful attractions of television is its ability to show an event as it happens—the Super Bowl, the funeral of an assassinated president or of a beloved princess, a man walking on the moon (delayed only a few seconds from space). Such live television can entertain, inform, inspire, help bring a grieving nation together, or fashion a sense of community among millions of scattered people. Decades ago radio brought much of that immediacy and connection with its live voices and sounds; television multiplied the effect with its sights.

Unfortunately, live radio and television sometimes can exact a toll on listeners. Shocked listeners heard the near-hysterical horror in the voice of a radio reporter in 1937 as he described the burning of the German zeppelin *Hindenburg* as it caught fire and crashed in flames at its mooring in Lakehurst, New Jersey. Forty-nine years later shocked viewers saw live and worldwide the horror on the faces of the parents of teacher Christa McAuliffe as the space shuttle *Challenger* exploded on takeoff, killing their daughter and six astronauts.

We have seen how difficult it can be to decide what sounds and images to broadcast or print when journalists have only minutes or hours to make decisions. The stakes are even higher when the broadcast is live. Although the benefit of the live shot is immediacy, a drawback is the meager time for editorial judgment to gauge how live footage of an event or interview will come across to viewers. The shock can be overwhelmingly personal if a family member or friend hears about a loved one's death over the air—or even sees it on a television screen as it happens.

Actually, considering the proliferation and competitive pressures of television news coverage, it may be surprising that more live televised killings have not occurred. American television watchers witnessed an actual killing for the first time in 1963, when Jack Ruby shot Lee Harvey Oswald, the accused assassin of John F. Kennedy.

It was not, however, until April 1998 that the first suicide on live television actually happened. Once again, the scene was a Los Angeles freeway. This time a disturbed man stopped on an overpass, at one point unfurling a banner that read, "HMOs are in it for the money! Live free, love safe, or die!" After setting his clothes, his pickup, and his dog on fire, the man placed a shotgun under his chin and pulled the trigger. Seven local stations and MS-NBC were showing the scene live. Two of the local stations interrupted children's programs for the occasion.

Now, the stations did not know at first that the man intended to kill himself. The live coverage started after police reported a sniper was driving along the freeway and stopping at various points. That certainly was a newsworthy event at afternoon rush hour on one of the most crowded thoroughfares in the United States, but did it have to be televised live? Even if the likelihood he would commit suicide was not immediately obvious, the knowledge that he was armed and apparently a sniper should have alerted news directors to the possibility that live coverage might show him committing violence.

Tom Goldstein, dean of the Columbia University School of Journalism, noted in a commentary for *TV Guide* shortly after the suicide that the stations had an alternative to live coverage: "Every live event is not newsworthy, and journalists are being asked to make quick editing judgments of what is important. It was easy not to show the suicide last month. Some stations demonstrated commendable strength by cutting away from the scene—or, better still, not going live" (1998:41).

Two subsequent letters to *TV Guide* from readers vigorously endorsed Goldstein's commentary, although one from a Pennsylvania woman also called the magazine hypocritical for putting a photo from the scene in the middle of the article. (It was a little photo taken from a television screen that showed the man getting out of his pickup before he shot himself.) The other letter, from an Illinois woman, summed up not only a general feeling about the particular event but a more general public anger over media coverage: "Amen, Mr. Goldstein, amen. Take note, all news anchors and newspeople— the thinking people of the world are rapidly becoming totally disenchanted with you. You have become a media full of sensationalism, violence, crudeness and bad manners. Congratulations to the stations who cut away from the suicide scene" (Gilliland 1998:86).

That reader perhaps had in mind both broadcast and print media in some of her comments, but the immediate television reporting was what triggered her passionate and thorough condemnation of reporting practices. After the suicide, some broadcast chieftains acknowledged they had sinned and vowed to do differently the next time. CNBC announced it henceforth would use a tape-delay of several seconds when airing live feeds with the potential to become violent.

One thoughtful reaction—during a Today Show roundup the day after the suicide—came from Stephen Cohen, news director of KCOP-TV in Los Angeles (whose station had interrupted adult programming to show the death the previous day): "I do think this will force a very real reconsideration of the use of live television and how quick we are to show everything that we're able to show, so that technology does not outstrip our journalistic ability to make decisions. And I think that'll be a good thing, and probably the only good thing, that'll come of this event."

Many stations that showed the event live pledged afterward to refrain from broadcasting the actual shooting again. Several, though, replayed tapes of the man with his clothes afire.

Guidelines

Given all the conflicting advice and situations, it may seem impossible to conclude there's any one "right" way to handle visuals when it comes to broadcasting death. However, we have some ideas about publishing a photo, airing a radio report, or telecasting a death.

Some of the most practical and blunt proposals come from professional organizations. For example, RTNDA has been a leader in exploring the topic in newsletters, meetings, and seminars. Similarly, *News Photographer* magazine for years has published vigorous internal debates and soul searching about who should be pictured, and how, in violent situations. Other intensive explorations have come from organizations with a teaching mission, among them the Poynter Institute for Media Studies.

We have put together a list of guidelines from the recommendations of these various organizations:

- Do not knowingly allow a live broadcast of a killing, whether homicide or suicide, especially in close-up and showing wounds and blood.
- Build in a delay of several seconds during live transmissions to allow a decision on whether to show something.
- Insist that photographers and photo and graphics editors join other editors or news directors in deciding what photos to publish or tapes to air.
- Be sure relatives have been notified before you announce or show the identity of a person who has been killed. (That may be impossible in rare instances such as Dwyer's suicide in Harrisburg—a well-known public official at a public forum—but even a few minutes' delay could help authorities notify key family members first.)
- Do not interrupt children's programming to show deaths.
- For television news reports, give viewers enough advance warning of what you are about to show so that someone can leave the room, remove children, or change channels.
- Remember that children may be able to see a photo in a newspaper left lying around or when adults have left the television on.
- For newspapers, think about the relative effects of photos published on the front page and inside pages. Something that might be too graphic for someone (especially a child) glancing at a front page could be less troublesome inside.
- No matter what photos or footage you decide to use, tell the whole story—before, during, and after—of what happened to the human being involved, not just the death.
- If you decide to show a tape of some part of a suicide or other death, do it once—say, on the first regular evening news—but do not use file tape in subsequent telecasts.
- If you have considered all these factors and still cannot decide what to do, try what the *Christian Science Monitor*'s Buffy Chindler calls the "Wheaties Test": Would it be suitable for the breakfast table?

- As soon as deadline pressures ease, discuss the decision, how it affected survivors and the public, and whether you should have handled anything differently. The more discussion there is of these experiences, the more likely you are to avoid thoughtless miscues in the future.
- Finally, do not assume that these, or any other guidelines or policies, will save you from agonizing over what to show and not show. They will not and perhaps should not.

War—The Ultimate Visual Frontier

One other special pictorial realm remains to be explored: the visual depiction of war. Whatever the intensity and importance of the discussions of violent local news, they pale when compared with war coverage. War has a way of combining threats to our individual existence with threats to our national survival and way of life. For photojournalists and broadcasters war brings extraordinary opportunities to show war and how it affects people on the battlefields and home fronts. With that comes the potential to bring more pain quickly and vividly to survivors.

Earlier we touched on the Civil War illustrations that drew thousands of eager and anxious readers and viewers to newspapers, magazines, and photo galleries. They were merely a tiny primitive taste, however, of what was to come pictorially. Newspaper and magazine photographs, movie newsreels, radio, and television followed in succession and accompanied fighting Americans on land, sea, and air.

During World War I (1914–1918), many Americans could for the first time see moving scenes of battlefield action. World War II, which erupted in Europe in 1939, brought radio prominently into war coverage for the first time. When Edward R. Murrow intoned, "This is London . . ." from the besieged British capital, the U.S. radio audience began to understand how civilians were suffering from the Nazi blitz and what might lie ahead for populations everywhere.

Japanese pilots used Honolulu radio station broadcasts to home in on their Pearl Harbor targets that infamous Sunday morning of December 7, 1941. After that, U.S. radio covered the war along with newspapers, magazines, and newsreels. A handful of television stations were broadcasting then, and New York City's WCBW announced bulletins on the Pearl Harbor attack and showed maps of the Hawaiian war zone to a few thousand viewers. A 1942 government freeze halted construction of new television stations; the historians Edwin Emery and Michael Emery found only six stations were still broadcasting when the war ended in 1945.

Security and sensitivity concerns largely blocked publication of photos or film of U.S. war dead during World War II. It is believed that photos of dead Americans were first published in 1943, halfway through the war, when *Life* magazine showed a helmeted GI face down, half-buried in New Guinea beach sand. Photos of American dead and wounded were published only rarely after that. Families of U.S. military personnel usually heard first from a dreaded telegram or knock on the door that a son or daughter or husband had been killed or hurt, but the Pentagon regularly released casualty lists, which were quickly printed in newspapers.

The Korean War saw the first widespread reliance on television for information on the whereabouts of fighting Americans, although newspapers, radio, and newsreels still provided the bulk of the coverage. Murrow, who had shifted from radio to television, led television's first full-length combat report in 1952. His heralded "Christmas in Korea" show depicted for Americans the hardships many soldiers endured in that stalemated war.

Vivid broadcast and photo coverage no doubt helped fuel public discontent about U.S. losses (33,629 dead) and the inconclusive end of the Korean fighting. It remained, however, for another Southeast Asian war to show the influence of television and print photography on U.S. voters, who very gradually decided the cost was too great. The coverage of fighting in Indochina stretched from early U.S. military aid to France in the 1950s through the huge build-up of forces in the 1960s to U.S. withdrawal and the surrender of Saigon by the South Vietnamese government to Communist soldiers in April 1975. From Vietnam Americans saw television film or photos of such horrifying scenes as the Buddhist monk setting himself on fire, the street execution of the Vietcong prisoner, the fleeing burned girl, and the burning of a Vietnamese village. Film reports also often showed U.S. troops feeding Vietnamese children or rebuilding village huts, but those scenes apparently did not stick in viewers' minds.

At home the political conflict sometimes seemed as bad or worse, indelibly highlighted as Americans watched Chicago police club and teargas youths during the infamous "Days of Rage" at the Democratic National Convention in 1968 and as National Guard troops killed four students at Kent State University in 1970.

People still argue why Vietnam was such a debacle, but television and photo coverage depicted and helped fuel the weariness, impatience, and (especially among youth) outrage that forced the United States to get out of the traumatic and seemingly unwinnable conflict. Scenes of suffering Vietnamese civilians and body bags containing U.S. military personnel (about fifty-five thousand Americans died there) were bad enough, but when the victims included protesting U.S. college students, it became clear to the country that it was time to get out of Vietnam.

Television Myths

Television undoubtedly played a prominent role in affecting U.S. voters' perceptions of the Vietnam War. Yet some myths that sprang up about media coverage bear examination. Certain notions, such as the idea that the media generally and television in particular, "caused" the loss of South Vietnam, are outside the scope of this volume. One other lingering misreading, though, is that television brought "the truth" about the death and violence of war into American living rooms. The implication is that television showed many dead people and often broadcast real combat action (Braestrup 1985).

CBS correspondent Morley Safer reflected such a view of television's influence during the Vietnam War in this part of a 1966 commentary that originally appeared in an Overseas Press Club publication: "The camera can describe in excruciating, harrowing detail what war is all about. The cry of pain, the shattered face—it's all there on film, and out it goes into millions of American homes during the dinner hour" (Braestrup 1985:67).

Actually, except for a few notable instances, such as Safer's own report of the burning of a hamlet in 1965, the networks seldom showed the dead or wounded. Lawrence W. Lichty noted in the book *Vietnam as History* that while about half the television reports filed from Vietnam concerned military action, most showed little actual fighting. Most filmed reports showed helicopters buzzing overhead, troops filing down jungle trails, or smoke or explosions in the distance (1984:158).

A different myth emerged from the Persian Gulf War in 1991. It became almost gospel that the conflict with Iraq was the "first war brought live into our living rooms." To be sure, some broadcast coverage was outstanding. CNN's Peter Arnett and Bernard Shaw won much praise for their flashbulb memory report of the opening allied air attack on Baghdad. Plaudits also went to other broadcast reporters. For example, CBS News's Bob McKeown drew attention for entering liberated Kuwait City just ahead of the coalition forces, and NBC's Arthur Kent was dubbed "the Scud Stud" for his live reports while under Scud missile attack.

Despite such vivid reporting, live television news showed little actual fighting and death in the Gulf War. No home viewers saw people dying before their eyes. Tapes tended to show military build-ups, missiles being launched from warships, destroyed buildings and Iraqi equipment, and news conferences with officers explaining aerial and ground successes. The military's control of information gathering and transmission (which, journalists complained, had reached unprecedented restrictions), as well as logistical and geographical restraints, limited news coverage. That suited many a Pentagon official and, judging by public opinion surveys at the time, many American news consumers. For example, the Times Mirror Center for the People and the Press polled Americans two weeks after the war began. Seventy-six percent said they knew the Pentagon censored news reports on the conflict (Gannett Foundation 1991:90–91). Indeed, 57 percent in the same poll said the military should exert *more* control over the media. That and similar surveys did not try, however, to plumb whether the public realized the extent of the censorship. After all, if citizens do not know something happened, how can they evaluate the importance of what they missed?

One of the most gruesome scenes from the Persian Gulf showed Iraqi soldiers burned to death around their vehicles as they tried to flee Kuwait City as the end of the conflict neared. Again, these were the enemy dead and they were far away. Because television crews could not get access to Iraq, viewers did not see live scenes of what happened when bombs fell on both military personnel and civilians—just as they had not seen Saddam Hussein's earlier bombing and gassing of ethnic Iraqi populations before the war or his treatment of occupied Kuwait. The easy win by the U.S.-led coalition brought relief and jubilation, but Americans still had not seen vivid television footage of the trauma of war.

The Rest of a Photo Story

One Vietnam War photo stands as both an example of the lasting power of visual journalism and its inability to tell the whole story. Thirty years after he took his Pulitzer Prize–winning picture, AP photographer Eddie Adams shared his thoughts as he focused his camera on Gen. Nguyen Ngoc Loan's execution of a Vietcong agent at point-blank range. The picture fortified public opinion against the war because so many people considered the general's action brutal and uncivilized. When Loan died in 1998, he was running a restaurant in Virginia, where he had moved his family after Saigon fell. In his obituary in *Time* magazine Adams commented: "Still photographs are the most powerful weapon in the world. People believe them, but photographs do lie, even without manipulation. They are only half-truths. What the photograph didn't say was, 'What would you do if you were the general at that time and place on that hot day, and you caught the so-called bad guy after he blew away one, two or three American soldiers?'" (1998:19).

Adams noted that the photograph also did not show that the general devoted much of his time to trying to get hospitals built to handle war casualties and was admired by his troops. In a way, Adams said, two people died in the photo: the Vietcong agent and the general. The picture "really messed up" the general's life, although Loan never blamed him personally, Adams wrote. (1998:19). The photo and Adams's comments illustrate how important it is to try to put a story in full context. A single photo or taped scene may burn into our consciousness; it may also signal that we need to know more about what we are seeing. Whether the location is a war-torn Vietnamese street or a body-littered U.S. schoolyard, powerful images need powerful handling.

Certainly the differences between still pictures and television footage are important. Still photography requires proximity. To be effective, photos must show facial expressions. Television can get by with less descriptive sights. CNN, for instance, showed little but flashing lights in its much-praised presence in Baghdad during the Gulf War. Of course, that display was not reporting restraint but an example of correspondents making the best out of being pinned down at a hotel.

Whatever television actually did is almost irrelevant; the perception of its enormous role in the Vietnam and Persian Gulf wars underlines the mighty influence of the medium in depicting violence. We have seen how strongly newspaper and magazine photos can affect readers. The reaction to violence and its aftermath may be revulsion or fascination, whether the cause is murder, suicide, or accident and whether the stage is a small room or a far-flung battlefield.

Clearly, many viewers and readers will react strongly to graphic images, whether the scene is an Oregon schoolyard, a Pennsylvania state office, an Oklahoma federal building, a Los Angeles freeway overpass, a Middle East war zone, or an East Coast airline crash site.

It behooves photojournalists and broadcasters both to celebrate the power for good under their command and to respect the harm it can do, unchained, to aggravate human suffering. Circulation and ratings are facts of journalistic life, but if they are all a station or paper considers, more and more outraged consumers may flip the page or hit the "off" button. Dramatic *and* compassionate visual and audio journalism does and will draw listeners and viewers, sell papers, and win honors. Photos and voices that vividly tell the whole story of ordinary people under extraordinary circumstances will have even more important roles in the new century. Coverage that ignores or debases the human factor will increasingly draw the contempt it deserves.

We also urge news organizations to recognize that their photographers are the most vulnerable of all employees to traumatic injury. Like many of the photographers themselves, editors accept the myth of the "camera as shield." We know that reporters who regularly cover violence may suffer from emotional stress. Although photographers have not been studied much, we strongly suspect that the effects may be even greater for some of them. As this book went to press in the spring of 2000, the National Press Photographers Association was about to make its first member survey of the extent of their exposure to violence and their own emotional responses. The study was designed to provide a benchmark assessment of the building toll of general assignment photography, and the association planned to use its findings in training its members and devising effective means of supporting photographers and videographers.

Lynne Dobson

Photos That Connect

The paramedic described him as "a human being in tatters," crisp skin hanging off in rags, more than 80 percent of his body burned. The fire, the work of an arsonist, took Emmett Jackson's hands, nose, ears, eyelids, and lips and killed his wife and baby daughter. Three years later photographer Lynne Dobson and reporter Michele Stanush of the *Austin American-Statesman* set out to learn how he had survived such loss and kept going. The result was an award-winning story, "The Test of Fire."

Lynne Dobson. PHOTO BY MS. DOBSON.

The photos are compelling, not just for the respectful way they reveal such horrible injuries but for the way they transform the reader. Dobson turns the voyeuristic impulse to simply *stare* at a disfigured human and back away into a sense of connection.

The first photo in "The Test of Fire" shows Jackson at nineteen in his army uniform, its frame propped next to a similarly framed photograph of his wife, Diathia, and baby girl, Pookie. Below, in the second photo, Jackson is alone at the window of his apartment. A ball cap covers his head, a patch his left eye. His ears are holes, his face and arms a patchwork of grafted skin. He leans toward the daylight. Before and after, the readers want to get closer, to understand the journey between and beyond.

For Dobson any discomfort she felt in Jackson's presence was short-lived. "He made it easier," she says. "He taught me to see through his appearance." Her photos, each a reminder of how much more a person is than face or hands, teach the same. She captures nuances of posture that are as expressive as a raised eyebrow or the crinkle in the corner of an eye. There's the set of Jackson's shoulders—all attention—as the therapist teaches him to use a headset. The stiff determined stride as he jogs. The exuberance in his raised metal forearms as he watches a football game to which he drove in his own car. And, most especially, there's the unexpected tenderness in Jackson's prosthetic claws as he holds a worn open Bible, its page marked by Diathia's picture and obituary. The layout itself is a progression that reflects the increments of Jackson's physical and spiritual recovery.

Dobson brought to this assignment fourteen years of experience and an ability to recognize commonalities with survivors. One of her early photo assignments was the funeral of a man who died in a military plane crash; in the frame of her camera's long lens she saw the man's young son, wrapped in his mother's arms, look up as a plane flew overhead. Dobson, whose father was killed in a plane crash when she was a girl, felt an immediate attachment. She also knew she had a great picture and would have to put her camera aside to ask the woman for her name. "I was crying when I approached her," Dobson says without a tinge of apology in her voice. "I'm a human first. A photojournalist second." Time and again, the human touch is what she remembers most. Describing photos she took of seven-year-old Jonna Daughn as she underwent treatment for a leukemia that proved fatal, Dobson pauses to note that the previous day would have been the little girl's birthday. Her rapport with Emmett Jackson began when she first learned about the fire, which occurred on her own birthday.

All this empathy would be lost without the technical skills to communicate it through photos. Listen to her describe other assignments and you come to understand where she learned, and continues to hone, many of her skills. Shooting fashion trains her eye for light, posture, and shape. On fashion shoots everything is controlled, and facial expressions—consistently vacant, even when the models smile—are not primary. Sports coverage keeps Dobson alert for decisive moments and forces her to trust her intuition to capture the one shot that tells the story of the entire event. "You flow as *they* flow."

For Dobson time can be as essential as camera, lenses, and film. During the six months she followed Jonna Daughn and her family, on some days she took no pictures at all, and on others she went through six or seven rolls of film. "The Test of Fire" took her and Stanush eighteen months to report. "You can't have a list," she says of her approach to such stories. "It's more like a blank slate and you let them [the subjects] fill it in."

When she covered accidents, violence, and natural disasters, Dobson appreciated the support she received at the *Austin American-Statesman*, especially its policy that it will not publish photos of dead bodies or body bags. (She left the paper in 1999 to concentrate on freelance photography.) At funerals she combined respect for the wishes of the family with good manners: she wore black, stayed in one place, and used a silent shutter. "I'm just a journalist, but I'm usually accepted," she says. Still, ethical dilemmas are unavoidable, such as the time she was told to get a picture of former U.S. representative Barbara Jordan on a gurney after a near drowning in 1988. "I hated taking those photos," Dobson says. After much debate about whether to print the pictures, the staff chose the most unobtrusive—Jordan is mostly hidden from view by the three emergency medical technicians who are helping her—and ran it on page 3.

Dobson is well aware of her potential to revictimize people in the course of crime coverage, even as she feels the competitive pull of pack journalism. "I try to keep my head on straight, to remember that the people involved have a life *beyond* the event." A long lens, unobtrusive angles, and putting her camera aside to connect with survivors helps, as does focusing on what readers will think and feel. "Readers *care* about people," she says. Because Dobson is aware that readers will be interested later, she always keeps an eye out for follow-up ideas. Her deference and restraint immediately after the arson, when Jackson's family and the hospital staff forbade all pictures, laid the foundation of trust she needed three years later for "The Test of Fire."

Like the survivors she photographs, Dobson has learned that to move forward, sometimes it is important to pull back. "You're a privileged witness to life on the edge," she says of her work. "You've got to think about what you're doing to those lives."

A framed photo of Emmett Jackson at 19, propped next to one of his wife and baby girl, quietly marks the past as it guides readers to consider how struggle and survival underlie the scarred image they will see in the other Dobson pictures. (Photo sequence courtesy of the photographer and the *Austin American-Statesman.*)

In his apartment, Jackson leaned toward the daylight inviting the reader to understand his journey. Dobson said Jackson had taught her to "see through his appearance," an effect she achieved in this and other pictures.

Jackson jogged, and Dobson's picture asserted both his physical strength and his confidence.

Dobson's camera caught Jackson's hands - the prostheses he used to read his Bible - and the bookmark made from his wife's obituary.

Jackson had become active in the High Praise Church
and said that God wanted him to be an example for others.

Jackson cheered at a Cowboys/Oilers scrimmage game,
his exuberance obvious in his raised metal forearms.

Dobson found ways to illuminate the milestones of Jackson's physical and spiritual recovery. In rehabilitation, when Jackson could barely walk, he vowed to one day climb a nearby hill. When he was able to complete the climb, therapists named the hill for him.

A team of therapists helped Jackson learn to do everything from using his prostheses to standing up. Here, he talked to three members of the team, Sara Dwyer, Rosa Cavazos, and Lynda Jennings.

A Dobson photo subtly underlined the importance of both technology and human caring in Jackson's recovery. A special phone lit up to alert him to incoming calls (damaged nerves in Jackson's ears robbed him of much of his hearing). Charlotte Missouri was one of his early care providers.

Michele Stanush

The Test of Fire

Over an eighteen-month period photographer Lynne Dobson and reporter Michele Stanush followed the recovery of arson victim Emmett Jackson. Despite the horrific details and images of the fire and his many losses, the resulting story portrays Jackson as a whole and engaging person. These photographs and story excerpts are taken from the two-part series "The Test of Fire," published in the Austin American-Statesman *on September 4 and 5, 1994.*

April 1993—Emmett Jackson sits rod-straight in the front row of a federal courtroom, a Dallas Cowboys cap guarding his scarred scalp and a black patch covering his left eye.

Metal claws have replaced Emmett's fingers. There are bare nasal cavities where he once had a nose and holes where there once were ears. His lips were rebuilt by doctors.

Emmett, 37, is anxious for this day to be over. It's the sentencing date for the man convicted of setting the October 1990 fire that changed Emmett's life—leaving him maimed and alone.

His wife and only child died.

The arsonist—a five-time felon nicknamed "Trigger"—enters the courtroom. He's a stocky 33-year-old with a defiant chin. He strolls to the front without even a sideways glance at Emmett.

Does he have any idea what he's done? Emmett thinks.

In his old life, Emmett Jackson was an easy-going supermarket baker who loved the feel of raw dough between his fingers. *Texture is the key,* he'd say.

He was a handsome man who dressed sharp, joked hard, and jogged fast. He had long, well-toned limbs and a low voice with lyrical cadence—like a poet or a preacher. Except Emmett didn't care much for church. He preferred to hang out with friends or spend time with his family.

He'd "rassle" with his little girl and bake cinnamon rolls for neighboring kids. And he was deeply in love with his wife, a pretty woman with almond-shaped eyes and a keen intellect. "I'd never experienced a woman like that before," he says.

The fire changed all that.

* * *

In February, Emmett gets a call from the Austin Fire Department. A videotape is being produced for troubled teens who have set fires. Safety officials figure young firebugs might be strongly affected by seeing someone like Emmett.

Would he be willing to tell his story?

Emmett finds the prospect daunting. There will be lights and cameras and lots of videotape to be filled. But at the same time, he's excited. This is just the kind of thing he figures he was saved for.

I survived a truly tragic fire.

There must be a reason.

As he prepares for the taping, he gets a little notebook and—with a pencil gripped in his prosthesis—writes down topics to discuss: the consequences of crime, the loss of freedom. In the mid-1980s, he spent almost three years in prison for his stint as a burglar and forger. And he hated it. He hated being told when to wake up. What to do during the day.

Do kids realize what it means to be locked away, Emmett wonders.

More importantly, do they realize the price their victims pay? Particularly for something like arson?

"I was incarcerated for two years and 10 months, and not one day of it felt like a week of this," Emmett says. "And not the whole time I was there, it didn't match this at all, what I'm going through right now."

The day of the taping is chilly. Emmett puts on his Cowboys cap, a striped shirt and blue jeans. As always, he wears the gold chain his mother bought after an operation gave Emmett back his neck; his chin was scarred down onto his chest.

Emmett meets the video crew in the hall, casually extending his prostheses to shake hands. He senses that they might be apprehensive about seeing him. Most people are when they meet him for the first time.

It's up to me to put them at ease, he thinks.

("I was expecting some monster," one crew member later admitted, "but that's just the imagination working overtime.")

Lights are set up, the camera is focused on Emmett's face, and the interview begins.

"You want to tell us a little bit about what happened?"

For the most part, Emmett is tired of telling the story. He's repeated it umpteen times: How Diathia heard crashing noises about 2 a.m.; how they quickly realized the complex was on fire; how he had no choice but to send his family through a wall of flames.

But maybe this time, Emmett thinks, it will be a lesson.

He tells the story in a deep, melodic voice—a voice better suited for reading a bedtime story:

"The fire was spreading so fast . . .

"The windows upstairs . . .

"We could hear them crashing and popping . . .

"The railings from the stairwell . . .

"They was twisting and cracking . . .

"The fire and the heat was so intense . . .

"I couldn't judge my distance . . .

"It was burning my eyelids . . ."

Emmett wonders if fire-happy kids have any idea how fast a blaze can spread and how much damage it can do. As the camera hums, he looks into space and describes emerging from the flames to see his wife:

"Her hair was singed to her. Her gown was seared to her, and she was different colors. And then she told me that she dropped the baby."

Emmett pauses and purses his lips. There was a time when he couldn't talk about his family without crying. But time has dulled the hurt. Now all he needs is a pause.

"And so," he continues, "we was telling each other not to hold each other 'cause we didn't want our skins to touch and lose what little skin we had left."

Did Diathia ever regain consciousness in the hospital?

"She opened her eyes only one time, I think, to have a chance to see her mother. But she never really gained consciousness, so she never really suffered.

"Which is good because getting well was not easy."

Sometimes, Emmett still thinks about his months in the hospital and rehab institute—the frightening hallucinations, the strange skin sensations, the excruciating pain.

"It was very painful just to take a bath," Emmett tells the camera. "That took an hour and a half. To wash an arm, I had to get another shot of morphine. To do the right arm, that was another shot. To do both legs, each would be another shot."

For a long time, Emmett had flashbacks of the fire. He also had strange nightmares. Once, he was surrounded by snails that grew as big as cats and multiplied when he tried to whack them to death.

The snails, a psychologist surmised, symbolized the fire.

The weird dreams are long gone. So are the flashbacks. And the pain. Still every day remains a series of challenges—from opening doors to carrying groceries to dressing.

Once that fire strikes you it goes deep, and it does it quickly, Emmett thinks. *I wish an arsonist would think about that.*

As much as Emmett hates to be dependent on other people, he still needs help with simple tasks, like buttoning clothes. If he wants to look nice for an early-morning appointment, before his helper arrives, he must sleep all night dressed up in a shirt and tie.

Meantime, as hard as he's worked to accept his new looks, reactions from other people can still pain him—particularly when children grab onto parents' shirttails, nervous and scared.

Can you grow hair? the woman from the fire department asks.

This time Emmett smiles.

"I had about six strings growing up there, and then it fell off," he says. "I just had a friend the other day tell me balding is in. Which was real good for me 'cause I can't help but have a complex about the way I look."

Chapter 7

Reporting on Rape Trauma

On a Sunday morning in February 1990, an emotional and extraordinary story gripped readers of the *Des Moines Register*. The first of a five-part series told the story of a twenty-nine-year-old woman who had been raped by a stranger. He had entered her car as she was studying for a licensing test early in the morning in a college parking lot. The story spared few details as it conveyed some of the horror of the attacker's words and actions. Even more to its credit, the newspaper gave Iowa readers a clear sense of the emotional aftermath of a rape and the cycles of traumatic symptoms. They learned how the woman's trauma was made more painful by waiting for the trial, delayed for months, and her having to testify about the attack as the defendant looked on. Although it was not the first newspaper profile of a rape survivor, it drew bags of supportive letters from readers and attracted national media attention. It underscored why so many who suffer rape do not go to the police in the first place. Countless rape survivors understood the woman's ordeal.

And readers of the newspaper also learned her name. Then and now newspapers regularly report rapes, but the usual practice is to withhold the name of the person who was attacked.

The *Register* had invited a rape survivor to tell her story. Its editorial judgment appeared to be that candor about rape and sensitivity to the woman's needs are compatible. The *Register* and its editor, Geneva Overholser, wanted to address the stigma of rape. "I understand," she had written in an open letter to readers the previous summer, "why newspapers tend not to use rape victims' names. No crime is more horribly invasive, more brutally intimate.

In no crime does the victim risk being blamed, and in so insidious a way: She asked for it, she wanted it. Perhaps worst of all, there's the judgment: She's damaged goods, less desirable, less marriageable" (1989:6A). The stigma was "enormously unfair," Overholser said, adding that her newspaper would continue to follow a policy of not naming rape victims. But, she added, the stigma will persist unless women speak publicly about their experience and identify themselves.

Nancy Ziegenmeyer responded to Overholser's call. A reporter, Jane Schorer, and a photographer, David Peterson, began a long collaboration with Ziegenmeyer that resulted in a series that won a Pulitzer Prize the next year. The story (Schorer 1990) was an important addition to the literature of the rape experience, which had been growing steadily in books, magazines, and newspapers since the 1960s. The Ziegenmeyer-Schorer report gave a realistic account of the rape survivor's first year of recovery and showed repeatedly how even minor incidents set off those painful trauma symptoms of anxiety, avoidance, and unwanted recollections. In its details, then, it truly helped Iowa readers understand what a person goes through in the months and years after a rape.

But the series raised other issues that show what difficult choices reporters and editors face when they cover the rape experience. Those other issues, rooted in centuries of U.S. social history, have confounded journalism's efforts to come to terms with the realities of rape.

The first point the critics made was that an African-American man had raped a white woman, an assault that is most likely to get press attention because it involves a stranger rape and plays into racist stereotypes. Critics wanted the public to know that kind of rape case is rare despite the media's fascination with it and the hold it has on popular culture.

Only one rape in five is committed by a stranger. Four out of five rapists are relatives or acquaintances of the victim. This powerful statistic appears to hold across a wide variety of national and local studies. Its import is that by far the most common rape experience is one in which a betrayal of trust accompanies physical violence and the shattering of the victim's emotional stability.

The Iowa story also was about interracial rape, a kind of assault that is even rarer than stranger rape. One study shows that men raping women of the same race account for 93 percent of all rapes. The newspaper had helped a rape survivor tell a rare and important story, but its telling had invoked race as an important factor in rape. Although Overholser answered the criticism directly, the reporting still reinforced harmful myths about rape fostered by the history of race relations in this country. Overholser wrote, "One of the sad facts of this rape case is that the woman is white, the man black. This, unhappily, perpetuates a stereotype that is utterly contrary to fact. . . . Nationally, only 4 percent of rapes involve a black man and a white woman. While race was an issue in this particular crime, as some parts of the story show, there is no truth to the cruel stereotype" (1990:1C). Still, the series had inadvertently emphasized race over trauma.

Public discussion of the Des Moines series unearthed other contradictory assumptions about people who are raped. Although the newspaper wanted to weaken the stigma of rape by allowing one survivor to tell her story, a critic argued that social stigma is not so much of an issue if the woman has all the "right" attributes. The Iowa woman was an easy choice, writes Helen Benedict in *Virgin or Vamp: How the Press Covers Sex Crimes* (1992). Ziegenmeyer was middle class, white, respectable, and raped by a black stranger. "I do not wish to detract from the courage she showed in coming forth to tell her story," Benedict writes, "but had she been black, poor, in a bar, or attacked by a man of her own race or higher class, she would not have received such sympathy from readers and the press; she may not, with reason, have even wanted to take the risk of exposing her story" (1992). Rejection and blame by others because of a rape certainly play a part in worsening trauma symptoms or in delaying recovery.

Even in reporting on the Iowa story, other media fostered the fiction that it was the first or one of the first voluntary accounts of the rape experience. They made little or no mention of the many women who, since the early 1960s, had turned rape into a public issue through testimony at "speakouts," sharing their stories in support groups and creating rape-counseling centers. Rape survivors themselves had found mutual support and raised important public safety, legal, and policy issues in the process, leaving journalists to catch up with both the social and mental health knowledge. Feminists working to support rape survivors had joined hands with women in mental health professions to put trauma at the core of the struggle to recover from a rape.

The Des Moines series showed that the most careful reporting may run afoul of biases against the survivor and foster rape myths based in our social history. News conventions will emphasize some victims while ignoring others, and journalists will run into barriers to reporting realistically what a rape survivor endures in the months and years after an attack. It is essential that care be given to the task. We need to understand the realities of rape trauma—1 in every 8 adult women in the United States has been raped—and the disabling aftermath: 8 in 10 will suffer post-traumatic stress disorder (PTSD).

Issues for Journalists

We have come to see that reporting on rape differs so greatly from documented patterns of sexual assault that the public is often ill informed about frequencies, circumstances, and most likely victims. Some of this disparity results from a news tradition of writing less about rape than about other serious crimes. To some extent, it reflects social values and attitudes rooted deeply in American history and race and gender relations. It also reflects the preoccupation of the news media with the issue of naming rape victims. A consensus that the news media not identify rape survivors—a policy we support—inadvertently has contributed to a dearth of information about the trauma that survivors endure and struggle to recover from.

This chapter describes rape trauma, from its immediate effects to those that still may intrude in the survivor's life months and years later. We use that knowledge to frame our support for more reporting about rape so long as it satisfies three ethical considerations that we outline in this chapter: It should place rape in a realistic context for the news outlet's community or region; it should name survivors only so long as they give fully informed consent to the use of their names; and it should give due attention to survivors' recovery and report accurately about the traumatic effects of the assault.

First, let's understand what rape is and is not.

We use the word *rape* to refer to forced violation of another person's body. Rape can occur between women and between men, as well as between a man and a woman. However, it is a striking marker of our society that men raping women is by far the more common pattern. Strangers, acquaintances, friends and spouses, adults and children rape and are raped. The act of rape may involve physical force, including the use of weapons, or psychological coercion, or both. This use of *rape* differs from the variety of definitions provided by state laws that define the crime and set the penalties. In California, for example, rape is a crime against a woman; the rape of a man is called *aggravated assault*. In such laws rape is sexual intercourse that is forced or coerced. Sexual intercourse is sometimes defined as "penetration with a penis or object (such as a finger or pencil), either orally, vaginally, or anally, and includes oral sex." Laws sometimes invoke greater penalties when the rape involves threat or harm with a deadly weapon, a kidnapping, or felonious entrance to a building or vehicle. Under such laws physical or mental incapacity of a victim may be an element in the degree or level of rape that is charged. These differences in laws affect the conduct of police investigations and the trials and punishments for rapists, but they do not help to predict the severity of rape trauma—the sudden extreme helplessness and loss of meaning that follow a coercive use of force. The injury in rape is instant and long lasting and may or may not be aggravated by the particular circumstances that some of these laws address.

Rape is not about sex in any usual sense of the word. The rapist uses and violates sexual organs and body openings used in sex, but the violent traumatic effects are alien to feelings we expect in consenting sexual relations. The behaviors characteristic of rapists—anger, violence, intimidation, use of force, and abuse of power—and the trauma suffered by the victim distinguish rape from a conventional sexual act. Still, whatever is reported about a rape is filtered through some readers' or viewers' assumptions that sexual gratification played a role in the assault or what led up to it. Victim advocates struggle to put such notions to rest. In the view of Judith Lewis Herman, a professor of psychiatry at the Harvard Medical School, literature from pornography to academic texts advanced the erroneously harmful view for much of the twentieth century that rape "fulfilled women's deepest desires" (1992:30). The trauma of a rape destroys that argument. The defining element of rape is the choice of one human being to destroy another's autonomy over her body, initiating an interminable, painful struggle to regain control of her life. The words apply as well to men who rape men. The act appears to validate their power only when they use it to control another man, an obsessive desire for many male rapists.

Herman describes rape as a calculated "physical, psychological, and moral violation of the person" (57). The rapist uses power "to terrorize, dominate, and humiliate" a victim, she writes. "Thus rape, by its nature, is intentionally designed to produce psychological trauma" (58).

What Is Rape Trauma?

What happens to the victim during the assault? The initial attack surprises the victim, often includes physical injury and use of physical force or a weapon, and imposes the threat of death. The victim, a captive, then endures the violation of her or his body. Self-defense often becomes or appears to be useless, even life threatening; the brain and nervous system are overwhelmed. The foundation is set for a lasting injury. Herman writes: "Each component of the ordinary response to danger, having lost its utility, tends to persist in an altered and exaggerated state long after the actual danger is over. Traumatic events produce profound and lasting changes in physiological arousal, emotion, cognition, and memory" (1992:34).

In her book Nancy Ziegenmeyer describes her assault: "It was as though someone had hit a switch, and my body had shut off. Only my mind was working, part of it insisting this isn't happening, this isn't happening, the other part oddly focused" (1992:16). Nancy Venable Raine, a poet and essayist whose memoir of rape recovery, *After Silence: Rape and My Journey Back*, was published in 1998, describes her shock and terror. Assaulted by a man who had slipped into her apartment unnoticed, she suffered rape and torment for three hours:

> During the attack my terror seemed to implode and compress until it was like a hard dry seed. Once I was free of this devouring fear, a cold, even calculating awareness took its place, illuminating everything all at once and destroying all capacity for emotion.... He decided what was and wasn't possible. His world was, by my former measures, insane. A universe of ferocity that was sustained by fear and pain. I had no emotional reaction to this universe and observed it with the detachment of a yogi. (13)

In wrenching language she describes what happened in the first minutes after the rapist fled. "Terror overwhelmed me. My body shook uncontrollably. My thoughts were flawed in structure, like cups without bottoms. Words fell through them. Words no longer referred to anything, even themselves. My shock was so great I could not walk" (15).

Herman calls the emotional detachment felt by some rape victims "one of nature's small mercies, a protection against unbearable pain" (1992:43). People who tell of being raped sometimes place themselves in the position of an observer who stands away from the assault. The victim knows what is happening but does not interpret or judge actions in the usual way. The person's sense of what is happening may be somewhat distorted.

Along with the shock and dissociation, accounts of rape survivors testify to the will to survive. Raine involuntarily "withdrew all reaction," although she sensed that the rapist wanted an emotional response from her. Narratives from other women reveal intuitively smart answers and reactions, life saving in many cases. In her book, *Still Loved by the Sun: A Rape Survivor's Journal*, Migael Scherer describes how, within the first minutes of her attack, survival instincts took over:

With the sound of that closing door several things happened inside me simultaneously. I remembered, all in a single piece a rape-prevention video seen while teaching high school twelve years ago. I remembered how I had broken up a fight between two boys in my classroom. I remembered a friend's escape from a rapist in Jamaica, when she distracted him with greed for her gold ring. Two messages sprang up: Stay calm. And: Use your wits; be clever. I forced myself to breathe more slowly. I forced my body to sag a bit against his. (1992:61).

The rape ended, the person who survives may face immediate contact with strangers, police, family, friends, and medical personnel. This occurs as she begins a lifetime of what Herman calls "the oscillating rhythm" of intrusive memories of the assault and the numbing constriction that follows the trauma. Balance, confidence, and control over reality disappear. In other sad outcomes the victim chooses to be silent about the assault, suffering the trauma without any help. Children raped or molested by parents, teachers, or neighbors often endure the trauma in silence for all or much of a lifetime, cloaking their pain in ways that block recovery.

Trauma effects continue for years. Even as they subside or become less frequent, the rape survivor faces the possibility that reminders of the assault will revive the trauma symptoms. Individuals vary greatly in their response to rape, but studies suggest that although some trauma symptoms may fade after several months, fear and anxiety persist much longer, leading in some survivors to nervous breakdowns, suicidal thoughts, and suicide attempts.

Women who tell of their recovery from rape show how their need for privacy is heightened. Besieged by fears for their personal safety and a sense that even the smallest matters are out of control, survivors begin to rebuild that essential sense of control by making choices, sometimes about things that appear trivial to anyone else. Every relationship poses new stresses, every encounter may set off new fears; even friends and family now respond with blank stares and faltering conversation. The process is a turbulent one, marked by feelings of guilt, then of hatred, then of fear. Nothing in the day is predictable, nothing in life is certain. For most of us privacy is simply a passive claim to keep things much as they are. Violations of our privacy are, at most, minor irritations. For the rape survivor privacy is an essential condition for taking steps toward recovery. Choosing to give personal information to police, friends, and reporters often is a step forward. Choosing to give their name or to withhold it has proved profoundly important to survivors. The journalist who denies or invades the privacy of a rape survivor interferes with that person's right to try to recover from the assault.

The Importance of Context in Rape Reporting

Rape recovery involves struggling against a raging current of mispercep- tions about the assault and its victims. The survivor finds her suffering "edited" in the words and responses of others, then confronts distorted rep- resentations of rape in the media. No amount of clarity or accuracy in news reporting will end the trauma of someone who has been raped, but care in reporting may avoid the infliction of fresh wounds through stories that ignore or misrepresent the survivor.

Begin by trying to provide a realistic idea of the extent and frequency of rape in the United States and in your community. Infrequent mention of rape in the news media contradicts the troubling statistics about the num- bers of Americans who have been raped. The cumulative national effect of rape, according to a 1992 study by Margaret Gordon and Stephanie Riger, is that 1 in every 5 to 8 adult women in urban areas will be raped in her life- time (1989:36). Rape of males is less frequent yet still accounts for 1 victim in 13, according to one study. Adult rape is mentioned most often in the news, yet teenagers, male and female, are more likely to be raped than are older persons. Judith Lewis Herman notes that half of all rape victims are twenty or younger when they are raped (1992:61). The rate of rapes of women is far higher in the United States than in other industrialized coun- tries, excluding nations involved in civil war or international conflict. The high rate of rape coincides with the evidence that 98 percent of rapists are not arrested and that those few who are convicted typically serve prison sen- tences of only a few months.

Gordon and Riger assembled a useful picture of rape patterns by com- paring the statistics in the U.S. Justice Department's Uniform Crime Reports with interviews of crime victims nationally and stories about rapes in daily newspapers in several major cities. In their book, *The Female Fear*, they report that interviews with crime victims yield the most accurate infor- mation but still understate the number of rapes (1989:35). The victim inter- views, conducted by the National Crime Survey in conjunction with the U.S. census, showed a rate of rape twice that which appeared in the Uniform Crime Reports, which are based on statistics from local police departments that regularly underrepresent rapes. Based on the number of rapes disclosed to interviewers, about 140 women in 100,000 are raped each year in the

United States. Rates of rape of women are substantially higher—in some cases three times as high—in the nation's biggest cities, according to the National Crime Survey.

It is easy to see why those who collect data on rape are uncertain about the true extent of the problem. Consider just three reasons for the misleading statistics. First, more than 80 percent of rapes are not reported to police, by one estimate. (A greater percentage of male victims than female victims do not report—perhaps as high as 90 percent.) Second, people raped by relatives and acquaintances are not likely to call police or even acknowledge their rape to the people who do the interviews. Third, survivors often choose to list rapes as assaults, even in surveys. Further questioning does not necessarily bring out that the assault was a rape. Gordon and Riger comment, "There is general agreement that all official or publicly ascertained rates are underestimates, but no one yet knows how much higher the true rate is" (1989:37).

As incomplete as the government data may be, newspaper reporting distorts the reality of rape even more, Gordon and Riger found. When they analyzed rape stories in leading newspapers, they concluded that readers who wanted to know about the risk of being raped in their own communities were likely to be misinformed. For example:

- Newspapers do not report most rapes reported to the police. (Remember that most rapes are not reported to the police, and you can see how hard it is to gain a clear idea of the frequency of rape in a particular community.)
- Newspapers rarely report attempted rapes. The national survey of victims shows that in every four attacks, three people escape without being raped. A content analysis by Gordon and Riger of newspapers in San Francisco, Chicago, and Philadelphia showed that in every fourteen reports about rape, thirteen stories were about completed rapes and only one about an attempted rape. Gordon and Riger comment, "This may be why women believe most rapes are completed, and that women have very little chance of getting away. The consequences of presenting such an inexorable view need to be considered" (1989:69–70).
- Newspaper reporting of rape tends to focus on older women, according to Gordon and Riger. As a result, the relatively high rate of rape among young women, especially teenagers, goes unreported.
- Victims report to census takers that 50 percent of rapes occur in the evening, between 6 P.M. and midnight. Only 5 percent of the newspaper stories studied by Gordon and Riger assigned a rape to that time period. The authors argue that rapes in that time period are more likely to be

committed by dates and acquaintances and that those rapes "are also quite likely to be underreported or declared unfounded" (1989:70).
· Rape stories are less likely to include details than are stories about murders or assaults. Thus readers may not learn the victim's age, occupation, or condition, whether the rapist used a weapon or even where the attack occurred. Stories rarely mention strategies that victims use to avert or lessen violence. Moreover, few stories provide statistics about rape patterns in the neighborhood, city, metropolitan region, or state. And news accounts too rarely emphasize strategies that might prevent rape, such as demanding identification documents from door-to-door salespersons or people coming to do repairs.
· News accounts often provide a distorted explanation of how the victim came to be raped. Reporters sometimes are misinformed or make wrong assumptions about the victim, the place, or other details. A rape that began with a meeting in a neighborhood bar may be reported in ways that imply that the victim was taking needless risks. Sometimes such details fit preconceptions held by a police officer or a reporter that no one questions until much later, if at all. They may also readily fit ill-informed ideas about rape held by many readers and viewers. Without care, reporting about rape can stigmatize the victim, making recovery more difficult, and misinform the public. News reporting that makes the victim seem responsible for the assault may simply foster more silence about the horror of rape.

These findings yield a set of guidelines for helpful reporting about rape cases.

1. Put the case in the context of patterns of sexual crimes in your community and state. At times, report these patterns as stories in their own right.
2. Avoid ways of describing details that serve to reinforce stereotypes.
3. Include details that may help others avoid assault.
4. Mention details that get across the seriousness and horror of the crime.
5. Name local agencies that help survivors and families and explain state laws on sexual offenses.

The Issue of Naming Rape Survivors

Although it may seem that issues of reporting about rape have been raised only in recent years, the struggle of journalists to come to terms with rape is at least a century old. That history may help you understand why naming survivors—the ethical issue most often raised in connection with rape coverage—remains so controversial.

Reports of rapes "are not wanted" by newspapers, the Associated Press told its correspondents, according to John Palmer Gavit in the 1903 *Reporter's Manual*, except when the perpetrator "is pursued and lynched by a mob or is rescued by authorities" (80). This brief statement conceals cruel assumptions about rape in our country's past. Men accused of rape who were pursued and lynched by mobs usually were African Americans (Collins 1991), and the murderous exercise of vigilante justice often involved some action interpreted by white men as an affront against a white woman. Actual rapes need not have taken place for lynching—typically, the capture, torture, humiliation, and killing of the targeted person by a mob—to follow. The reporting mentioned the accused perpetrator, dead by that time and beyond fair justice, and the nature of his alleged actions but rarely named the woman who was said to have suffered the assault.

We need to understand the racial dynamic of lynching and reporting about it. The historian Patricia Hill Collins writes, "Lynching emerged as the specific form of sexual violence visited on Black men, with the myth of the Black rapist as its ideological justification" (1991:177). The vengeance brought down on black men obscured another form of racist "social control"—rapes of African-American women by white men as an element of slavery before the Civil War and one that continued afterward.

Through much of the first half of the twentieth century, the news media paid little attention to allegations of rape or to those who were raped, except in cases involving well-known people. By the 1950s debates about what drove men to rape had completely eclipsed any discussion of survivors' needs. Debates in law enforcement, courts, and mental health circles as well as the news business invariably were about offenders. Victims were rarely mentioned until the 1960s and then, in the words of Elizabeth Koehler, "only in the most derogatory, condescending and dismissive of terms" (1995:53). The near absolute omission of concern for survivors reflected the common prejudice that the woman who was raped "invited" the assault in some way.

Beginning in the 1950s, the press, the legal system, and medical experts began to question some of those assumptions. A few judges and some journalists asked whether rape victims needed special protection in legal proceedings.

In the 1960s and 1970s feminists did the most to convince the public and journalists about the trauma of rape. They made the case for the victims' suffering and challenged stigmatization, then framed the argument that rape was part of a system of violent behavior, generally carried out by men against women. Feminists argued that the way sexual violence was reported inscribed myths about rape, about women, and about male power and contributed to the stigmatizing of victims while helping to lessen the legal and social penalties for perpetrators. The myths were so pervasive that they were as likely to influence the thinking and writing of a female reporter as of a male reporter, feminists argued. Susan Brownmiller's important 1975 book, *Against Our Will: Men, Women, and Rape* shaped public understanding that rape was a crime of violence. The book followed more than a decade of feminist efforts to call attention to the rape crisis through self-education, speakouts, and victim-assistance centers. "Rape, after all, was one of the biggest causes of the 1960s women's movement," Benedict told us.

Feminist teaching about rape gained credibility as it was linked to the evidence of the first clinical studies of rape survivors. These researchers described the trauma of rape and the lasting grip it had on the confidence and capacity of women. In 1972 Ann Burgess and Lynda Holmstrom began to study the women who came to the emergency room of Boston City Hospital. In time they proposed a model of rape trauma that includes a first phase of acute disruption in one's life and a second, long-term process of recovery (see Burgess and Holmstrom 1979). The victims' symptoms, they note, resemble those seen in Vietnam combat veterans. In the same decade hundreds of rape crisis centers opened around the country, offering legal and emotional support. Judith Lewis Herman notes that early attention focused on rape committed by strangers, followed by growing concern for rape in relationships and marriage. She also credits the women's movement for the subsequent concern about domestic violence and sexual abuse of children (1992:29–31).

The news media inevitably reflected the new thinking about violence against women. As "lifestyle" sections of newspapers became forums for such topics, journalism began to seriously examine its own assumptions about rape and did so in open debate. The most significant result was the nearly universal acceptance of the idea that news stories should not name survivors of rape. The rule, though, usually was not linked to the trauma of rape. Indeed, the standard on names often appeared to reflect the convention of the early part of the century, that women who were "involuntarily involved" in the loss of chastity would face great difficulty regaining their reputations. In other words, the woman wasn't named because of the assumption that she would encounter hostility from the public if she were named; stigma rather than trauma supported the convention of not printing names.

Several highly publicized rape cases in the 1980s and early 1990s shattered the news media's consensus about not naming rape victims. Each of these cases—including the accusations against William Kennedy Smith, the Rideout marital rape case, the Preppy Murder story, and the Central Park jogger—was national news and attracted hordes of reporters spurred by the increasingly competitive character of news, especially about sensational occurrences or famous people. Each case, like that of Nancy Ziegenmeyer in Iowa, raised myriad ethical issues and forced some news organizations to confront opposition from their staffs and their audiences to the way the stories were handled. Rape changed from a local crime covered with some care by local media to one with the potential to set off frantic international media coverage. In the rush, conventions about publishing or broadcasting names fell by the wayside.

In her book, *Virgin or Vamp* (1992), Helen Benedict isolates the details that helped spin coverage well beyond the routine. In one of those cases, the rape of a woman by four men in a bar in New Bedford, Massachusetts, in 1983, she found these characteristics of newspaper coverage:

- Men wrote most of the stories that appeared in newspapers and magazines.
- Media attention to the ethnicity of the defendants distracted attention from the brutal assault against the woman. The concerted reaction of the community under attack prolonged the focus on ethnicity.
- The initial stories emphasized the victim's innocence, in part because the rapists "fit all the worst stereotypes." In time, though, defendants, reporters, and others helped to frame coverage to imply that the woman invited the assault.
- A near consensus to withhold the name of the victim held until the trial. Even then, some media respected the rule even though several newspapers and a local television station named her. The decisions stirred public and media debate about using survivors' names in news accounts.
- The trial, in which the woman testified standing up for fifteen hours over three days because no chair was provided for her, brought sympathetic coverage at first, followed by stories reporting testimony about graphic details of the rapes that, Benedict argues, "invaded her privacy, humiliated, and stigmatized her" (1992:124).
- By the time of the first verdicts against the defendants, community opinion had turned with fury against the victim. The press did little to change the hostility that hounded the woman out of the city.

Benedict, who remains "emphatically" opposed to naming victims without their consent, concludes that community and press fury turned against the woman because of several biasing characteristics—details that essentially ignored her trauma and what she had suffered and instead served to feed a prejudice that she too should be punished. "She knew the assailants . . .; no weapon was used . . .; she was of the same race, class, and ethnic group as the assailants; she was young; she was attractive, and, above all, she deviated from the norm of a 'good woman' by being alone in a bar full of men, drinking, when the attack occurred" (1992:142). In this and other cases, Benedict has argued, suspicion of the victim is latent in our thinking, awaiting only certain details in news coverage to bring it to life.

Two more recent cases have shown that media coverage of rape remains bound to such social factors as race and class. In the first case, a young woman who was running in Manhattan's Central Park at night was raped and beaten by several boys, most younger than sixteen, who were participating in what the media called a "wilding" rampage. Raped by at least seven boys, beaten, and cut, the woman lost much of her blood while she lay unnoticed in the park for several hours. Then she lay in a coma in a hospital for weeks afterward. The national media covered every detail of the horrific crime yet carefully omitted her name from every story. To the world, she was "the Central Park jogger." The journalists' sensitivity to her right to privacy appeared to say that they would continue to respect the convention of withholding the identity of rape victims. A few criticisms of the reporting surfaced. The woman was white and fairly affluent—a stock broker. Critics said her identity played a part in both the extraordinary attention and the refusal to report her name.

Two years later, to the month, a member of the Kennedy family was accused of rape, and the consensus about withholding the victim's name came apart. Because the Kennedy family was involved, the story got saturation coverage around the world. The naming began in the British "scandal sheet," the *Globe,* a tabloid sold in U.S. supermarkets, then moved quickly to *NBC News* and finally to the *New York Times.* The *Times* not only named the woman but profiled her in ways that horrified many readers. The story mentioned her traffic violations, her mediocre school record, the illegitimacy of her child, her divorce, and other personal matters (Butterfield and Tabor 1991:A17). Some staff members, among them the columnist Anna Quindlen, reacted so angrily that *Times* editors were forced to answer their objections in a meeting covered by the newspaper and widely reported elsewhere (Glaberson 1991:A14). Fox Butterfield, one of the five reporters for the profile, later said the story was done, in part, because the woman had hired attorneys who appeared to be trying to "court publicity" (Butterfield 1991:5). Also, the reporters were intrigued by the story of a woman who was not like the Central Park jogger. Almost as an aside, though, Butterfield framed the dilemma that faces journalists assigned to report on rape: What story do you tell about the victim? "None of this behavior, of course, is relevant to whether or not she was raped. Our story was not intended to prove or disprove the rape" (1991:5). Quindlen wrote in her column for the *Times*, "I imagined one of the editors for whom I have worked asking, 'How does all this [the personal details] advance the story?' The answer is that it does not. It is the minutiae of skepticism" (1991:E17).

Naming Survivors: Pro and Con

We believe that journalists may harm women, men, and children who are raped if their names appear in news reports without their consent. Before we make this argument, let's consider the arguments made by those who support using the names of survivors.

First, they assert that information that is central to the reporting of a crime and is on the public record should be disclosed. Journalists always have preferred disclosure to suppression of information. Second, not naming reinforces the stigma against those who are raped. They need to be noticed and respected in their communities. Third, the media routinely name other victims—victims of auto accidents, muggers, burglars, and murderers. One category of victims should not be made an exception. Finally, some people make false accusations of rape. A person who makes false charges does not deserve the special privilege of anonymity. (Rapes are falsely reported. A careful study by the *Columbia Journalism Review* shows that no credible estimate of that percentage exists—it may be 8 to 10 percent, about the same as other major crimes except murder. Police agencies vary greatly in how they identify and report false and credible rapes (Haws 1997:16).

We are persuaded that naming victims against their will can intensify the trauma of rape. Strangely, debates about rape today rarely mention trauma; people talk about the press's duty to disclose information and inconsistencies in protecting some victims and not others but not about trauma. Yet we are convinced by the knowledge gained about trauma in the past thirty years.

The trauma following a rape is severely disorienting and likely to last for a long time. The victim loses the sense of control so necessary to survival and will regain it only after many setbacks, false gains, and unbelievable emotional pain. We know men and women who have been raped, and we have watched their long fights to regain control over their lives. We have seen the devastation in the personalities of students who have been raped while they were in our universities. And we have watched dear friends suffer deeply when, years later, they were forced to review in some ways the terror of the attack. We are fully persuaded by Judith Lewis Herman's conclusion that rape is intended "to produce psychological trauma." Of course, the degree and severity of trauma vary from crime to crime and person to person, but in general clinical evidence suggests that the victim of rape endures a degree of suffering deserving of special treatment. In writing this, we know that victims of other crimes also feel violated and anxious; indeed, they may suffer severe traumatic symptoms.

People in the media have a right to claim neutrality on controversial matters, but when it comes to helping public and private agencies address the needs of those traumatized by rape, media owners and journalists alike ought to be giving support. People tell of the hurt and anger they experience from seeing news reports containing their names and personal information framed in ways that make the victim into a villain. "No wonder most rapes are never reported," writes Migael Scherer of the news coverage of her attack. "The unpredictable public scrutiny, the implication of blame, the focus on the suspect that shifts attention away from his victims—all add to our private anguish. And the realization that it is not the rape that is newsworthy, but the rapist and the investigation, is deeply disturbing" (1992:123).

As Nancy Ziegenmeyer and many other women have done, survivors are gaining the strength and confidence to tell their stories publicly (Ziegenmeyer, however, came to regret the way her story was told). Some, like Scherer, our colleague in the writing of this book, and Raine, have told their stories in books. Others, like Kathy Sitarski (1996), have used magazines or newspapers as their forum for disclosure. These women have shown us a way of talking about rape that serves them and the public well. Each such speaking out demands the same extraordinary degree of courage and commitment shown by the women who first told their stories in small support groups back in the 1960s. But each story also conveys a truth about rape that the public needs to understand. As Sitarski writes, "One reason violence isolates is because personal violence makes us ashamed. . . . The result is often painful isolation and patterns of quietness, invisibility, shyness, and other hiding behaviors. The very thing we need to talk about in order to heal instead gets buried deeper and deeper" (1996:23).

Helen Benedict makes a different argument for not naming victims and for protecting their privacy in the aftermath of a rape. It may not be shame that underlies the need of a victim for privacy and protection. "I believe that, because rapists use victims' sexual organs as the targets of their attacks, rape is a more intimate violation than any other type of crime. A victim should have the right to protect herself or himself from being publicly described in the act of being sexually tortured because of this violation of their private bodies," Benedict told us.

We believe that this country is coming to honor those survivors of rape who choose to speak publicly; their examples offer support for others. Because we have these models of disclosure, based as they are on personal decisions anchored in the recovery process, we can afford to protect other rape survivors until they too are ready to speak out. (Discovery of a false rape accusation, of course, changes the journalist's obligation.)

The Reporter, the Survivor, and the Trial

Long after the rape, the trial of the accused forces the survivor to relive and recount the details of the assault, often in view of the attacker and an audience of observers, reporters, and court personnel. For most, the emotional burden is like a second assault and has been called that often. Although the survivor may receive support from prosecutors and the police in a trial, she will not be represented by an attorney, may find that things she said to investigators will be used to discredit her testimony, and she will not benefit from the same presumption of innocence given the defendant. The risk of an acquittal or plea bargain is high (conviction rates for rapes are low), and retaliation by the rapist is a real fear.

In the Seattle trial of an accused rapist, a newspaper reporter played up the survivor's misidentification of the color of her attacker's eyes. Indeed, even after a jury convicted the man, the reporter persisted in saying the jury had done so although the victim had the color of his eyes wrong in her statements to the police. The news stories deeply troubled the woman because they implied that the jury's conviction of the man was not warranted. Moreover, it misinformed readers by leaving the impression that a rape victim knows every detail about an attacker. Although memory experts disagree on how our brains record the details of a traumatic experience, they seem to agree that the level of emotional stress affects the reliability of the memories. In other words, although defense attorneys may persist in playing up discrepancies in a victim's account to try to influence jurors, reporters ought to be aware that the story can be authentic, if not accurate in every detail.

We offer these suggestions for reporters who are covering trials of accused rapists:

1. Respect the survivor's almost inevitable emotional relapse because of having to testify against and be in the presence of the person whom she believes committed the rape. "For days after the trial, I wandered around the house in a fog," Ziegenmeyer says, suggesting the effects of the trial experience (Ziegenmeyer and Warren 1992:124). It makes no sense to try to add to courtroom testimony by interviewing the survivor at the trial or even soon after.

2. Consciously incorporate your knowledge of trauma in the coverage of the legal maneuvering and argumentation in the trial. The survivor is not an ordinary witness, slightly nervous but well primed with information. Your stories should cover the shock waves of trauma evident in the people they hit—victim, family, coworkers, friends— as well as the arguments about evidence that will occupy the judge and attorneys.

3. The details of a rape may occupy a good deal of the court's attention. When you consider including graphic and invasive details, think about whether they will help a reader or viewer understand the horror of rape or whether they may encourage a bias against the victim.

4. You may conclude, as some journalists do, that once a survivor testifies in open court, you should use her name along with her words. We believe that in many cases trial reports should not name the person who testifies about being raped for the reasons we have discussed in this chapter.

"Recovered Memories" of Childhood Rape and Incest

All that we have said about the trauma of rape and the need to protect its victims from press attention and identification applies as well to the child or teenager. Traumatic events are often harder on children than on adults. Children who are raped should not be interviewed or identified in news stories. News organizations generally respect this rule.

The rule is no different if the rape occurs within a family. Again, certain numbers are hard to come by, but records of hospitals and child protective services support the claim that roughly half of the hundreds of thousands of child rapes each year are committed by fathers, stepfathers, or other relatives. Most incest victims are quite young—five or six years are common ages for incest, and the abuse may continue over a long period. News stories about incest cases will depend on information from police and prosecutors, and journalists still will have to decide how to identify the accused.

Anyone who doubts the toll that incest takes on the lives of its victims should consider the reporting by Debra McKinney for the *Anchorage Daily News*. She portrayed three women's struggle to confront the trauma they had suffered several decades earlier because of assaults by their fathers or an uncle. All three had been unable to cope with the pain, shame, anger, and emotional crippling that followed them into adulthood. For two of the women, not even the deaths of the relatives responsible did much to ease their trauma until the trio bonded in their therapy group. All found that their relatives had a hard time believing their accusations of incest.

In recent years a different sort of story about incest has perplexed journalists and has furious debate raging in medical and legal circles as well. The issue can be illustrated with a fictitious example.

Troubled by emotions, dreams, and unwanted thoughts, a man seeks help from a psychiatrist or therapist. In the course of treatment, he appears to remember being sexually abused by his father during early childhood. He had evidently blocked out any memory of the rapes. Supported by this "recovered memory," the man tries to confront the attacker, tell others about the assumed assault, or take part in criminal or civil action against the accused. The discovery may pit the man against his parent or parents who deny being sexual abusers and may divide families and friends.

The journalist, whether covering accusations or the legal actions that result from the memory recovery, will be in the middle of a fiercely argued issue. On the one hand, some scholars and clinicians of various backgrounds say memories cannot be lost and then recovered. They often argue that the memory is not actually recovered but is suggested by a cue from the therapist or attorney, a story in the news media, or some other source. On the other hand, other convinced and competent experts argue that memory can be lost and regained, that the trauma to a child that results from sexual abuse may have that result, and that incest and child rape are so frequent that we must take recovered memory cases seriously.

Some reporters, taking the side of the skeptics of recovered memory, have concluded that most such claims are fraudulent. That stance is a disservice to the many victims of child abuse.

In 1998 a panel convened by the International Society for Traumatic Stress Studies published its conclusions about the recovered memory claims. The panelists, representing the psychiatrists, psychologists, and social workers who work with trauma survivors, offered this even-handed conclusion:

> While there is some evidence that recovered memories of childhood abuse can be as accurate as never-forgotten memories of childhood abuse, there is also evidence that memory is reconstructive and imperfect, that people can make very glaring errors in memory, that people are suggestible under some circumstances to social influence or persuasion when reporting memories for past events and that at least under some circumstances inaccurate memories can be strongly believed and convincingly described. While traumatic memories may be different than ordinary memories, we currently do not have conclusive scientific consensus on this issue. Likewise, it is not currently known how traumatic memories are forgotten or later recovered. (1998:23)

The report, *Childhood Trauma Remembered,* should convince reporters that they should not judge claims of recovered memory as right or wrong at the outset. Each case requires the considerable effort of all those involved to reach the truth. The journalist can help by studying that process rather than the bombastic arguments of those organized on either side of the issue.

Rape at any age robs one of confidence in life. Recovery is the patient struggle to regain that confidence. If journalists respect that struggle, survivors will know that it is an honorable one. The poet Martha Ramsey in a memoir, *Where I Stopped: Remembering Rape at Thirteen,* wrote about shedding the memory of her trauma. "In each year of my life I can look forward to shedding more. Each time I stumble—at the dentist's, at the garage, or with Eric—the memory grows easier, for I find I can also hold the others—all the men, the witnesses, mother and father, everyone who did not know how to help me—in that river of my awakened heart" (1995:325).

Debra McKinney

Charting the Course of Recovery

Getting on with their lives. Putting the pieces back together again. With "Malignant Memories," *Anchorage Daily News* reporter Debra McKinney transcends these clichés to give readers an honest look at recovery from childhood sexual abuse.

That she took on the story at all is amazing. McKinney had recently completed "A Story of Incest." The perpetrator was a Baptist preacher, the victims his three small daughters. Six years after sentencing, the entire family—

Debra McKinney. PHOTO BY MICHAL THOMPSON

including his wife, who had turned him in—seemed to have been sentenced as well. "They would live the rest of their lives without feeling whole," concluded McKinney. "He had raped their souls." With no comforting end in sight, she felt drained herself: "All I wanted to write about for a while was the latest trend in breakfast food."

Then she met Ezraella—Ezzie—a survivor of incest who told McKinney how she and her friends, Margie and Vivian, met every week for lunch. They called themselves the Marvellas, a combination of their names. For McKinney its upbeat, you-can't-stop-me spirit was irresistible.

She took no notes during those first meetings with the Marvellas, letting them get to know her, following at their pace. While covering the preacher's family for "A Story of Incest," she'd learned the importance of trust; without it "you have a story without a pulse." After some misgivings (Margie was the most concerned, mainly for her kids), the Marvellas included McKinney in about half their get-togethers and—remarkably—Vivian's confrontation with her family and Margie's return to the farm where her uncle had sexually assaulted her.

Trust goes both ways. For her part, McKinney offered them the chance to see their story before it landed on neighbors' doorsteps. She had used the same ground rules with the preacher's wife: Except for errors, the preview was not about changing the story; it was about easing the shock of seeing themselves in print. As for the possibility that they might, at that point, back down—"That was in the rules too. They understood they were committed before they read." McKinney and her editor defend showing the text of the story to the women. "We felt a strong sense of responsibility to them for trusting us with their stories," McKinney explains, "and it didn't end with the last of the interviews."

The aftermath of childhood sexual assault is full of pain and rage, destructive behavior, searing memory, and total denial—McKinney had seen it all with the preacher's family. She had tried, with them, to sift through the pieces, to comprehend the damage. There were glimmers of hope, most notably the wife's courage in coming forward publicly, but they were overshadowed by such bleak realities as the youngest daughter, a prostitute who had a baby with a man who left teeth marks all over the woman's flesh. The Marvellas showed what healing could look like thirty years after the abuse. "I needed the Marvellas so bad," McKinney says. So, she reasoned, did her readers.

Early on she knew the story was recovery—not the incest per se—and such recovery occurs in small steps over a lifetime. McKinney, a fourth-generation journalist, had more than an ear for language and an eye for detail; she had the patience to wait and watch as the Marvellas revealed their stories. Working around other assignments, she also had the luxury of time.

For the actual writing, she credits instructors at the Poynter Institute and her editor ("flexible *and* demanding") for keeping her on track—writing for readers, not her sources. McKinney introduces the Marvellas as she met them, adult women with families, jobs, and a capacity for fun. She describes their lunches—the teasing, the terrors they share, the rich desserts they order. McKinney respects both the anguish of remembering torture no child should ever experience and the difficulty readers have in accepting what they do not want to believe. She continually shifts the focus back to Margie, Vivian, and Ezzie as they are now: celebrating Ezzie's conversion to Judaism with a potluck and slumber party; soaking together in a hot tub after Vivian confronts her family; leaving the barn Margie's uncle had forced her into, skipping arm-in-arm like schoolgirls.

What McKinney struggled with most was the issue of repressed memories. Vivian's father had confessed, but Ezzie's father and Margie's uncle were dead. In the end, McKinney says, it didn't matter whether she could verify the memories. The story was not about the perpetrators, she reminded herself, or about the details of abuse; "it was about getting healthy and reclaiming stolen childhoods."

The vital first step to recovery is remembering, and McKinney invites readers into the process. She braids the women's stories together, letting readers discover with her the extent of the violence. With Vivian, McKinney is able to show memory's elusive nature: Vivian did not remember her father barging in on her in the bathroom, as he had confessed, only that she was always constipated as a child. With Margie, McKinney describes remembering as a process like seeing in fog—blurred forms, strained senses, sudden clarity. As Ezzie and Vivian attempt to follow Margie's uncertain directions to her uncle's farm, McKinney notes the wrong turns, the dead ends, the guesses and doubts. Standing with the Marvellas in the farmhouse, Margie speaks in the voice of a little girl, remembers what her uncle did, cries at long last. Readers, standing there as well, understand.

Though McKinney admits, with relief, that she has never experienced such trauma in her life, she brought considerable knowledge of sexual assault to this story. In addition to the story of the preacher's family, she had covered rape support groups and was familiar with a range of resources: therapists, detectives, attorneys, the head of Alaska's sex-offender treatment program. "Malignant Memories" is infused with solid information.

To feel emotion and still be strong—McKinney's summation of the Marvellas also applies to her. Instead of toughening or turning away, she turned back and looked again. Like a reporter who follows soldiers in the field, exposed to combat and the trauma that follows, McKinney followed those who had been wounded in secret by the very adults who should have protected them. Carefully charting the course of recovery, she discovered the heroes.

By Debra McKinney

Malignant Memories:
It's a Long Road Back to Recovery from Incest

Debra McKinney's account of the mutual support of three women as they faced down memories of the incest they had suffered was framed by her account of the trip to the farm where an uncle had assaulted one of the women. These excerpts focus on that visit. Although the article emphasizes what McKinney and the women call "the Dark Ages"— the ordeal of opening old wounds—its ending affirms the substantial distance they all have traveled and the optimism they gained in the process. The entire story was pub-lished in the Anchorage Daily News *on June 6, 1993.*

SEATTLE—Twenty-five years have come and gone since Margie last visited the old man's farm. She's not sure she can even find the place. She's not sure she wants to.

The 51-year-old Anchorage travel agent has made a lot of progress lately confronting her fears. But she still has trouble talking about what happened in the barn.

So fragmented are the memories. She remembers her Uncle George car-rying her piggyback across the horse pasture, her bony legs, black patent-leather shoes and white-lace socks poking out from under his arms. She remembers staring up at the barn's rafters, and how the hay scratched her skin. She remembers her ankles being strapped down, legs apart.

And then there's the time she was tied by her wrists and hoisted.

Did things like this happen a couple of times? Every visit? Why didn't her aunt come looking for them? Did she not want to know?

Margie wants to remember more. No, she wants to forget. But she knows she has to go back there if she ever wants peace. And so she studies a local map.

Although Uncle George has been dead for more than 20 years, the courage to go through with this comes from two friends.

A year ago they were strangers—Vivian Dietz-Clark, 41; Ezraella "Ezzie" Bassera, 44; and Margie (to protect their own privacy, her children asked that the family name not be used). Now they call themselves sisters.

Their demons brought them together. Within the past few years, memories have surfaced, forcing them to deal with what had long been buried— the sexual abuse they're convinced they experienced as children.

A tremendous amount of energy goes into locking things up inside, Ezzie's therapist, Joan Bender, explained. It's like sitting on a huge, bulging chest to keep it from popping open. Any added stress drains energy from that chore. The lid creaks open. Memories escape.

The three Anchorage women met in a support group for adult survivors of childhood sexual abuse offered by STAR (Standing Together Against Rape). And when that group ended, they continued to meet on their own.

The Marvellas, a combination of their first three names, is what they call themselves now that they're a team. The melding of their identities is a metaphor for the journey they've taken together.

* * *

Their efforts took them to the Seattle area this spring to confront family and fears, and to be there for each other.

The first attempt at finding Uncle George's place ended in the Big Brothers Bingo parking lot. Could the farm have been paved over? No, this wasn't right. Margie tried hard to remember. The next hill over looked familiar.

Vivian turned the rental car around, crossed over the freeway, took a left at the top of the hill and ended up in the middle of a subdivision.

What now? They drove on.

At the end of the last row of houses was a gravel road. They took it. Halfway down Margie turned white.

"That's it," she said.

Vivian stopped the car at the top of a long driveway. The three of them sat in silence a moment.

"Let's go down there," Vivian said.

Margie groaned.

"We're going," said Ezzie.

Slowly the car headed down the gravel drive. At the bottom, Vivian stopped in front of a little yellow farm house, the kind you'd expect to have an apple pie cooling in the windowsill.

"Amazing," Margie said.

The place was just the way she remembered it. There was the chicken coop. And the old chopping block. And the big pear tree the guinea hens used to roost in. And there, behind the little house, beyond the gate with the "Keep Out" sign, was the barn.

"I don't want to get out," Margie said.

Vivian put an arm around her and hugged her. Ezzie gently rubbed her back.

They all got out of the car.

* * *

At Uncle George's farm, Vivian knocks on the door of the little yellow house, and explains to the woman who answers that her friend used to stay there as a girl. Would it be OK to look around?

Margie, who's stayed by the car, needs a cigarette. She lights one, hoping the woman will say no. She doesn't.

Vivian and Ezzie push because they want their friend to remember. If she can remember, if she can confront her fears, she can learn to be strong.

They escort her to the top of the driveway, as if she were a schoolgirl again just getting off the bus to visit her now late aunt and uncle.

"He would walk with me to the back of the barn like this," Margie said, cinching her arm around Ezzie's waist. "He held me very tight and the horse would follow because he had sugar or something. I'd be squirming because I didn't like being held. And he would tell me if I didn't stop squirming the horse would stomp on me.

"And so I was always afraid of horses."

"But you showed me a picture of you sitting on a horse, and he was next to you," Vivian recalled. "You said you could remember your thighs being chafed after being here because you'd ride your horse."

"No," Margie says.

"From him?"

"Wasn't that just the perfect excuse to be sore down there?" Margie said.

Nothing shocks the Marvellas anymore. They agreed. Yup, the perfect excuse. Then they put their arms around each other's shoulders. Next, they were skipping down the driveway, giggling like kids, not caring what anybody might think.

Margie remembers only bits and pieces of being fondled in bed at night. Vivian decided to walk her through it, using those fragments to pry more memories loose.

"You sleep right here in this corner?" Vivian asked, gesturing toward a small window.

"Uh-huh. I remember times when I was sleeping in that little bedroom and he would go in and stoke the fire, and he'd come in my room and she would call out to him, 'George, aren't you coming to bed? What are you doing?' His whiskers were long late at night."

Margie's cheeks began to flush.

"So, you're laying in your little bed and what's he doing? Touching you?"

Silence.

"Kissing you?"

Margie stared at the ground. Her cheeks were now bright red.

"I mean, you're getting whisker burns. And you've talked about his breath. Do you feel his breath?"

Margie couldn't answer.

By then, Vivian had her by the shoulders and was staring into her face. The prodding was more than Margie could handle.

"I just want him to go away," she said in a little girl's voice. She burst into tears, put her head on Vivian's shoulder and sobbed, her body shaking.

At last.

Margie had always said she'd crack a bottle of champagne the day she finally cried. But since she no longer drinks, the Marvellas made do later with chocolate.

"Oh my," Margie said, pulling herself together. "That's enough for me right now."

Later, thinking the Marvellas were on a nostalgia tour, the farm's new owner led them through the barn. While he chatted away cheerfully, Margie systematically looked things over. Looking down on the stalls instead of up, she realized how small she was back then. The barn, which seemed cavernous back then, seemed so tiny.

But no new memories came.

An hour and a half after first pulling down that driveway, the Marvellas were back in the car, debriefing.

"It wasn't scary going into the barn because you were with me," Margie told her friends.

And the scene under the bedroom window?

"I just wanted you to stop," she told Vivian. "I just went, 'No, don't. I don't want to remember this.'

"I feel a little heavy chested. But I do feel like I went and conquered something."

Chapter 8

Reporting About Children

"They're okay!" shouts the rescuer. "She's okay," says the doctor after the accident. "Kids Okay," says the headline after a shooter menaces a school playground. Until the 1970s Americans tried hard to believe that children who were not injured physically suffered only brief and minimal emotional harm in disasters and violent events. Not much was known about how children react to tragedies except what parents reported. And parents, caring and loving as they were, often turned out to be unreliable observers of their children's emotional states. Over a few months, parents typically said, trauma symptoms rapidly disappeared.

Researchers rarely questioned the children, and their parents' hopeful observations lent support to both a government and therapeutic view that children truly were lucky survivors of disasters and violent events. Research on the resiliency of children in stressful situations, such as extended illnesses and marriage breakups, fed the assumption that youngsters could handle anything, including trauma. So "they're okay" seemed the right thing to say after disasters, so long as no one suffered bleeding wounds or broken bones.

Today we are beginning to understand that the phrase, hopeful as it is, is misleading. Promoting the error through news stories is a disservice to the children whose emotions are under siege and to those in the community who are trying to help children.

Getting the story about children right is difficult, in part because we have so many complicated ideas about them. Cute and appealing as news subjects, they also call up for us a lot of assumptions about what a child is and how a child is to be valued. One can understand why the notion of the resilient child eased the consciences of adults during the Great Depression of the 1930s, World War II, and the Korean War. Adults were preoccupied with the demands of the time; it helped to think that once the crisis was over, everyone would return to normal. War and depression had separated children and parents and made children witnesses to the horrors of war. Yet as recently as the 1940s it was still widely believed that children were not much affected.

Images of children encode many of our hopes and fears about ourselves. During a war or famine and after a natural disaster or act of violence, journalists find children to photograph or interview. They know intuitively that a child's plight rivets the attention of readers and viewers. If we can see the physical harm to the most vulnerable of us, we will take note of the crisis. Starved frightened children, bones etching deep lines in stretched skin, remind us repeatedly of the horrors of famine, genocide, brutal civil war, and the AIDS plague in Africa. Stunning images of American children stay in our memories long after we have forgotten most other news pictures. We remember a dead child in a firefighter's arms in Oklahoma City and the aerial view of the ghostly naked body of a boy lying on the bed of a pickup after the searing blast of the eruption of Mount St. Helens in Washington State. But the living, cherubic child is an equally powerful image. The face of Jessica McClure, the baby freed from an abandoned water well in Midland, Texas, in 1987, lifted spirits across the country.

We dote on messages that say that innocent and helpless children can confront terror and survive. The "okay" boy or girl reassures us. The child in obvious distress troubles us and for good reason. Concern for our own children helps us identify with any child's plight. Journalists are as vulnerable to those feelings as anyone.

The emphasis on child victims in news coverage is universal, if not often acknowledged by journalists. But once in a while a reporter will say that children are important in the packaging of news. Children are important bearers of the values of our society. That is why newspeople seek them out and why we all pay attention to stories about them. And that may help us understand the desire to say apparently whole children are "okay" after they have confronted some form of violence.

New knowledge about the emotional damage children suffer contradicts the cliché. A thoughtful physician is not likely to to dismiss the possibility that the child is suffering from trauma; a reporter should be as careful.

Since the early 1970s new ways of studying trauma in children argue that children are likely to suffer long-term trauma symptoms from a variety of violent events. These newer studies, using tested diagnostic questionnaires, place a greater value on children's reports about what they feel. Many of these studies conclude that children who have survived hurricanes, earthquakes, and tornadoes or have witnessed school shootings and other acts of human violence will have traumatic symptoms long after. The youngest children—those in the first ten years of their lives—are most likely to be deeply affected by trauma, although their symptoms may differ from those of older children and adults.

The critical change in the thinking of mental health experts, psychiatrist Lenore Terr argues (1990:11–12), came when they accepted that real events cause traumatic effects in children. Thus, evolving knowledge about trauma gives a better understanding of the sweet, wise, and photogenic children who may be the first candidates for interviews and pictures as journalists arrive at the scene. We have learned from a series of horrifying, violent episodes endured by American children since the early 1970s and from the natural calamities and countless wars that other children around the globe have survived.

How Does Trauma Affect Children?

Small children may be traumatized by a sudden unexpected event that injures or kills their classmates, parents, or other relatives and robs them of all sense of security. The natural disaster or the violent incident, such as a school shooting or a kidnapping, may take its toll in different ways than a sustained or repeated sexual or physical assault by a parent or other adult. This section draws on recent research about children who suffer in the single, unexpected event.

In 1984, when a sniper opened fire on a crowded Los Angeles elementary school playground from his home across the street, he killed a child and a passerby and wounded a staff member and several children. Children who had been at play watched friends cut down, sensed the danger to their own lives, and saw human bodies mangled. A bullet cut through the side of one girl, taking out lung and heart tissue. As the passerby was killed, children saw his intestines burst from his abdomen. Inside the school, as teachers hastily taped paper over windows and told children to hide in closets or under desks, many children thought gang members were attacking the school and would kill them. Bullets shattered the windows of some classrooms. Although many children had already gone home, others were separated from their families, and for a time police denied parents access to their children.

Therapists who treated the children found devastating effects. Kathleen Nader, one of the therapists, later wrote: "One month after the sniper attack, 77% of children present on the playground under direct attack and 67% of children in the school had moderate to severe post-traumatic stress disorder (PTSD)." Children who knew the girl who was killed had significantly more trauma symptoms. Fourteen months later, children exposed to the shootings still had significantly more symptoms and more severe reactions than the children who had left the school early, were told by teachers to hide under their desks, or were on vacation at the time.

The children, of course, suffered the same trauma symptoms as adults: unwanted memories of the shootings, heightened anxiety, and, over time, decreased interest in people, some aspects of their lives, and the future. For some, such symptoms as bad dreams and fears faded quickly. Some children, in contrast, received help for as long as two years after the shootings. A loss of interest in life may endure much longer.

What should a journalist who is covering child disaster survivors know? A recent survey of studies of children in disasters over two decades offered this guidance: The children who are nearest to people who are killed or injured or who are directly threatened with loss of life are most likely to show extreme trauma symptoms. They are most likely to suffer anxiety, depression, and PTSD, including symptoms of avoidance. Even mild levels of exposure will lead some children to experience intrusive reminders of the event.

The journalist might keep this commonsense scale in mind when children are involved in newsworthy events: If the child suffers directly in the traumatic event, the degree of trauma is likely to be high. If the child only witnesses injury, death, or terror as it affects others, the child witness will suffer. The more the child cares about those who are most affected, the more likely the child is to show symptoms of trauma. After the explosion of the space shuttle *Challenger* killed Christa McAuliffe, a schoolteacher, and six astronauts in 1986, researchers interviewed children in McAuliffe's hometown who did not know her and children in a city three thousand miles away. The study found that because children were likely to care about her, they also were likely to develop such trauma symptoms as new or exaggerated fears of flying or of death and dying or dreams about McAuliffe or the deaths of others in their lives (Terr 1990:327).

In such single-event traumas children place more of their trust than usual in the adults around them—teachers, parents, and administrators.

Those same adults also may be reeling from what happened, less able than usual to give emotional support to the young. Often children wait, while school staffs, emergency workers, and others find ways to regain control over their chaotic situations. The parents' roles are especially critical, particularly for infants and preschoolers. The mother or father often serves as the protector in whose care the child can try to understand the event. Children deprived of contact with parents during and after disasters later fear being separated from their parents even in routine ways.

Some experts on children's trauma believe that long-term symptoms may be related to such social factors as whether the community or school organized quickly to deal with the emotional damage, whether and how long the child was separated from parents, and how adults individually responded. A community's preparation for a natural disaster is likely to reduce the likelihood of lasting emotional disorders among the children. Normal routines, even in wartime, and open, frank discussions of risks, ways to deal with them, and the possibility of death and injury may reduce stress enough to limit long-term effects among children.

A different emotional response may occur in children who are victimized by another person, rather than by a natural disaster. Trauma specialists note a variety of forms of anger and rage that may follow an event in which a human force blocks the child's innate ability to resist or escape injury. The adrenaline that encourages survival may lead to a build-up of both fear and aggression if the child cannot take action. If these horrors are repeated, anger may overwhelm the fear. Over time, the anger may evolve into one of three behavior forms: identification with the aggressor, retreat into victimization, or general control marked by occasional outbursts or wild rages (Terr 1990:63).

When relatives or other children die in violent circumstances, trauma often confounds the natural and lengthy process of grieving. Unable to work through the usual stages of grieving—often identified as denial, protest, despair, and resolution—a child may become locked into one of the early stages for several years.

It is not unusual, though, for a child caught in a single event to already be suffering from some type of prolonged trauma, such as homelessness following a parent's death, a disability or disfigurement, sexual or physical abuse, survival of a war, refugee status, or the aftermath of a car crash. Responding to the combination of traumatic experiences, the child may take on other emotional traits. One kind of response is to disappear into a cocoon and stay there. This kind of self-protection may be labeled denial, dissociation, or repression, and it may take such emotional forms as a lack of feelings, rage, and unbroken sadness. (Some research shows that children caught in a disaster are less likely than adults to pass through the emotional phase called denial; that is, they are more realistic about what has happened to them.)

Dissociation refers to wrapping one's emotions in a "cast," to use psychiatrist Sandra Bloom's description, to keep from suffering. Adults, including reporters and photographers, may do this when they confront troubling scenes. Most adults, though, know rationally what happened to them even as they shut off their emotions. They have clear memories of the event and can recount its details with a fair degree of accuracy.

Those who treat trauma in children say that dissociation is a much more powerful response in them, one that may completely eclipse the child's memory of the reality of the event. "Given the powerlessness and defenselessness of children, dissociation is often the only thing they can do to protect themselves," Bloom writes (1997:37). The result of locking up the emotional stress of an event may be, in some cases, a complete inability to contend with or understand reality.

Children are more vulnerable to trauma than adults because they have not yet learned ways to cope with trouble. They may be resourceful in sizing up their situation and in finding practical ways to deal with it, but they will not be as able to prepare themselves for the emotional injuries they will suffer. "Children who are traumatized do not have developed coping skills, a developed sense of self, or a developed sense of their self in relation to others," Bloom adds (37). These observations especially fit children aged ten or younger and apply in some degree to older children as well. A shooting at a high school may not be as traumatizing as it would be at an elementary school, but traumatic symptoms will occur nevertheless. Columbine High School students interviewed on television after the April 1999 shootings in Littleton, Colorado, showed signs of the confusion, agitation, and numbness that come with acute stress. In general, even at high school age symptoms of trauma are likely to be more severe than for adults. Some children exposed to violence or its effects may simply find it hard to communicate or may communicate incoherently, child psychologist Donna Gaffney told us.

When the trauma is prolonged, as in repetitive physical and sexual abuse, the child's identity may be so affected that it exists only in fragments that have no integration with each other. Memories and emotions tied to one event may exist entirely separate from those of another event.

Like victims of single events, such as shootings, tornadoes, and fires, children caught in warfare suffer emotional injury. Researchers studied a group of Kuwaiti children after the occupying military forces of Iraq were expelled in 1991. These children showed levels of traumatic reaction similar to those of survivors of the 1989 earthquake that leveled Armenia and those who witnessed or were under fire from the school sniper in Los Angeles. Most of the Kuwaiti children knew someone who had been captured, injured, or killed; a majority had seen dead or injured people in the streets; and a third had witnessed the killing of humans.

Lessons for the Journalist: At the Scene

Journalists should consider ahead of time which of their actions at the scene may be harmful and which may help children. Strange adults—reporters—and unfamiliar gear—cameras—may add extra stress for children who are trying to deal with the frightening images of the event as well as their own troubling emotional responses. Caught in a frenzy of media attention, children may find reporters are frightening. A reporter who covered a sniper attack on children in a Stockton, California, schoolyard remembered that the children, already frightened by blood and bullets, were "being chased by a mob, microphone poles extended like weapons, cameras trained on them, people shouting at them to stop. Some reporters even tried to interview them as they fled, yelling, 'Did you see it? Did you see it?'" (Libow 1992:380).

News personnel at the scene risk being part of the contagion of fear and trauma that will affect children. Emotional stress is contagious. Fear can be heightened by the reactions of people the child trusts—teachers, parents, and siblings. We have suggested that small children are especially vulnerable to the effects of contagion. How is it communicated? A look of panic or fear on a mother's face as she arrives at a congested school site may become one of the images a child captures as part of the trauma. The anger of a parent who does not know whether a child has been harmed will affect the child who is watching. A reporter or camera operator, shouting in the tumult of a chaotic scene, also contributes to this confusion and contagion. When administrators have time to follow their disaster plans after a violent event at a school, teachers and others greet the parents and help them calm down before they see their children.

After a murderous shooting spree in a Fort Worth, Texas, church in September 1999, police acted quickly to isolate the child witnesses and relatives from the media as crisis counselors rushed to the scene. Yet when reporters finally were allowed to conduct interviews, aggressive individuals still intimidated some children with their lights, cameras, and intense questioning.

It has become common for parents, hospital staff, police, and school officials to ask for or insist on isolation of traumatized children from the media. We think such actions serve the needs of the children by allowing them and their parents to begin to recover from what happened before they handle questions from reporters. In Springfield, Oregon, after a school shooting in 1998, hospitals set up media centers where reporters could interview wounded children but only as they were being discharged and then only if they wished to talk to the media.

Lessons for Journalists: Interviews and Photographs

As a general rule, we believe that journalists should not interview or photograph children aged ten or younger in connection with devastation, disaster, homicide, and accidents. We base this argument, which we know many in the media oppose, on our knowledge that trauma is likely to affect most children who are victims or witnesses. Interviews of traumatized adults also may be harmful; each interview requires a thoughtful judgment by the reporter about the need for an interview. The possibility of traumatic harm is sufficiently great with young children that few interviews are defensible. The child who is the only eyewitness may give important information, but most children will have little to add to accounts that are available from older witnesses. Traumatized children need to recall the event but in ways that pay attention to their emotional responses to memories. The typical journalist's interview will not help the child do that; indeed, it may make it harder for the child to deal with the trauma.

If you decide that your reporting requires the child's words or picture, discuss this need openly with both the child and a parent. Parents provide critical emotional support when the child is frightened. In general, without a parent's permission and assistance, reporters and photographers should not approach children of any age who may be traumatized. Do not leave the decision about talking to the child solely to the parents, though. Parents may be under stress too and may find it difficult to decide whether to expose a child to media attention. They may think the child is "okay," may not know what harm has been done to the child, have a sense of whether a press conference or interview would be helpful or harmful, or understand that the media event may actually have adverse effects. Some parents grant interviews to show gratitude for public support or to encourage financial donations. An author of a textbook on interviewing wrote that journalists should not interview children without a parent's consent "except at a news event." If the "news event" has affected the child, we believe that journalists have a responsibility to participate in protecting the child from unnecessary stress. In other words, journalists are not justified in talking to children or photographing them simply because the confusion of the scene makes them accessible.

Finally, ask the child if he or she wants the attention. Elsewhere, we have endorsed the recommendation of some editors that interview subjects be given the equivalent of an informed consent form, a detailed statement about what the reporter or photographer wants and what might actually appear in the newspaper or on television. The needs of a child make this negotiation much more difficult but no less ethically necessary. The child is trying to gain control of a confusing world. Deciding whether and how to participate in news coverage can be a part of regaining control. Some children want and will enjoy the experience, while others will be upset by it. Still others will have delayed negative reactions. Neither you nor the children will know how they will respond to the interview.

Make a point of raising with the child and parents the possibility that even talking about the event may cause unpleasant feelings and a belated sense of a loss of privacy. Attention the child gets may be appealing at first, but the family may not anticipate that the child will be scolded or teased by classmates. Judith Libow, who treated traumatized children in a California hospital, warns that personal disasters and publicity—even media attention that exalts the child as a hero—may turn out to be harmful. "Many children react to personal disaster with intense pessimism about their future, expecting their lives to be shortened and new disasters to befall them," she says (1992:382). The child, then, has a hard time reconciling the upbeat news approach with his or her internal sense of the traumatic aftermath. It is a mistake, though, to think that a child, especially one younger than ten, cannot be part of a decision about talking to a reporter. There is no ready answer to the dilemma a reporter or photographer faces with a child at a disaster scene. No one can say with certainty that some or any of the consequences will occur. We are arguing for an informed negotiation with child and adults, one that restores some degree of control to the child and lets everyone know that troublesome consequences may arise.

Be realistic when you talk to the child and parents about whether your publication will use photographs and how much of the interview your story might use. Children whose trust in adults has been undermined may not understand why a thirty-minute interview turns into a thirty-second story or why a distracting photo session never yields a picture in the newspaper or on television. Libow describes the disappointment of a boy taped for a story on a local news program about his fight against leukemia. "He was ready on the designated night, his hospital room filled with friends and family to watch his story," she says. "He was seriously depressed for days afterwards when his story was bumped, without warning, to make way for a more pressing news item. His story was never televised" (383). Some reporters make a point of repeating several times during an interview that a picture or story may not be used.

In chapter 4 we listed ways that journalists can reduce stress for an adult who is being interviewed. These ideas apply as well to interviews of children or teenagers. Find someone to give them support while you talk; take them away from the sights and sounds of rescues, medical aid, destruction, and fire fighting; and sit with them, keeping at their eye level.

If the interview takes place some hours or days after the event, consider seeking the help of someone trained in interviewing trauma victims. That person may be able to help you gain useful information.

Anticipate that the child's version of the event may differ from that of an adult observer. An adult might think of a tornado's strike as a single event, but small children sometimes remember several different traumatic events, each distinct and not necessarily linked in the child's mind. A psychiatrist who studied twenty-six children who were kidnapped, then buried alive in a truck-trailer, in Chowchilla, California, in 1976, found that, unlike adults, the children apparently did not go through the stage of denying what had occurred (Terr 1990:78). A reporter might interview a parent who is grateful for a child's safety and in denial about the child's losses, such as friends' deaths. The child, needing and wanting to grieve for those losses, may be bewildered by the parent's responses. Children also may feel extraordinary guilt about their role in the event, and that guilt may be reinforced by questions or references to details of what happened. Guilt can be based on a failure to act, being safe when others were hurt, or acting in ways that endangered others. Some experts have noted that small children may be confused about times and physical characteristics (particularly of strangers). On the other hand, they may remember details peripheral to the center of the action better than some adults because the children are not as adept at focusing on the salient details of what happened.

Few reporting textbooks say anything about interviewing children, implying that all interviewees are pretty much alike. One of the few writers who makes a distinction between adults and children, Shirley Biagi, makes these suggestions about interviewing children:

- Ask open-ended questions. You are more likely to obtain information by asking what happened, rather than "Did you see the car hit the boy?"
- Ask the same question several times. "Information that remains the same through several sessions is more likely to be accurate," she adds.
- Independently verify what children tell you.
- Interview each child privately. (1992:83)

And think about how the things you take for granted in your work may affect a newly traumatized child. Flashes and cameras may be reminders of what happened. You are likely to be much larger and taller than the child; be aware that the child may fear a violent adult and so may shrink from rapidly approaching strangers and loud voices. You have learned to act quickly and assertively in your work. But that loud bang, quick pace, and assertive voice that work so well around adults may trigger fears and memories in the child.

Lessons for Journalists: As You Write and Edit

Avoid the "poster child" trap. Appealing, photogenic children invite your attention and too often they are quite willing to cooperate. Some children, though, do not understand why they attracted the attention, and many of their peers may be hurt or confused by being ignored in favor of the chosen one. The "poster child" represents only one identity, one gender, and a unique part of the event; using only this child ignores all others.

When shots were fired in a Seattle high school, wounding a boy and a girl, television reporters were able to interview the girl in her hospital room in time for evening newscasts; police kept the media away from the boy while they questioned him. The media coverage, which emphasized extensive interviews with and photographs of the white girl and completely ignored the African-American boy, angered other students. In the balanced attention they paid the two victims in their school paper, student reporters asked why the boy was not interviewed when the police finally finished questioning him. The answer most likely was that it was too late that day to do an interview and by the next day more current stories had eclipsed the shooting. A familiar variation on the poster child report is a focus on the gifts, money, and attention from the public. Ask yourself whether barraging a child with such attention really is a helpful act at that stage.

Reporting sometimes places too much emphasis on a single traumatic symptom, such as attempted or completed suicides. When these examples receive extensive news coverage, or are translated into fictional dramatic treatments in movies or on television, copy cats often follow. If the copy cat case is newsworthy, place it in a broader context by calling on experts, examining trends, and looking at prevention efforts.

Respect the child's need for privacy. Being shown on television or in news photographs in pajamas or hospital gowns bothers some children. A boy who was injured in a drive-by shooting was afraid to return to school because he had to wear an eye patch. A boy whose picture appeared in a Seattle newspaper was identified in the caption as a resident of a homeless shelter, which the accompanying story said he did not want classmates to know. Children's fears sometimes disappear with careful help from trauma specialists, teachers, parents, and journalists. When a girl about to begin school was badly burned in a campfire, such intervention, aided by a local newspaper's effective stories and photographs, enabled her to prepare to enter school.

Do you need to name children described or quoted in the story? Traditional news practice argues for full and accurate identification. An awareness of what a child might endure from public knowledge of his or her experience suggests a compromise. Alex Kotlowitz, who has reported about children for the *Wall Street Journal* and in several books, asks the child or a parent for permission to use a true first or last name. "You need to consider the well-being of that child you are writing about," he argued in a meeting with other reporters at the Casey Journalism Center for Children and Families. Other reporters have regretted using real names for children.

Do not assume that children are in denial about a traumatic event because they do not talk much about it. Denial, as we have noted, is more likely to be an adult symptom after a devastating event. Children often act quite thoughtfully and selflessly in threatening circumstances. In some cases, though, they may find themselves helpless to do anything and that very knowledge may affect their later recovery. In contrast to the few children who can be heroic in a threatening situation—the student who wrestles a weapon out of the hands of a shooter, for example—most children can do little to affect the crisis that surrounds them. But it is often misleading to say that the children, individually or as a group, behaved "helplessly." When a woman shot herself in front of a fifth-grade class, she did so after the children, at their teacher's urging, had begged her not to take her life, then prayed for her. Kathleen Nader, a child trauma expert, tells of an eight-year-old boy who watched as a woman killed several of his classmates in a schoolroom, then noticed and shot the boy's friend Bobby. "When she had turned her focus to Bobby, he had promptly run for cover and slid like a baseball player behind the file cabinet, effectively saving himself." The boy's self-image was shattered until he began to accept "the competence with which he had saved his own life" (1997:166).

The children who endured the Chowchilla kidnapping acted thoughtfully throughout their capture, Lenore Terr, the psychiatrist, concluded. At each stage the children assessed their risks and acted deliberately to save their resources and to escape their "jail." The same children told Terr, though, about what they felt in the most frightening moments—the fear of helplessness. She found that the residents' hasty creation of a rock monument to honor the freed children only caused them more pain. "The kids of Chowchilla hated their notoriety. They hated what had happened to them. They hated their story. And so they hated 'The Rock'" (1990:110). The monument exposed them publicly, Terr argues, as young, ineffectual, and helpless.

Educate readers and viewers about the long-term character of trauma. "Only one child came out of the Dunblane school gym physically unharmed," read a newspaper dispatch about the killing of a teacher and sixteen kindergarten pupils in a Scottish school in 1996. This variation on the "okay" cliché harmfully separates physical from emotional injuries. The reporter should have recognized the likelihood of severe traumatic injury to that child whose "clothes were drenched in the blood of his classmates" and explained it in stories soon after the event.

Do not include vivid and startling images in your coverage. We do not know exactly where to draw the line between acceptable coverage of a death scene, for example, and coverage that goes too far. Expect that many children you may have observed at the scene will later become glued to the television set, watching replays of their own traumatic experiences or connecting the newest event to one they have experienced. That coverage will remind them, above all, that the world is an unsafe place. The images you show will trigger the troubling images in their memories, adding to the difficulty they have dealing with the trauma. Images mentioned but not shown can be harmful. In a television report about a train wreck the reporter mentioned that one of the last acts of rescuers was to pull the body of a very young child from the water. Children who knew the victim might imagine the victim's death and appearance, might ask whether she had died instantly or how long she had been alive in the water, whether she was scared or in pain, and why no adult helped her in time to save her life. A mother complained bitterly when a newspaper story included an eyewitness's description of her son's last futile struggle to break out of a car as it sank into a lake. While the mother will continue to struggle with that horrible image, classmates of the boy also may be plagued by those few printed words.

Finally, think seriously about the tone of your report. Most news is about bad things, and some media, especially television news shows, actually go to the extreme of banning good news. In doing so, they often work at odds with school officials, health experts, and parents who are trying to restore a sense of safety for traumatized children. Even after children appear to be out of the way of direct harm, their sense of danger will persist. If media reporting continues to focus on the death, injury, and danger without taking into account the efforts to restore safety, children will only be supported in their fears. Some Seattle mental health experts responded angrily when a local television station that had covered a devastating fire refused to send a news team to cover the firefighters who returned to the neighborhood to reassure the children about their safety. News reports not only tell us how bad things have been but also can help us to learn how to respond in case of another event. A television weather reporter calmed small children in a school that had been struck by a tornado when he visited them to explain what causes a tornado and what protective actions to take during a storm.

We have argued that children should be protected from media attention, especially if they are ten or younger. If they have been directly affected by a devastating event at any age, they need protection. What we have suggested contradicts the values of many journalists who believe that journalists' first obligation is to tell all they could learn about an event, even if it means using children to do so and naming those children. Children are traumatized by violent events. The closer they are to danger, the more likely it is that they will have post-traumatic stress disorder or many of its symptoms. A major event may leave a neighborhood or community with a long-term problem of recovery because of the suffering of its children. Journalists need to sacrifice images of and quotes from some of the cherubic faces they find at disaster scenes and, in the interest of supporting the long-term health of those children and their communities, rethink the ways they present news of violence.

Chapter 9

Using the Spotlight with Precision and Sensitivity

An uncle of Roger Simpson's was a wonderful friend in his childhood and teen years, easy going, creative, and caring. He was a veteran of World War I, a fact never discussed in family gatherings. After his death relatives constructed the story of a man sent into combat who emerged physically whole but evidently never spoke to anyone about what he had seen and done. He had grown into adulthood at a time when even speaking about combat experience put one at odds with both medical authorities and other citizens who thought any sign of emotion about war identified "a constitutionally inferior human being," in the words of the psychiatrist Judith Lewis Herman. Some physicians argued that war trauma could have psychological effects, but the issue and interest faded quickly when the war ended. Although medical understanding of trauma had become much more sophisticated by 1945 and the end of World War II, the veteran's silence remained a hallmark of later wars and of the experience of later groups.

Chapters 7 and 8 offer guidelines for reporting about rape and about children's trauma. The thesis of this chapter is that our communities and news beats are filled with other silent survivors of traumatic experiences. Not all of them insist on silence. In many cases the survivors are not heard because the media overlook them and their stories. They are not part of any breaking news—no fire, landslide, or shooting brings them to our attention. Eric Schlosser wrote in the *Atlantic Monthly* in 1997: "Americans are fascinated by murders and murderers but not by the families of the people who are killed—an amazingly numerous group, whose members can turn only to one another for sympathy and understanding" (37). Schlosser's remarkable twenty-two-thousand–word article provides a rare account of how the silence of being a homicide survivor pervades the lives of those family members. Many of those people that the news media overlook represent the qualities of character that we admire—tenacity, courage, self-sacrifice, strength. Their lives speak to sweeping changes across the globe or in our own towns and cities. Yet too often they are left in the shadows of public awareness.

When silence is the result of news media avoidance and not a choice by an individual, journalists can challenge that silence. But the reporting must be respectful, sensitive to private matters, and concerned about recovery and survival more than the awful events that created a victim in the first place.

The poet Peter Balakian explores another kind of silence in his memoir, *Black Dog of Fate* (1997). Some of his relatives had escaped the Turkish government's genocide of hundred of thousands of Armenian people early in the century. Yet Balakian described a childhood with grandparents, parents, and aunts who never spoke of the massacres by Turkish authorities between 1910 and 1915. The book was the poet's assault on the silence produced by the trauma of the genocide experience. Survivors of the Holocaust, the Cambodian genocide of the early 1970s, the Balkans wars, and the Rwandan slaughter in the 1990s know about those silences. Balakian wonders how a state action that killed so many and scattered many others to refuges throughout the world could become lost to memory. As the survivors committed their suffering to silence, the genocide of Armenians faded from the world's collective awareness.

Other people have sought to understand silences of different kinds. Judith Lewis Herman writes that social mores silenced the traumatic sources of women's suffering in the nineteenth and early twentieth centuries. "The cherished value of privacy created a powerful barrier to consciousness and rendered women's reality practically invisible. To speak about experiences in sexual or domestic life was to invite public humiliation, ridicule, and disbelief. Women were silenced by fear and shame, and the silence of women gave license to every form of sexual and domestic exploitation," Herman writes in *Trauma and Recovery* (1992:28). Grasping her own critical need to speak about what happened to her, Nancy Venable Raine, a rape survivor, titled her 1998 memoir about recovery *After Silence*.

Today we talk more openly about domestic violence than ever before, yet we often fail to see the oppressive character of many relationships. Herman writes:

A man's home is his castle; rarely is it understood that the same home may be a prison for women and children. In domestic captivity, physical barriers to escape are rare. In most homes, even the most oppressive, there are no bars on the windows, no barbed wire fences. Women and children are not ordinarily chained, though even this occurs more often than one might think. The barriers to escape are generally invisible. They are nonetheless extremely powerful. (1992:74)

Conflict that appears to be rooted in differences of skin color or ethnic origin is often noisy, confrontational, and even violent. Once the conflict subsides, those who fought may choose silence because of weariness or because of symptoms of trauma. The great and effective civil rights actions in our recent history took place in the 1950s and 1960s. Yet those activists can be found today among the many silent victims of prejudice and social conflict in every community. U.S. Rep. John Lewis of Georgia, in his 1998 memoir, *Walking with the Wind*, describes the summer of 1964 in Mississippi when he and other African Americans and their allies physically challenged the brute force of southern resistance to desegregation. The summer gave civil rights leaders "a purpose, a goal, an object of hope," writes Lewis (1998:274), who was beaten by a mob in Montgomery, Alabama, in 1961 and knocked unconscious by Alabama state troopers in March 1965 in Selma. Of the veterans of the civil rights action, Lewis writes: "Like the soldiers who would begin coming home from Vietnam within a year, the veterans of Mississippi Summer were affected for the rest of their lives by what they went through and what they witnessed. Their spirits, as well as many of their bodies, were broken. Some remained casualties from then on. Many simply dropped out of the system. Others surrendered to overwhelming anger and irrational behavior" (273). Unlike the veterans who might have asked for and found clinical help in the 1960s, civil rights activists found little help and scarcely any understanding that they too had been in combat. "Get over it, their friends and families would tell them," Lewis writes (273).

The Legacy of War

Paul Fussell, the war historian, has written that most of us do not want to hear about the horrors of war. Yet in 1998 the director Steven Spielberg created a remarkable film about the Allies' 1944 invasion of France that included nearly an hour of simulated but horrifying and realistic images of men in the landing force being killed and maimed. We do not know whether people went to the film because, as a whole, it was another entertaining story told in cinematic form or because they wanted to know more about the violence of war. Critics praised Spielberg for the gritty honesty of the film, but few, if any, used trauma knowledge in appraising the film. And none that we found appeared to be aware that some of those who survived the assault would continue to experience its effects long afterward. After the war the traumas of both combatants and civilians were dismissed far too readily. Civilians suffered more than half the casualties in World War II (compared with only 5 percent in World War I), but even those unscathed lost homes and possessions as well as friends and relatives.

Peacetime is a good time to report on war, because the spotlight does not stay focused on the day-to-day action of a particular conflict. When the spotlight can sweep around more and seek out those who are often missed, what stories might journalists be able to tell?

The pessimistic accounts are already there in such great numbers that they have become clichés. Veterans of Vietnam ignored in their communities turn to drugs and crime. The suicide rate among veterans is stunningly high for people in that age group. Decorated veterans turn up in homeless shelters, sleeping in parks, or dead in city alleys. If the story is about one person, it is likely to describe a slide from success and achievement into weakness and failure, if not death. The stories feed on a stereotype about veterans, the Hollywood notion that war survivors are destined to find success after the war ends. Those that fail to return to conventional lives must somehow be flawed, an echo of the strange thinking in the medical profession at the time of World War I.

Yet the struggle—the real story—for some men who fought in Vietnam was to recover from the traumas of combat and the subsequent emotional assaults of rejection at home and failures in their postwar lives. Although a failure to survive these pressures, represented by a suicide or committing a crime, is a sure-fire story, the recovery story gets little attention. The omission is not due to a lack of information; veterans and therapists will readily tell us what it entails. One finds little evidence in the news about how one recovers from a war, the day-by-day effort whose results are scarcely noticeable, the two-steps-forward, one-step-back character of the process. Veterans with PTSD who have taken our classes have been able teachers, reminding us from time to time that a traumatized person may have difficulty dealing with course material that will spark no special emotional reaction in most students.

Jonathan Shay, a psychiatrist for a group of Vietnam War combat veterans in the Boston area, describes the barriers they faced in recovery in his book,

Achilles in Vietnam (1994). For years, as he counseled the veterans, he considered the similarities of their combat experience to that described by Homer in the Greek classic *The Iliad*. Interweaving the stories from *The Iliad* with those told by the Vietnam veterans suffering severe post-traumatic stress disorder, Shay tries to find ways to prevent psychological injuries.

What the former combatants faced each day, Shay writes, was a set of symptoms that ruined the character and personality of the victims most affected. The litany of effects includes loss of authority over mental function; persistent mobilization for danger; a persistent focus on survival; persistence of betrayal, isolation, thoughts of suicide, and meaninglessness; and destruction of the capacity for democratic participation (1994:170–181).

Shay does not offer recovery as a guarantee. But, he says, "recovery is possible in many areas of life, perhaps in the most important ones for a fulfilling existence" (186). Yet some of the most active veterans "remain highly symptomatic." The veterans, then, dare to regain their place in their families and communities despite the long-lasting effects of trauma. The journalist who approaches the war survivor must be alert to both the dangers and opportunities in asking for a narrative. Do not assume that asking the veteran about combat experience will be therapeutic. Telling the story under the wrong conditions may be terribly harmful.

Journalists and therapists educe the stories of war trauma for very different reasons, and their ways of eliciting the narratives differ in important ways. Whereas therapists working with veterans often encourage them to tell their stories, the narrative of war experience is a delicate instrument. "Narrative heals personality changes only if the survivor finds or creates a trustworthy community of listeners for it," Shay writes (1994:188). Often, those listeners have endured similar traumas but not always. Indeed, Shay argues for more sharing of veterans' narratives in a wider community. Any audience for the narratives must be able to listen without being injured by the accounts and without blaming the victim or denying the story's reality, according to Shay. A good listener will refrain from judgment, respect the narrator, and be willing to experience some of the terror, grief, and rage.

How do these expectations apply to a journalist whose reporting of the war narrative will be passed on to an audience and who cannot assure that any of these standards will be met? Should the reporter, whose own capacity to listen with respect and without judgment may be limited, even solicit such stories? Because we believe that news reports can be a bridge for understanding between those who fought in our wars and the public, we encourage reporters to write about combat veterans but in ways that do no further harm.

In casual interviews or those in which the reporter and the subject of the story meet only once, reporters should not ask victims of violence, including combat trauma, to recount what happened to them during the trauma. A Vietnam veteran who spoke at the University of Washington said he would talk freely about the history, policies, and aftermath of the war but would take no questions about what happened to him during the war. He had learned on many occasions how troubling it can be to tell that story to an audience that is not prepared in the way Shay describes. And it can also prompt unwanted memories for the veteran. (When the veteran and the reporter have time to come to trust each other, the veteran may make disclosures about trauma.) But, of course, there are exceptions to this advice. Some veterans can recount their combat history in extensive detail. If you are interested in a compelling example of a combat narrative, read Robert Kotlowitz's *Before Their Time* (1997). Kotlowitz, one of three in his platoon who survived an irrational and failed assault on an entrenched German unit in France during World War II, tells the story of his survival and the aftermath in fascinating detail.

But the news story can tell how a person found his or her way back into civilian life or moved further toward personal goals after the war. And it can explain what recovery involves.

In 1998 a Seattle reporter compiled an extraordinary account of war experience in World War I, based on the recollections and letters of her 105-year-old grandmother. Trust was not an issue when Carol Smith, the *Seattle Post-Intelligencer* reporter, interviewed Laura Frost Smith, who had served as an army nurse on five of the bloodiest fronts of the war. The nurses witnessed the many amputations, brain and head injuries, and deaths even as they, the first women to participate in the U.S. military, fought prejudice and bureaucratic pettiness at the front. Carol Smith writes that her grandmother rarely mentioned the war after she returned to the United States. "Though many of the nurses' experiences were more dramatic than those of their husbands, boyfriends or brothers, they didn't talk for fear of embarrassing the men. Social pressures against women doing 'men's work' also enforced their silence. But the war's imprint remained. It would influence my grandmother's outlooks and actions for the rest of her life" (1998:E5). Smith's story, which her newspaper presented on three full pages, went on to describe the many connections between war experience and later actions, emphasizing not the trauma but its importance in a person's later life.

Our communities are rich with the contributions of veterans of Vietnam, the Gulf War, or older conflicts. One Vietnam veteran who lives in a Seattle suburb spends his time working with scouts and applies the lessons of the war in a remarkable way. Alarmed by the overuse of video games by boys, he developed a program of working with parents and boys who are observed using video games compulsively.

Survivors of Genocide

In 1946 the United Nations General Assembly passed a resolution on genocide: "Genocide is a denial of the right of existence of entire human groups . . . . Many instances of such crimes have occurred, when racial, religious, political and other groups have been destroyed, entirely or in part." Two years later the UN adopted a convention identifying genocide as acts intended to destroy "national, ethnical, racial or religious" groups. A squabble over terms led to the omission of political groups from the definition, although killing for political reasons was a major form of genocide in the twentieth century. Mass killings may have the same causes but differ from genocide in that they are not part of a campaign to destroy an entire group.

The Holocaust, the extermination of six million Jews by the Germans during World War II, is the example of genocide most studied. The Nazi regime in Germany killed several million other people, including political opponents, Catholics, Gypsies, homosexuals, mentally ill persons, and citizens of other nations. The genocide was not part of combat; it was carried out as a policy of the regime.

Other genocides mark the history of the twentieth century. In 1915 the Turkish government carried out the killing of more than 800,000 Armenians in Turkey (Staub 1989:10). In 1975 the Khmer Rouge government of Cambodia targeted potential enemies of the state. Millions of people were taken from cities and forced to build new villages in the countryside under harsh conditions. The death toll from executions and starvation before 1979 has been estimated at two million people. In 1976 the military government of Argentina began wholesale murders of political opponents. Estimates of those killed range from nine thousand to thirty thousand. In more recent times we have seen the genocide against Bosnian Muslims by the Serb government and the 1994 genocide of 800,000 in the Tutsi minority in Rwanda.

Genocides and mass killings have scattered refugee-survivors throughout the world. They join refugees from combat zones in our communities. Their stories are compelling and need to be told so that we all can under-

stand the consequences of nationalistic and regional violence. Yet interviewing such survivors and telling their stories with understanding is very
difficult. When the reporter does not speak the survivor's language, a skilled
interpreter can help. Let the interpreter help alert you to the cultural differences that shaped the survivor's response to the trauma of war or mass
killing. You will have to seek the right help or do the research required for
an effective interview. You will need to listen for signs that a particular
object, act, or event is understood differently by you and the other person.
And you will need to be sensitive to the likelihood that your questions about
a traumatic event may do further harm to the other person.

Anne Fadiman's fascinating study of the treatment of a child in a family
of Hmong refugees from Laos offers many examples of how failure to bridge
cultural differences caused unwarranted fear and harm. In the book, *The
Spirit Catches You and You Fall Down* (1997), she recounts how medical personnel in a California hospital asked the child's parents to sign a release
before taking the child home to die. The family found the prediction of
death offensive. "In the Hmong moral code, foretelling a death is strongly
taboo," Fadiman writes (177). An interpreter tells Fadiman, "In Laos, that
means you're going to kill a person. Maybe poison him. Because how do you
know for certain he's going to die unless you're going to kill him?" (178).

Personal stories give the community a chance to ponder the critical roles
played by people enveloped in genocide or mass-killing horrors. Each event
confronts us with the actions of three kinds of participants: perpetrators,
survivors, and bystanders. Historians have little trouble constructing the
actions of the perpetrators. Many victims will not be able to tell their stories
because they are dead or too severely injured, and few will try. The examples
of the survivors and the bystanders may help us to learn how to deal with
these unimaginable human atrocities.

The narratives of refugees can illuminate how people in fear for their
lives find ways to survive. A Holocaust survivor told the students in one of
our classes how she escaped prison camp guards several times by relying on
the aid of other prisoners and her own craftiness. Agate Nesaule, now a professor at the University of Wisconsin–Whitewater, tells in a memoir how she
and her family had fled Latvia during a Russian advance in World War II and
were then captured by brutal Russian troops. During an interrogation
Nesaule's mother survived by speaking Russian. "My mother began talking.
It is one of the things I most admire about her, that at this moment she could
talk, and that she knew what to say," Nesaule says (1995:72).

The survivors live among us, and their stories can both inspire and instruct us. But what about the bystanders, those who witnessed the killings, who may have tried to halt them or may have assisted in them? Students of genocide have placed the bystander role in the spotlight increasingly in recent years. They argue against an assumption that bystanders can and will do little to prevent violence or mass killing; to the contrary, they say, we need to educate ourselves about the potential for moral action among bystanders. Two bystanders whose stories have assumed heroic status emerged during World War II. Oscar Schindler's resourceful campaign to rescue Jews from the German genocide on the pretense of employing them in a factory has been told in books and in a popular movie, *Schindler's List*. Raoul Wallenberg, a Swedish businessman, gained a diplomatic appointment to Hungary in 1944. During the next six months he saved tens of thousands of Jews, relying on bribery, threats, and the issuance of "protective passes" that allowed a safe exit from Hungary to Sweden. (Wallenberg evidently was arrested by the Soviets late in the war and was not heard from again.)

Ervin Staub, professor of psychology at the University of Massachusetts–Amherst, has studied bystander options as part of his effort to understand how to prevent genocide and other group violence. He distinguishes "internal bystanders," members of the perpetrator group who are not perpetrators themselves, from "external bystanders," witnesses who are not members of the perpetrator group. Staub writes:

> Bystanders can exert powerful influence. They can define the meaning of events and move others toward empathy or indifference. . . . Why then are bystanders so often passive and silent? . . . Lack of divergent views, just world thinking, and their own participation or passivity change bystanders' perception of self and reality so as to allow and justify cruelty. (1989:88)

For the reporter the lesson in Staub's analysis is that any situation that might result in violence has the potential to be short-circuited by a thoughtful bystander, especially early in the cycle of events. At the same time, if the passive bystander is the model for everyone involved, escalation to violence is more likely. News stories can focus on the interventions of active bystanders. Survivors and refugees from violence elsewhere in the world can be witness to the efforts and failures of bystanders, as well as the acts of perpetrators and the plight of victims. Reporters, by telling stories that reflect action against violence, also move from passivity to moral action.

Survivors of Domestic Violence

When relationships turn violent and violence kills and injures, the news media often report what happened in ways that confuse readers and viewers and contribute to harmful stereotypes. Stories about domestic violence seldom reflect any knowledge of this pathology. Consider two recent stories from the Seattle area. A Cambodian man killed his wife. The second-day story noted a pattern of violence and abuse by the man toward his family yet undercut that key idea by implying, through quoted comments from neighbors, that the killing could be understood as a result of "a clash between traditional Khmer culture and a more liberal American society." In another example newspapers reported that an emergency room physician had killed his wife, staged a car accident to try to cover up the killing, then tried to kill himself. Instead of keeping the focus directly on the killer, his victim, and the problem of domestic violence, news stories offered a bizarre interpretation that would lead readers to conclude that an otherwise normal man had gone berserk one day for inexplicable reasons. One headline said, "Residents Wonder If Small-Town Life Has Left Their Town." The lead of another story began, "In a place the neighbors say is so quiet you can hear a pin drop . . ." Another story emphasized a comment from a neighbor: "This would be normal for California, but not here."

Judith Lewis Herman, the psychiatrist, argues that many of us are disturbed by the apparent normality of the killer and his family situation. Perhaps for that reason reporters emphasize the ironies as they try to offer quick answers to the why question. The Cambodian killer, one newspaper said, "was an immigrant success story." Another newspaper described the murderous physician and his wife as " 'gentle' and 'generous' people who once lent storage space to a neighbor whose home had been destroyed." A neighbor was quoted as saying, "They just seemed like a real nice couple."

According to Herman, the victim of violent abuse suffers captivity in the same way as a person held in a slave-labor camp. Yet to all outward appearances the man, woman, and children are "real nice" and "normal." Herman describes the batterers as "exquisitely sensitive to the realities of power and to social norms." She adds, "His demeanor provides an excellent camouflage, for few people believe that extraordinary crimes can be committed by men of such conventional appearance" (1992:75). The men in these cases coerce their partners and children into being victims; indeed, the perpetrators thrive on their ability to control other people. Such control requires cutting the victimized family member off from contact with anyone else.

"The more frightened she is, the more she is tempted to cling to the one relationship that is permitted: the relationship with the perpetrator," Herman adds (81). The experience traumatizes the victims, fosters changes in identity and emotional responses essential to survival, and burdens victims with intense rage long after the relationship ends.

Deaths from domestic violence are not uncommon. According to the FBI's Uniform Crime Reports for 1995, 26 percent of female murder victims were killed by husbands or boyfriends. Studies of particular cities or regions have placed the percentage as high as 50 percent. Wives or girlfriends killed 3 percent of all male murder victims. Children are often killed along with the spouse or partner. Some of the children who survive are witnesses to the killings of others.

You can find victims of domestic violence who have escaped abusive relationships throughout the community. But before you approach a woman who has suffered at the hands of a husband or boyfriend, take these ideas into account:

- The threat from the perpetrator may not have ended. Speaking out in any way or being identified in a news story may increase the degree of danger she faces.
- Take your own identity and physical presence into account. Size, demeanor, and verbal behavior may trigger fear in someone for whom such cues have accompanied violence.
- Domestic violence may create traumatic effects that the person will have to address over a long period of time. Be as sensitive to what recovery entails as you would be for a person who has been raped.
- Recognize that the criminal justice system may do little for the abused partner or spouse of a violent person.
- Do not write about the woman's experience in ways that imply she was responsible for her victimization. We have outlined how batterers often coerce others in their families; the relationship is a complex one, never explained simply by a single action that might have provoked a violent response. Another example from a Seattle-area newspaper illustrates this point. A story about the trial of a man charged with killing his former girlfriend and her baby included this paragraph: "Though they had sex just minutes before he killed her, she apparently told him the relationship was finished, prosecutors have said." While readers may take different meanings from the sentence, some are likely to see the woman as duplicitous, willing to have sex before breaking off a relationship. The sentence has little to do with the power represented by the killer and the gun that he held.

- Talk to experts on domestic violence as you do your reporting. One article included this quote: "I don't think we'll ever know what precipitated this situation." Maybe not, but people who work with victims of domestic violence could make a good guess.
- Finally, respect all people who are willing to tell their stories about domestic violence. Amazing insights about this experience appear in newspapers for the homeless, in an array of performance pieces about domestic violence, and in the stories of those who have suffered. A reporter's careful and sensitive interviewing of a survivor of domestic violence could help to destroy the myths that perpetrators of such acts are normal people and that the victims should take the blame for violence.

How Discrimination Compels Silence and Resists Narratives

This chapter has been about people whose stories have been missing from the news, in part because their suffering encourages their silence and in part because the rest of us are too unwilling to take their experience into account. Each group we have discussed—combat veterans, genocide survivors and refugees, victims of domestic violence—has a high ratio of traumatic exposure and a high risk of post-traumatic stress disorder for some period after. With a good deal of preparation a journalist can help release these personal narratives from the cocoon of trauma in which they are often wrapped.

As we drafted this book, a woman student of color challenged us to extend its reach to include people who live with stress that rarely abates—stress engendered by fear, lack of means, coping with prejudice, and health problems that do not receive adequate attention. In some cases, traumatic injury results from or is complicated by these conditions. In other instances, stress simply reduces the quality of life and erodes optimism and energy. The threat of violence can be so great that its victims rarely experience relief from the stress of living. A climate of prejudice takes its toll in fear, alienation, and resignation from an active life. The writer James Baldwin reminds his white readers of the power of racial terror in the lives of African Americans who regularly confront prejudice and violence. In the fall of 1998 Americans were reminded that lesbian, gay, and transsexual people may face violence and prejudice; a gay University of Wyoming student, Matthew Shepard, died after being beaten fiercely, then tied to a fence and left exposed to the cold in a cornfield. His death, in concert with other murders of gays and lesbians in recent years—including some in the military—was a reminder that violence based on sexual orientation is not uncommon in the United States. Even when violence does not occur, the fear of homophobic prejudice drives some men, women, and teenagers to compromise their own identities and aspirations. Yet the news media often ignore both the violence and the manifestations of prejudice.

We believe journalists can help remove the veil of silence that surrounds the emotional injuries suffered by these groups. As with the victims of the shock waves of the single horrible event, these people have stories to tell that will help them and inform others. However, journalists have to approach them as wisely and respectfully as they would approach a trauma victim.

We offer these suggestions about how to report these stories:

- First, recognize the vitality and resiliency in all communities. Honor the diversity of experiences in every group and disdain easy assumptions about whether people are able to cope with their conditions. Do not assume any particular person suffers either stress or trauma.
- Respect the wisdom represented in often-neglected communities and include their members regularly in your reporting. Their voices add a dimension of experience often missing in news stories.
- Seek ways to enable people to tell of their experiences. We have read compelling accounts by or about people coping with AIDS or cancer, single parents raising children, and families flourishing in dangerous neighborhoods. Yet such stories are rare enough that when they do appear they receive unusual attention. Such stories are not routinely reported.
- Trust the authentic voice of a person who has experienced difficult conditions. The *Seattle Times* invited a young man with AIDS to write a regular column; the personal perspective was both fresh and startling in its candor. Homeless people write for and sell newspapers. Many of the articles are compelling stories about the experiences of homelessness.
- Report about subtle as well as obvious forms of prejudice, but learn about both from the perspective of people who see them as threats in their own lives.
- Beware of news conventions that routinely provide a political or religious "balance" to stories but end up serving only to demean what the victim has said. When a lesbian or gay person is featured in a news report, for example, it isn't unusual for a "balancing" source to be quoted as well, often to provide a negative characterization of the person's identity. The practice is reminiscent of a ploy used by some Southern television stations during the civil rights ferment of the early 1960s. After a network news program described a march for economic or political justice, for example, the affiliate would present a local segregationist who would provide "the truth" about African Americans' demands for civil equality.
- Respect people's desire for silence, but do more to encourage those who want to speak to tell their stories with your help.

Chapter 10

Oklahoma City: "Terror in the Heartland"

In a single horrific event Oklahoma City illustrates vividly nearly every key point this book has been making about human cruelty, its ramifications, and the vital role the media play in reporting and interpreting it all. This chapter tells a story that is at once terrible and inspiring. Much of the focus is through the eyes, minds, and hearts of the people at one newspaper and how they affected—and were affected by—a community and nation in shock and recovery.

9:02 a.m.

It was sunny that morning. Most newsroom staffers at the *Daily Oklahoman* were well into their regular routines as they worked on stories for the next morning's edition. At 9:02 A.M. they heard a thunderous noise and the building shook. Joe Hight, the community editor, and reporters Ellie Sutter, Allison Day, Carla Hinton, and Bryan Painter looked out a window to see a fountain of dust bursting into the blue sky from the downtown area a few miles away.

One hundred sixty-eight men, women, and children died on the spot or within hours or days of the blast, which caved in a third of the nine-story federal building. Several structures near the Murrah building were heavily hit. Other damage was reported as far as fifteen miles from the blast.

The human damage appalled and stunned the city and nation. The final toll included 853 injured. Many victims worked for or were visiting one of the several federal agencies with offices in the building, such as the Social Security Administration, Secret Service, Veterans Administration, and Bureau of Alcohol, Tobacco, and Firearms.

On the second floor, though, most of the occupants in one area were much younger and smaller. They were the preschoolers in the building's day-care center, located just above the spot where the bomb exploded. The center had been built a few years earlier to give government workers a place to keep their children nearby and, they had reason to believe, safe. In addition to the nineteen children killed—fifteen in the day-care center and four elsewhere in the building—police ultimately calculated that thirty were orphaned and more than two hundred lost at least one parent.

Instant Coverage

The *Oklahoman*'s coverage began literally before the dust had settled. The Murrah building was only about six miles away from the newspaper's office, and reporters and photographers rushed to the scene. Staff writer Diana Baldwin went to the site with photographer Jim Argo; in her high heels, she circled the smoking and burning building, listening to everything that went on. Reporter Clytie Bunyan already was close to the Murrah building when the bomb went off—too close. She was injured when the blast shook the nearby post office she was visiting. Off-duty reporters and editors automatically went to the office to begin shifts that never seemed to end.

"I have a lasting image of reporters clearing their throats and wiping away tears in order to write, edit, photograph, and create," says Ed Kelley, who was managing editor at the time. "Maybe our readers did get to see that through our stories. They were written not only by talented people but by people who care about their community." Kelley notes that 150 newsroom employees worked overtime—copy messengers and clerks, reporters and editors, the fashion writer and the sports columnist, and management.

We have emphasized in this book that journalists should respect the privacy of victims and their families in any story. At best, it is a daunting effort to do that when thousands of people are directly or indirectly involved and a whole city and nation want to know what happened. Somehow, the *Oklahoman* did it day after day and week after week, as the horror struck, sank in, and had to be faced in daily struggles for survival and recovery.

Having a formal policy about covering victims is always helpful, but in this case it was not necessary, Kelley says: "There was never any declaration from me or anyone else saying, 'This is how we'll treat these people who have been victimized.' There was a collective sense by our top editors and reporters that these are *our* people. These are people we send our kids to school with, attend church with."

Still, it was clear that to do their jobs the reporters and photographers had to contact survivors, their families, and friends at precisely the times they were suffering the most and might be most inclined to withdraw. Baldwin says she and her colleagues realized that, took it into account, and still got the necessary stories and pictures. "You have to be patient," she says. "You don't have to beat them over the head to get the story. In fact, you'll probably get the story that others wouldn't if you are patient."

That approach was especially helpful in the sad job of chronicling the deaths. Rather than run standard obituaries, the *Oklahoman* published "profiles of life," one for each of the 168 people who died in the bombing. "We wanted these vignettes to focus more on their lives, not on their deaths," Kelley says.

One of the first profiles, by staff writer Jim Killackey, was of Michael Carillo, a forty-eight-year-old employee of the U.S. Department of Transportation. He was presumed dead, although his body had yet to be recovered from the rubble of the Murrah building. The story focused on his brother's search for dental records to help identify Michael when the time came and on his family and life: "He was a great American . . . who loved his country so very much," the brother told the paper. "Dr. Margaret Louise 'Peggy' Clark loved her horses and loved her kids," read the lead to one of the last profiles several weeks later that noted the life of a Department of Agriculture veterinarian. Between those accounts 166 other tributes told why the man, woman, or child was someone special, someone loved and missed.

Gathering information for the profiles was part of a style of interviewing that emphasized knowledge of the deceased before contacting the family to ask for the interview and then talking about details of the person's life rather than effects of his or her death, as well as accepting that some people would not want to talk. Some staff members became friends of victims' families, relationships that everyone agreed were appropriate, so long as they were limited by a style of professional responsibility.

One of the victims who attracted the most attention was among the youngest, year-old Baylee Almon. An AP photo that the *Oklahoman* and thousands of other papers around the world printed on page one showed a firefighter tenderly carrying the limp baby away from the bomb site. It was not until the next day that the hospital confirmed that little Baylee had died.

Baylee's picture became the most famous Oklahoma City photograph. Many others, though, played important roles in showing not only the massive destruction and grief but also the communal sharing of grief, outpourings of help and compassion, and the informal but heartrending shrines that people erected. Some of the most touching items in the shrines came from children. One photo showed a poster sent by Texas youngsters that read: "We care. For the children who left mommy's, daddy's, family & friends. . . . For the children who were left without mommy's, daddy's, family and friends. Love from children in Texas." It was decorated with pictures of teddy bears and flowers and signed by five children. Another picture showed a drawing by kindergartener Courtney Craig of a sad stick figure that said, "I'm sad because the building blew up."

One photo by staff photographer Steve Sisney even helped solve the mystery of what caused the death of Rebecca Anderson, a nurse. She was not in the explosion but was one of the first medical volunteers to enter the building afterward. She collapsed after leaving the rubble and died four days later in the hospital. The medical examiner finally determined that she had been struck in the head by falling concrete debris. Doctors said the positions of her hands in the photo told them she had suffered a neurological trauma. One more loss, although still painful, was given some closure.

The *Daily Oklahoman* served as the community's unofficial clearinghouse and coordinator in many ways after the bombing. Most immediately, the paper established a "Searching for Survivors" column in response to pleas from the state Health Department for help in counting those involved. The more than 225 published responses put the agency in contact with more survivors. Other special columns helped victims' families, survivors, and the public, including "How to Help," "How to Get Help," and "Acts of Kindness." For example, in one of the "Kindness" columns were notes about merchants, organizations, and individuals that provided coffee for rescue workers around the clock for several days and free long-distance phone calls for families directly affected. An internationally known portrait painter offered to paint a free portrait from a photograph of any child killed in the bombing.

Such stories and columns helped ameliorate the immediate immense problems faced by survivors and local and state officials as they tried to cope. The paper also helped survivors, families, and the whole community—however large that became—to understand more about what trauma does to people, especially when it is the result of deliberate human cruelty. Even the *Oklahoman*'s section headings helped convey the information that trauma and recovery are a continuing process.

The first few days after the bombing the heading was "Terror in the Heartland." That was an appropriate label for the initial stages of a severe trauma, especially an intentional criminal act in an environment where people had felt safe from such an attack. For several weeks after that, the heading became "Together in the Heartland," as the paper chronicled how community members and organizations marshaled their resources to help others and themselves. That fits into the longer-term trauma recovery period when survivors of any event search for meaning and help in recovery.

For one of the "Together" pages a story by staff writer Bryan Painter focused on post-traumatic stress disorder (PTSD). Experts told how it can be harder for individuals, or a whole community, to recover from the shock of a violent criminal act than from a natural disaster such as an earthquake or tornado. Bruce Hiley-Young of the National Center for Post-Traumatic Stress Disorder in Palo Alto, California, offered the *Oklahoman* this explanation of the difference: "People were confronted with the tearing away of the illusion of security. We don't generally feel the fear of our mortality. In Oklahoma City, that stopped happening, so people are vulnerable, unlike a natural disaster, because this was an intentional crime. That strikes a chord in people, a deep chord, so I think the recovery process will take longer" (Painter 1995:8).

Hiley-Young notes that dealing with the disillusionment stage varies according to the individuals and how much they are affected: "For the victims, it is not an issue of being mentally ill, rather it's an issue of having a normal response to an abnormal event." Dr. Ken Thompson, a psychiatrist at the University of Pittsburgh quoted in the same story, says: "It's important that the people who need to recover more slowly are not made to feel that there's something wrong with them" (Painter 1995:8).

The story was accompanied by a graphic that showed the four stages in the community's reaction to the disaster—"heroic," "honeymoon," "disillusionment," and "recovery"—and a "coping" chart listed eighteen things people might do to deal with their emotional aftershocks. Some suggestions were highly physical, such as "do strenuous exercise" and "eat well-balanced and regular meals." Others touched on psychological matters, such as alerting survivors that repeated dreams or flashbacks are normal and are likely to become less frequent and painful over time. The paper also tried to tell readers about seemingly trivial things that might increase their trauma, providing, for example, warnings about movies that had unusually violent content.

While working to help survivors and the community cope, the *Oklahoman* also heeded the needs of its own people in several big and little ways.

The paper made a therapist available to staffers for a year after the bombing, an opportunity that mostly attracted women. The women continued to meet and support each other in the months that followed. Right after the blast the paper relaxed its rules for its state-of-the-art newsroom, allowing pizza and other food to be brought in for those who were working long shifts.

Some staffers talked about their experiences or tried to. Clytie Bunyan, the reporter hurt at the post office, recalls her anger when she tried to tell a colleague what had happened to her and she realized she "couldn't get through to him." A factual error in the story about her injury troubled her deeply. That happened even though the paper had assigned an editor specifically to avoid and correct errors, saving the *Oklahoman* from publishing mistakes that might have added to distraught readers' trauma.

About two weeks after the bombing Kelley, the managing editor, issued a staff memo in response to the fear some had that their work was not very important in the great scheme of things and that they were "trafficking in the misery of the victims' families." In the memo he noted that many staff members had had to do things they were not trained for or prepared for, but he emphasized the kind of volunteer heroism they represented. "But you are among the only 170 or so people in a metropolitan area of 1 million who could, in depth, make sense of what happened, and why, and explain what lies ahead," he told them.

The *Oklahoman* focused heavily and appropriately on the victims and survivors in its coverage, but the paper also demonstrated the need to report on the bombers, and especially who they were not. Editors at the *Oklahoman* made it clear to us that the paper had been determined to have "ownership" all along of two stories—the victims' story and the crime story. Indeed, the newspaper covered the investigations and trials to the hilt.

The way the paper covered the crime aspect, however, was deliberate. From the start the *Oklahoman* sought not to focus on the culprit at the expense of losing the focus on those dead or suffering. It would have been easy—too easy—to go in the other direction. Much of the coverage elsewhere dwelt on who, or what, might be responsible. The *Oklahoman* and other media in the city might be forgiven for being so angry that they would scream for the arrest and punishment of the bomber or bombers. At times they did and properly so. Whoever killed dozens outright and injured hundreds of others had to be found, both for justice and to ensure they could not strike again.

Early speculation after the bombing centered on a suspicion that Middle East terrorists were probably responsible for the Oklahoma City blast. After all, some Middle Eastern extremist groups had vowed for years to attack Americans. The *Oklahoman* did not jump to that judgment, even when law enforcement personnel detained and questioned some Middle Eastern residents of the area.

Two days after the bombing police and FBI officials arrested not an international terrorist but Timothy James McVeigh, a twenty-six-year-old former U.S. soldier. The bombing occurred on the second anniversary of the fiery destruction of the Branch Davidian compound near Waco, Texas. Authorities said McVeigh had shown "extreme anger" in regard to the government's handling of that situation, in which about eighty men, women, and children died after a fifty-one-day standoff.

As the story unfolded, the world learned a lot about McVeigh and those who worked with him or knew about his deadly plans. McVeigh's arrest, as well as significant subsequent developments in the investigation, were front-page news for many days. The *Oklahoman* and other local media continued their intensive coverage through McVeigh's trial in Denver, his conviction, and his sentence of death. Other stories followed what happened to the two other men convicted in the case: Terry Nichols was sentenced to life without possibility of parole for conspiracy and involuntary manslaughter. Michael Fortier, the government's key witness in the case, drew a twelve-year prison term for not warning anyone about the plot and for lying to the FBI.

Other Media

We have focused on the work of the *Daily Oklahoman* because it was the hometown paper and did so many things so well, but other coverage was extensive, of course. The bombing drew throngs of journalists from around Oklahoma, the United States, and the world. Most showed respect for the survivors and their need for privacy. Others did not.

City and state authorities quickly realized, literally before the dust and smoke had settled from the explosion, that media coverage would be intense. Journalists from around the world soon converged on Oklahoma City, seeking news and competitive advantages. The parachutists often push local media out of the way.

Two months later the *Oklahoman* ran a story about a meeting of local officials held to reflect on the media coverage; most concluded it was a positive experience. In Oklahoma City, remarkably, officials said the local media set the stage early for the largely respectful coverage that soon prevailed. Media inquiries from around the nation at first often focused on such questions as how much looting was going on, Red Cross officials said. That tone changed within twenty-four hours, when national correspondents asked more about "the goodness of the community" (Hinton 1995:12).

The officials themselves also were important in encouraging that tone of respect and cooperation. Assistant Fire Chief Jon Hansen said that officials decided soon after the blast that reporters should be closer to the scene, not kept as far away as possible—something that often happens elsewhere. A big reason for the decision was that the public was becoming skeptical that rescue and recovery efforts were proceeding fast enough. "Things were going slow," Hansen said. "We felt it was necessary to get journalists into the building" (Hinton 1995:12). A pool of reporters went in and came out to explain the laborious, careful work necessary to clear the debris.

John Cox, deputy press secretary to Oklahoma governor Frank Ketting, said that the governor received two hundred requests for interviews the first day. "This may have been the biggest spot news since the Kennedy assassination," Cox allowed. Police spokesman Bill Citty realized the tremendous media interest when he went to the first briefing and was confronted by seventy-five television cameras. "It scared me," he said. But dealing with the media turned out to be "a wonderful experience" overall. In the midst of the bombing horror "we also saw some of the kindest things" (Hinton 1995:12).

The Fake Priest and Other Frauds

Not all media experiences were so wonderful for survivors and officials. Howard Witt and Hugh Dellios, whose column is syndicated through the *Chicago Tribune*, reported other types in a story that the *Oklahoman* headlined "Local TV Disagrees with Tabloids." As Witt and Dellios put it: "In a city where not a single looter was reported to have ventured inside the five-square-block area of destruction, police were kept busy chasing out visiting tabloid reporters with a lust for exclusive gore" (1995:20). One visiting tabloid reporter donned a priest's vestments to try to sneak into a church where distraught relatives of bombing victims had been brought to await confirmations of the deaths of their loved ones. The "priest" was caught when someone noticed that he did not have the proper vestment belt in his disguise.

Another tabloid television reporter, Witt and Dellios recounted, posed as a firefighter in an attempt to shoot video inside the bombed-out federal building as workers pulled bodies from the rubble. He was charged with grand larceny, impersonating a firefighter, and obstruction of justice. Another reporter dressed as a firefighter was escorted from the area when someone noticed he was not wearing regular firefighting boots. He even had given interviews to other reporters as part of his ruse. Security guards had to chase out intrusive reporters even at the hospital where most of the critically wounded victims were being treated. As one camera crew from a national tabloid television program was escorted from the hospital, a reporter from a New York City newspaper slipped in behind (Witt and Dellios 1995:20).

By contrast, the Chicago writers comment, local journalists had not "mimicked the national press willingness to thrust microphones into the faces of the bereaved." They note, for example, that Oklahoma City television reporters read homespun poems to calm anxious viewers and skipped reading sports scores because they suddenly seemed frivolous.

"Our philosophy is, we're not going to sensationalize this tragedy that truly happened to our own people," Michelle Fink, spokeswoman for Oklahoma City's NBC affiliate, KFOR-TV, told Witt and Dellios. When its reporters were not invited to funerals for bombing victims, the station stayed away. "We tried to imagine every story in terms of how we would react if we were the family," Fink said.

Even some national media stars came in for some criticism. Connie Chung drew heat from many viewers who thought she sounded condescending in an interview with Assistant Chief Hansen, the fire department's spokesman during the disaster. The critics complained that Chung, then coanchor of the *CBS Evening News,* seemed to disparage community leaders' resources and expertise in dealing with the disaster. The fire chief's calm, reasoned reply apparently satisfied many people that officials and the community generally were doing all that could be done.

No staffers at the *Oklahoman* have said they were content with the paper's coverage of the bombing, but their peers have recognized the paper's skilled and compassionate reporting with several journalistic honors for stories, photos, or overall work, including the 1996 Dart Award for Excellence in Reporting on Victims of Violence.

In the weeks after the bombing there were 168 individual funerals, each precious to family and friends. In addition, two other events served in some important ways as funerals for all survivors and the national extended family of Oklahoma City. Both drew heavy, and largely respectful, news coverage.

One news event was the destruction of the remains of the Alfred P. Murrah Federal Building. Indeed, many people who viewed the implosion of the structure on May 24, 1995—about a month after the bombing—said they felt as if they were at a funeral. Some said they realized the demolition marked the end of one stage in the process of grieving and recovery from trauma. That is a milestone familiar to mental health professionals and generally a healthy sign that survivors are coping and functioning better.

Still, one more communal "funeral" stirred even more emotions and more symbolism for many people on the long road to recovery from the bombing. That occurred in late October 1998, when the fence around the building site was removed and ceremonially carried off by hundreds of survivors and family members. The fence had been studded with photographs of victims, flowers, posters, and letters. It was, in a very real sense, a shrine. The removal made way for construction to begin on a permanent memorial, to feature 168 empty concrete chairs and an interactive museum exhibit.

Again, participants and onlookers said it seemed the end of another stage of recovery and the beginning of another. How many stages were still to come, or how long they would take, nobody could be sure.

The next day, and about fifteen hundred miles away in New York City, visitors from around the nation were in the crowd outside the studios of a popular network television morning show. The program daily turns the cameras on the onlookers, most of whom are tourists, who often wave, cheer, or hold up signs addressed to the folks back home. This time the cameras zoomed in on a sign held by one little group. The sign said simply: "Oklahoma City Is OK."

Chapter 11

Conclusions

Throughout this book we have contended that covering violence is a challenging endeavor but one with few journalistic equals in compelling interest and potential benefit to the public and those who suffer physical and emotional trauma.

We have provided a framework to help journalists prepare to interview, photograph, and write about people overwhelmed by violence. Journalists often acknowledge that covering such a story is the toughest assignment they get. That view is superseded only by the frequent public outrage about brutish or intrusive coverage of people who already have been subjected to murder, mayhem, rape, or other criminal violence and the horrors of natural disasters.

There are vast differences between covering public figures who want, expect, or at least endure news coverage and ordinary people who simply are caught up in extraordinary events. Reporters and photographers get used to whipping out a pen or sticking a microphone or camera lens in someone's face to get that "great stuff" on deadline. Too often they fail to realize that the techniques that served them well in covering, say, a candidate on the stump or a Hollywood or gridiron star, can frighten, overwhelm, or anger someone who has just been devastated by a horrifying experience.

Survivors, including relatives of the dead or injured, may be in shock or radiating confusion or rage. Others may project a deceptive sense of being calm, cool, and collected when they are actually in the throes of deep trauma.

Many times, though, victims remember all too well their encounters with news media. That is particularly so in notorious events that draw hordes of journalists to the scene or to the homes of relatives and friends. Residents of the little community of Jonesboro, Arkansas, found themselves swamped by more than two hundred reporters, photographers, and crews from about seventy U.S. and foreign news organizations when two boys murdered their schoolmates in 1998. Residents were appalled by the intrusions and antics of some of the journalists who swooped in and out of town but generally gave good marks to local media.

Avoid Avoidance

While some journalists seem to go to almost any length to get a sensational quote, video, or sound bite, the opposite also happens: Some try hard to avoid contact with deeply troubled people. This reflects the reporter's personal discomfort, and it may be insensitively dismissed by editors and coworkers.

We are not suggesting that journalists should not cover violence. The journalist's obligation to represent the public means, above all, going where human beings are most at risk. For better or worse violence is an important part of the report that we want journalists to bring back to us. Our aim, rather, is to encourage more of the better and less of the worse. That goes beyond the often cynical and self-serving tabloid notion that "inquiring minds want to know." Rather, citizens in a democracy *must* know about violence if they are to make responsible decisions about how to protect themselves, their families, and their communities. The job of the media is to tell them, accurately, fairly, and comprehensively.

Journalists and Trauma

Journalists are not psychologists, psychiatrists, or social workers. Few newspeople have such professional training, and journalists' prime job is to inform—not diagnose, treat, and heal physical and mental ills. Nonetheless, journalism can be one of the "helping professions." One way is, as physicians pledge, to "seek to do no harm." One way to do that—and to produce more compelling human interest stories—is to understand some of the basic facts about what trauma is and what it does.

The most prominent type of trauma is post-traumatic stress disorder (PTSD). It is signified by three reactions that last at least a month and occur together after an event that terrifies, horrifies, or renders someone helpless. The first of the three reactions—which can surface days, months, or even years after the horrific event—is recurring recollections that hit somebody who is trying hard to forget what happened. That can include bad dreams, hallucinations, or flashbacks, the vivid feeling that you are once again seeing, hearing, feeling, or smelling the very thing that is so repellent.

By contrast, a second PTSD element is emotional numbing and constriction of normal activities. The trauma victim tries to survive the unwanted memory attacks by erecting an emotional wall and avoiding anything that might reignite the recollections. That can temporarily protect someone from overwhelming distress, but it also can steal the joy, love, and hope from life. Pleasure disappears. Life is hollow.

In the third PTSD reaction the term *jumpy* takes on new meaning. The person's bodily alarm system undergoes a physical shift. The normal mechanism that warns us of danger becomes hair-trigger—set off easily and mistakenly by sudden noises or other unexpected sights or sounds. Something that once might have caused someone to be, at most, momentarily startled now sets off a shudder, jump, or even panic.

Whatever the signs of trauma, we emphasize that journalists should be aware that the distress can last a long time and be reflected in both obvious and subtle ways. Different people handle trauma in different ways. Children especially have their own methods of coping with terrible things that happen to them.

When the reporter or photographer arrives at the scene of a crime or disaster, the immediate effects of trauma usually are all too apparent. The cause may be an act of God—flood, earthquake, or volcanic eruption. It may be the result of human cruelty in a shooting, bombing, or arson. We have seen how the journalist at the scene has unusual power to shape what we remember about these events forever. We have explored how breaking news coverage can be an important resource for those who suffer in the aftermath of the event, as well as for the news audience.

Nothing can fully prepare a reporter to cover a disaster, but planning can improve the quality and accuracy of the reporting. That is true even if the only time you have is the time it takes to reach the scene. Do expect that you will see people injured physically and suffering psychological shock. The victims, aid workers, and you will all be affected. Nobody, including a journalist, is exempt.

Find emergency response and public safety personnel who are likely to have credible information later. Determine what other places someone will need to check, such as hospitals, morgues, and official public information offices. Finally, stay out of the way as rescue and relief work goes on.

You will deal with several types of public safety and emergency personnel. Reporters and photographers often move among emergency workers immediately after an event, but journalists are expected to stay clear of boundary markers once they are established. Most often a local or state police agency will be in charge, but in some cases a federal agency such as the FBI may coordinate activity at the scene. Identify key personnel with these agencies and stay in contact with them as you work. The Red Cross is at nearly every disaster or major accident scene, providing first aid, shelter, and comfort to victims and disaster workers. You are increasingly likely to work with a volunteer serving on a Red Cross public affairs team that may screen and coordinate interviews with reporters.

Do not weaken your reporting from the scene with the myths and clichés that often spring from reporting of accidents and disasters. One myth is a huge need for immediate contributions of all types. Do not, for instance, automatically issue calls for contributions of blankets, food, or other items that someone mentions are needed. Too often well-meaning people then flood the area with things that no one can use, clogging rescue and relief efforts. Wait for the Red Cross or officials to pinpoint exactly what people really need and how to provide it.

Another myth is that looting, price gouging, and panic always accompany a disaster. Studies show the reverse often is true, with survivors, community officials, and businesses doing what they can to help people and relieve suffering. On the other hand, do not assume that relief agencies are more rational and better organized than they may be. Confusion and head bumping among agencies at the scene often occur until things are sorted out and coordinated.

Do not repeat or give credence to the cliché that "things will get better as time goes on" for those most affected by the event. Tincture of time can be a great medicine, but those most affected may hit a wall of trauma at some point as their energies wane or disillusionment with their efforts sets in. Not everyone reacts the same way, and the media can help by reporting that continuing story. That is illustrated, for example, in the anniversary coverage of the Oklahoma City bombing. Months and years later people are still suffering. Recovery is news, however long it takes.

Interviewing

There is no substitute for interviewing survivors and their families. The interview with victims is a staple of news because it puts us in touch with the voice, face, and emotions of a person who is suffering. Yet what is a necessary interview to journalists often is seen as an intrusion or outright attack by those on the other side of the pen, camera, or microphone. That does not have to happen. One way to avoid it is to exercise empathy, the ability to identify intellectually or emotionally with another person.

The first step to an empathic interview is mental preparation as you drive to the scene. Remind yourself that many of the survivors, witnesses, friends, and family members will not have the same degree of self-control and ability to take in and deal with new information that you and trained police and emergency workers have.

Respect the other person's efforts to regain balance after a horrible experience. The person is likely to be confused, angry, or grieving, or all three. Offer as much support to the victim as conditions allow. Ask whether the interviewee would like to have a friend, neighbor, or relative stand by. Consider where to do the interview. Try to find a place away from the activity of the scene and sit down with the interviewee.

For that matter, make sure the person understands that you are a reporter and which publication or station you work for. Three opening comments always will be appropriate: "I'm sorry this happened to you"; "I'm glad you were not killed"; "It is not your fault." Do not ask, "How do you feel?" That enrages or stuns more victims that any other question reporters ask. Instead, ask what the person needs.

Remember that you may have information the other person does not. Do not be quick to volunteer information about someone's injury or death, especially if you have not yet confirmed the information. Gently learn what the person knows by asking such questions as "When did you hear the news?" and "When did the police arrive?" Help the interviewee contact individuals or agencies that can offer assistance.

In ending the interview, whether the person has given you much or little information, offer to be available later in person or by telephone.

Finally, give some attention to yourself. Recognize your own response to the interview, talk about it with others, or give yourself a chance to reflect on it.

Those are all pointers for interviews soon after the event. Follow-up interviews days, weeks, or months later involve the same guidelines, plus a few others. Remember that asking the person to go over details again may trigger painful recollections and reactions. Alert the person that that could happen. It may be helpful to the survivor to say that you wish to focus on recovery and the aftermath of an event, rather than on the details.

Writing the Story

If the interview has gone well, the reporter next plunges into the equal challenge of writing the story. A key word here is *story*. Remember that this type of writing is not simply a news story but an account of a particular human being and the traumatic events in that life. Like storytellers for thousands of years, the writer must quickly capture the audience's attention, hold it throughout a compelling narration, and wrap up with vivid images that go to the heart of it all.

Accuracy counts heavily in telling a survivor's story. Accuracy is vital in any journalism, of course, but victims of violence often feel the sting of mistakes even more keenly than other news subjects. Their lives already have been turned upside down, unwillingly and painfully. Errors such as misspelled names or wrong ages, addresses, or job descriptions add another layer to survivors' feelings of powerlessness and violation.

How you write the story also hinges on the timing. We call the various situations Act I and Act II. Act I includes the immediate reporting of the breaking story that focuses on the traditional "5Ws"—who, what, when, where, and why. Most stories about victims fall into this category. The reporter must concentrate on explaining who did what to whom, identifying the victim or survivor, and telling whether the attacker—in the case of a criminal act—is under arrest or still at large.

Act II stories, by contrast, portray the longer-term aftermath of trauma months or years later, profiling the victims and how they cope for better or worse in the continuing recovery process. This is an opportunity to explore in depth the devastating effects of human cruelty (or the whims of nature), but the focus is heavily on the victim or survivor, not the criminal or act of God that caused the trauma. Personality profiles usually form the foundation for Act II stories, as with many human interest features. A profile typically consists of the subject's background; telling anecdotes; relevant quotes from friends, relatives, coworkers, and neighbors; the reporter's observations; and a news peg.

Whatever the ingredients, the best profile of this type often uses techniques found in the best fiction writing: rich colorful details and narration that makes the individuals involved come alive and that drop the reader into

the action. That goes doubly for the lead of the story. As with any journalistic story, the lead should grab the reader and set the scene for everything to
follow. It does not have to be the hit-'em-hard lead generally associated with
news stories, but it should quickly enchant the reader in some way.

Details are the key to the body of the survivor's story—not tedious ency-
clopedic details but accurate, illuminating, and dramatic facts, quotes, and
observations that reinforce each point about the person's trauma and recovery. That can mean reporting details that show the person is not—sur-
prise!—a saint but has human weaknesses and eccentricities. Do avoid
details that unnecessarily wound or offend the survivor or family members
just for the sake of some "colorful" or scintillating tidbits. If a detail is necessary to portray and explain the event or the person truly, include it. If not,
ditch it.

Like any good story, fact or fiction, the survivor's chronicle should end
with a good kicker. A final revealing quote or anecdote may be the crowning
touch for one story. The reporter's observation may brilliantly wrap up
another story. Consider what memory or feeling you want to leave the
reader with and choose the type of walk-off accordingly.

We believe the Act I and Act II concepts are useful in crafting most stories about victims, but sometimes those frameworks seem inadequate for
capturing a wider perspective. These stories, dubbed Act III, go to a still
deeper level, placing specific traumatic incidents within broader historical
or economic contexts. Act III reporting might even be a way to help readers
understand the origins and aftermath of wars. The health or survival of
whole societies and nations may hinge on a better understanding of violence and victimization on the massive scale of war.

If It Bleeds . . .

All news media get angry complaints about insensitive reporting of victims,
but photographic and broadcasting coverage often draws the most outrage.
That is not surprising. Photography, television, and radio immediately hit
our senses. Pictures and sounds can be powerful tools for good journalism
in reporting on violence, or they can further wound suffering people and
misinform and mislead viewers and listeners.

Many TV stations feed such problems with the practice of starting virtually every news program with a report of a crime or other violence: "If it
bleeds, it leads." Sometimes that is exactly what stations should do. If there
is a wave of violence or a mounting disaster, the community must be

alerted. Other times, however, stations sacrifice or downplay news of more importance to viewers in favor of something more "visual." Regularly leading with news of violence may instill in the audience the impression that the community harbors much more violent crime and danger than actually exists.

Complaints also are abundant about the way broadcast journalists interview victims and family members. Nearly everyone has seen a reporter shove a microphone in the face of a grieving or shocked survivor and ask, "So how do you feel now?" Frequently, that microphone is just one in a forest of electronic equipment that surrounds the hapless subject. Television and still cameras do intimidate and frighten people. Some people are dumbstruck when the camera or mike is turned on them. Others react angrily. Still others may feel they almost have an official obligation to talk to a broadcast reporter, rather than simply saying, "Now's not the time. Please give us some privacy."

Only rarely is it necessary to report on individual suicides; when it is, you will find suicide is particularly difficult to cover visually. Photographers and broadcasters are wise, we believe, to consider how much to cover and to be especially alert and selective if they are broadcasting live. Consider too whether children are likely to see the footage if it interrupts regular programming or is shown on early evening newscasts.

Among other points in covering suicide, we suggest that stations as a matter of policy build in a delay of several seconds during live transmissions to allow a decision to cut something. Newspapers, for their part, can consider the possible harm of front-page photos of a suicide or other violent death.

Rape Trauma

Reporting about rape is one of the most controversial and difficult forms of reporting on trauma. It is also one of the most *under*reported forms of violence (see chapter 7).

We emphasize that rape is not about sex in any usual sense. It is not a "sexual act." It is an act of violence. News reporting that implies the victim is somehow responsible for the assault may foster more silence about the horror of rape.

Rape survivors who want to come forward, be named, and talk about their experiences should be supported. We strongly believe, however, that journalists may harm women, men, and children who are raped—and survive—if their names are used in news reports without their consent. Trauma persuades us that names should be withheld.

If a rape case goes to trial, we still think fairness supports not identifying the victim in court stories. We also urge reporters covering a rape trial to consider whether reporting the most graphic and invasive details is essential to the story.

The recent issue of the validity of "recovered memories" is still contested among medical experts. We think, though, that a recent study should convince reporters that claims of recovered memory should not be judged right or wrong at the outset. Automatically assuming that most such claims are fraudulent is, we believe, a disservice to the many victims of child abuse.

Child Victims

Children deserve special attention when they have just had a traumatic experience. Children are traumatized much more and longer than once assumed and should be interviewed and reported on differently than adults.

We argue that children should be protected from media attention, especially if they are aged ten or younger. As a general rule, we believe children of that age should not be interviewed or photographed in connection with events involving devastation, disaster, homicide or suicide, or accidents.

Children of any age are in particular need of therapeutic attention if they have been directly affected by a devastating event. The closer they are to danger, the more likely they are to suffer post-traumatic stress disorder or many PTSD symptoms. If interviews do seem crucial, involve both the child and a parent in the decision first; do not "ambush" a child. Quietly explain what you want and how the information might be used.

Using children's full names often exposes them to publicity or harassment that is especially hard for them to endure. We suggest that reporters consider using only a true or fictitious first name. Electronic screening should be considered for some children interviewed for television news.

Other Victims

Is silence news? We have discussed several types of rather obvious trauma, but our communities and news beats are filled with other silent survivors of traumatic experiences. In many cases the survivors are unheard because the media overlook them and their advice. Reporters can find such people in situations of poverty, discrimination, combat, and military siege; others have been held hostage or are refugees.

When silence is the result of news media avoidance and not a choice by an individual, we believe that journalists should challenge that silence with precise reporting. The reporting, though, must be respectful, sensitive to private matters, and concerned about recovery and survival more than the awful events that created a victim in the first place.

Combat veterans form one of the biggest groups of survivors who traditionally have remained silent about their traumatic experiences. We have noted how, going back at least to World War I, it was considered unseemly for veterans to discuss their emotions and problems resulting from combat. That has changed considerably since the Vietnam War, but many veterans still refuse to talk about what they saw and felt. We believe that news reports can be a bridge for understanding between those who fought in wars and the public but in ways that do not further harm the veteran.

Reporters should not ask combat veterans to recount what happened to them when the trauma occurred. That applies to interviewing any victims of violence in casual interviews or those in which the reporter and subject meet only once, but it is particularly important with combat survivors. We have recounted that victims often want and need to tell their stories but doing so may put them at great risk of psychological harm. Only when a reporter has built trust and demonstrated that the veteran can expect a sympathetic audience is the veteran likely to disclose traumatic events and his or her reactions to them.

Equally challenging but potentially beneficial are interviews with survivors of genocide or mass killings (today often wrapped in the semantic evasion of "ethnic cleansing"). Their stories are compelling and need to be told so that we all can understand the consequences of nationalistic and regional violence. Again, however, reporters need to take extra care to understand survivors' experiences and not harm them further. A skilled interpreter can help when the reporter does not speak the survivor's language, both to translate words and alert the journalist to any cultural differences that bear on the subject's responses to the trauma.

Whatever else they did, the O. J. Simpson criminal and civil trials awakened media interest in the domestic violence that often has been ignored or dismissed as a "family matter." Too often we cannot even talk about survivors, only victims, because the abuser kills the wife, girlfriend, or child. The attackers overwhelmingly are men. Careful and sensitive interviewing of a domestic violence survivor can help destroy the myths that the perpetrators are normal people and that the survivor is to blame for violence.

We also, finally, urge coverage of usually silent communities whose ethnicity, sexual orientation, or disability expose them to obvious and subtle forms of violence and prejudice. Too often individuals from such groups make the news only when they are killed or a comparative handful participate in a public demonstration.

Journalists and Secondary Trauma

One of the most revealing things we found in researching this book was the remarkable contrast between the tradition that "journalists can take it and not show it" and the incidence of considerable trauma among reporters and photographers exposed to violence as part of their jobs. As we have shown, journalists may need to deal with the same symptoms of secondary trauma as emergency and public safety workers and the therapists who work with victims of violence.

Some journalists apparently can absorb repeated exposure, do their work, and not be seriously troubled. Just as among victims of direct trauma, however, some journalists are affected so much that it seriously disturbs their work and personal lives.

One of the first solid gauges of trauma's effect on journalists came in a 1996 survey of 130 reporters, editors, and photographers at several daily newspapers in Washington State and Michigan (Simpson and Boggs 1999). The journalists disclosed a level of stress symptoms one might find among public safety workers recently engaged in a traumatic event.

Just as unsettling in the survey was that few of the responding journalists said they found ready newsroom support when assignments trouble them or had chosen to get any professional "debriefing" or counseling. Police officers and emergency workers often have such help available and even are required to use it, but few journalists do.

Our suggestions for dealing with secondary trauma start with acknowledging that you may see and hear things for which you are not prepared. Talking with another reporter or with an editor about what to expect can help. During the on-scene interview or in talking later with family and friends, try to monitor your reactions, maintain eye contact, and otherwise communicate your own emotion and empathy to the person.

After covering a troubling traumatic event, find ways to share your feelings with someone. That may be with a professional debriefer. We know many journalists who have been helped by a psychiatrist or psychologist. If that is not possible or necessary, seek out colleagues or talk with other friends and family. If the stress gets obvious, perhaps ask for time off.

Above all, simply remember that journalists are not exempt from human emotions and their effects.

Today's journalists have more potential power than ever. New ways to gather, process, and disseminate news would amaze and make envious journalists from earlier times. The media also now have the benefit of new insights into how people are affected by violence and human cruelty. It would be sad—and, we believe, indefensible—if journalists do not use that knowledge to devise new ways of covering victims and trauma.

We often noted in these pages how and why so much of the public is angry or bitter about news coverage that tramples and feeds on the raw emotions of people in trouble. Certainly those critics think it is past time for the media to act differently. Many journalists apparently agree, considering the healthy soul searching and debate within the profession on the ethics and practical effects of such coverage. We presented troubling examples of what we consider harmful coverage and held up inspiring illustrations of outstanding print and broadcast reporting that can and is being done.

Our aim is not to obstruct or hamper journalists. On the contrary, we want the profession we love to thrive and have the respect, trust, and support of those we serve. Treating with dignity and respect the suffering people we encounter produces some of the most compelling human interest journalism ever crafted and earns the profession respect and trust.

For those already engaged in the "helping profession" of journalism, the knowledge and tools are at hand. For those entering the field, great opportunities lie ahead to influence and shape this important aspect of journalism.

The Dart Award for Excellence
in Reporting on Victims of Violence

Since 1994 the Dart Award has recognized exemplary newspaper reports on violence and its victims. The recipients have included staff efforts—the reporting by the *Daily Oklahoman* of the aftermath of the bombing of the Oklahoma City federal building in 1995—as well as outstanding individual efforts.

The $10,000 award is administered by the Dart Center for Journalism and Trauma at the University of Washington School of Communications in Seattle.

Winners of the Dart Award

2000: "Who Killed John McCloskey?" *Roanoke Times.* For its compelling series on the suspicious death of an 18-year-old arrested and placed in the care of a mental institution, the cover-up that followed, and the family's grief and confusion. Honorable Mention: The *Denver Post* and *Rocky Mountain News* (Denver).

1999: "A Stolen Soul," *Portland* (Maine) *Press Herald.* For the sensitive and thorough portrayal of Yong Jones's struggle to bring her son's murderer to justice against the backdrop of her cultural beliefs. Honorable mention: *Palm Beach* (Florida) *Post.*

1998: "Children of the Underground," *Pittsburgh Post-Gazette.* For the complex and unsettling account of the hidden network that shelters youngsters escaping from sexual or physical abuse at home—real or alleged—and from a judicial system perceived as unwilling or unable to help them. Honorable mentions: *Westword* (Denver, Colo.) and *Nashville Banner.*

1997: "The Path of a Bullet," (Long Beach, Calif.) *Press-Telegram.* For its chronicle of the toll that a single 22-cent bullet exacted on individual victims and the broader community. Honorable mention: *Sunday* (Milwaukee) *Journal Sentinel.*

1996: *Daily* (Oklahoma City) *Oklahoman.* For its extensive coverage of the aftermath of the bombing of the Alfred P. Murrah Federal Building, coverage that helped readers connect to the lives of individual victims, survivors, and families.

1995: "The Test of Fire," *Austin American-Statesman.* For its unsentimental focus on Emmett Jackson's recovery from the arson death of his wife and child and his own extensive injuries. Honorable mention: (Munster, Indiana) *Times.*

1994: "Malignant Memories," *Anchorage Daily News.* For documenting the spirited growth of three women as they transcend the tragedies of incest that have haunted their lives. Honorable mentions: *Orlando Sentinel, Sheboygan Daily Tribune, San Francisco Chronicle,* and (Long Beach, Calif.) *Press-Telegram.*

A Note About Trauma Training

Learning about trauma can be stressful, for journalism students as well as working professionals who have experienced violence themselves or seen too much of it as part of their work.

We want to alert editors and instructors to some problems in training others about trauma and to suggest how to handle stressful reactions.

When we teach about trauma in the university classroom, we tell students that some people may find the subject too intense and may want to leave then or later. We try to take some of the edge off unexpected feelings of anxiety by saying in advance that in any group of fifteen to twenty students, one or more are likely to have suffered some form of trauma. (We also tell the students about the trauma training at least one class session in advance. Those who miss the training often give us some clue to their reasons, and invariably they have gone through a trauma that still troubles them.)

We tell students that if they should have unanticipated reactions, we can talk with them informally during or after the session or connect them with someone who can provide formal support. Both of us have experienced a student's suddenly leaving the room in tears or later disclosing a strong, unsettling reaction to the training. It is important to have a training team so that one member can talk to the person who is upset by the training while another instructor continues with the class.

The Victims and the Media Program at the Michigan State University School of Journalism introduces students in the first-level reporting course to the subject through written materials, lectures, and videos in which professional actors portray victims. In the advanced news-writing course, volunteer survivors appear in person to tell their stories and to be interviewed.

The Journalism and Trauma Program at the University of Washington School of Communications enables all students to do one or more interviews with an actor playing the part of a person who has experienced trauma. The interviews, carefully monitored by instructors who then offer supportive coaching, follow a session that simply orients journalism students to the nature of trauma and its effects on the people they interview.

Both programs provide time for debriefing after each class session. In all these training situations students may suffer unwanted reactions.

Editors who want to conduct in-house trauma workshops for staffers may wish to consider somewhat similar precautions. Even journalists who think they handle stress well sometimes find themselves affected when the topic is discussed openly.

Many newspapers and broadcast stations have a consulting psychologist available for debriefing who can also be asked to assist in the training. If the company does not have a regular consultant, we recommend one be made available for at least the workshop period.

Introduce the information gradually, allowing ample time for questions and comments. A common reaction when the topic of trauma is raised without adequate preparation is that some listeners simply "close down," overwhelmed by the ideas discussed.

If an event that has affected several or all staff members or students has prompted the training, consider seeking the help of a trauma response team (sometimes called a critical incident stress management team). Such teams are available in some communities and often are willing to travel some distance. Both of us have organized such teams to help news organizations in our regions.

In short, we believe journalists and students need to learn about trauma and violence, but we are equally eager not to harm them in the doing.

Bibliography

Adams, Eddie. 1998. "Eulogy." *Time*, July 27, p. 19.

Aiken, Charlotte. 1996. "Reporters Are Victims, Too." *Nieman Reports* 50 (3): 30–32.

Balakian, Peter. 1997. *Black Dog of Fate: A Memoir*. New York: Basic.

Benedict, Helen. 1992. *Virgin or Vamp: How the Press Covers Sex Crimes*. New York: Oxford University Press.

———. 1994. *Recovery: How to Survive Sexual Assault for Women, Men, Teenagers, Their Friends, and Families*. New York: Columbia University Press.

Biagi, Shirley. 1992. *Interviews That Work: A Practical Guide for Journalists*. 2d ed. Belmont, Calif.: Wadsworth.

Bloom, S. L. 1997. *Creating Sanctuary: Toward an Evolution of Sane Societies*. New York: Routledge.

Bloom, S. L. and Michael Reichert. 1998. *Bearing Witness: Violence and Collective Responsibility*. New York: Haworth Maltreatment and Trauma Press.

Borden, S. L. 1993. "Empathic Listening: The Interviewer's Betrayal." *Journal of Mass Media Ethics* 8 (4): 219–26.

Brady, John. 1977. *The Craft of Interviewing*. New York: Vintage.

Braestrup, Peter. 1985. *Battle Lines*. New York: Priority Press.

Bragg, Rick. 1997. *All over but the Shoutin'*. New York: Pantheon.

Brownmiller, Susan. 1975. *Against Our Will: Men, Women, and Rape*. New York: Simon and Schuster.

Buchanan, Edna. 1987. *The Corpse Had a Familiar Face*. New York: Charter Books.

Burgess, A. W. 1992. *Child Trauma I: Issues and Research*. New York: Garland.

Burgess, A. W., ed. 1985. *Rape and Sexual Assault: A Research Handbook*. New York: Garland.

———. 1988. *Rape and Sexual Assault II*. New York: Garland.

———. 1991. *Rape and Sexual Assault III: A Research Handbook*. New York: Garland.

Burgess, A. W. and L. L. Holmstrom. 1979. *Rape, Crisis, and Recovery.* Bowie, Md.: R. J. Brady.

Butterfield, Fox. 1991. "What the Media All Missed." *FineLine,* July–August, pp. 1, 5.

Butterfield, Fox and Mary B. W. Tabor. 1991. "Woman in Florida Rape Inquiry Fought Adversity and Sought Acceptance." *New York Times,* April 17, p. A17.

Carey, James W. 1997. "Why and How: The Dark Continent of American Journalism." In Robert Manoff and Michael Schudson, eds., *Reading the News.* New York: Pantheon.

Casey, Ginger. 1994. "When a Job Rips Out Your Heart." *Radio-Television News Directors Association Communicator,* September 1994, pp. 37–38.

Collins, P. H. 1991. *Black Feminist Thought: Knowledge, Consciousness, and the Politics of Empowerment.* New York: Routledge.

Coté, William and Bonnie Bucqueroux. 1996. "Tips on Interviewing Victims." *Nieman Reports* 50 (3): 27.

Crowell, N. A. and A. W. Burgess, eds. 1996. *Understanding Violence Against Women.* Panel on Research on Violence Against Women, Committee on Law and Justice, Commission on Behavioral and Social Sciences and Education, National Research Council. Washington, D.C.: National Academy Press.

De La Cruz, Ralph. 1996. "Path of a Bullet." *(Long Beach, Calif.) Press-Telegram,* November 10, pp. K1–12.

Deppa, Joan, Maria Russel, Donna Hayes, and Elizabeth Flocke. 1993. *The Media and Disasters: Pan Am 103.* London: Fulton.

Dezern, Craig. 1993. "The Miracle of Philip Chandler." *Orlando Sentinel,* December 26, *Florida* magazine special edition.

Dorfman, Lori, Katie Woodruff, Vivan Chavez, and Lawrence Wallack. 1997. "Youth and Violence on Local Television News in California." *American Journal of Public Health* 87 (August): 1311–16.

Fadiman, Ann. 1997. *The Spirit Catches You and You Fall Down: A Hmong Child, Her American Doctors, and the Collision of Two Cultures.* New York: Farrar, Straus, and Giroux.

Figley, C. R., ed. 1985. *Trauma and Its Wake.* New York: Brunner/Mazel.

——. 1995. *Compassion Fatigue: Coping with Secondary Traumatic Stress Disorder in Those Who Treat the Traumatized.* New York: Brunner/Mazel.

Figley, Charles, Brian Bride, and Nicholas Mazza, eds. 1997. *Death and Trauma: The Traumatology of Grieving.* Washington, D.C.: Taylor and Francis.

Fischer, H. W. III. 1994. *Response to Disaster: Fact Versus Fiction and Its Perpetuation: The Sociology of Disaster.* Lanham, Md.: University Press of America.

Freedom Forum. 1998. *Jonesboro: Were the Media Fair?* booklet, n.p.

Freinkel, Andrew, Cheryl Koopman, and David Spiegel. 1994. "Dissociative Symptoms in Media Eyewitnesses of an Execution." *American Journal of Psychiatry* 151, no. 9 (September 1994): 1335–39.

Fussell, Paul. 1989. *Wartime: Understanding and Behavior in the Second World War.* New York: Oxford University Press.

Gaffney. Donna. 1999. "Interviewing Children: How to Capture Their Words and Tell Their Stories." *Children's Beat,* Summer, pp. 24–26.

Gannett Foundation Media Center. 1991. *The Media at War.* New York: Gannett Foundation.

Gassaway, Bob. 1989. "Making Sense of War: An Autobiographical Account of a Vietnam War Correspondent." *Journal of Applied Behavior Science* 25(4): 327–49.

Gavit, John Palmer. 1903. *The Reporter's Manual: A Handbook for Newspapermen.* Albany, N.Y.: Author.

Gilliland, Mary A. 1998. Letter to the editor. *TV Guide,* May 23, Flint-Lansing, Mich., ed., p. 86.

Glaberson, William. 1991. "Times Article Naming Rape Accuser Ignites Debate on Journalistic Values." *New York Times,* April 26, p. A14.

Goldstein, Tom. 1998. "Dramatic Footage, Yes—But Is It News?" *TV Guide,* May 23, 1998, p. 41.

Goleman, Daniel. 1995. *Emotional Intelligence.* New York: Bantam.

Gordon, M. T. and Stephanie Riger. 1989. *The Female Fear.* New York: Free Press.

Guillen, Tomas. 1990. "Privacy and the Media Amid the Serial Killer Phenomenon: A Case Study of the Green River Serial Murders." Master's Thesis, Communications Department, University of Washington, Seattle.

Haws, Dick. 1997. "The Elusive Numbers on False Rape." *Columbia Journalism Review,* November–December, pp. 16–17.

Herman, Judith L. 1992. *Trauma and Recovery.* New York: Basic.

Harrigan, Jane. 1997. "On the Other End of the Story." *American Journalism Review,* January–February 1997, p. 46.

Higgins, Marguerite. 1955. *News Is a Singular Thing.* Garden City, N.Y.: Doubleday.

Hinton, Mick. 1995. "Group Reviews Media Coverage After Bombing." *Daily Oklahoman,* June 22, p. 12.

Huston, Aletha et al. 1992. *Big World, Small Screen: The Role of Television in American Society.* Lincoln: University of Nebraska Press.

Ignatieff, Michael. 1985. "Is Nothing Sacred? The Ethics of Television." *Daedalus,* Fall, pp. 57–78.

——. 1998. *The Warrior's Honor: Ethnic War and the Modern Conscience.* New York: Metropolitan.

International Society for Traumatic Stress Studies. 1998. *Childhood Trauma Remembered: A Report on the Current Scientific Knowledge Base and Its Applications.* Northbrook, Ill.: Author.

Kleber, R. J., C. R. Figley, and B. P. R. Gersons, eds. 1995. *Beyond Trauma: Cultural and Societal Dynamics.* New York: Plenum.

Koehler, Elizabeth. 1995. "Emergence of a Standard: The Rape Victim Identification Debate Prior to 1970." Master's thesis, Communications Department, University of Washington, Seattle.

Kotlowitz, Robert. 1997. *Before Their Time: A Memoir.* New York: Knopf.

Lachowicz, Steve. 1995. "Learning to Cope with Tragedy." *Wenatchee World,* July 16, p. 2.

Ledingham, John A. and Lynne Masel Walters. 1989. "The Sound and the Fury: Mass Media and Hurricanes." In Lynne Masel Walters, Lee Wilkins, and Tim Walters, eds., *Bad Tidings: Communication and Catastrophe.* Hillsdale, N.J.: Erlbaum.

Lewis, John, with Michael D'Orso. 1998. *Walking with the Wind: A Memoir of the Movement.* New York: Simon and Schuster.

Libow, Judith. 1992. "Traumatized Children and the News Media: Clinical Considerations." *American Journal of Orthopsychiatry,* July, pp. 379–86.

Lichty, Lawrence W. 1984. "Comments on the Influence of Television on Public Opinion." In Peter Braestrup, ed., *Vietnam as History.* Washington, D.C.: University Press of America.

Maass, Peter. 1996. *Love Thy Neighbor: A Story of War.* New York: Knopf.

McKinney, Debra. 1993. "Malignant Memories." *Anchorage Daily News,* June 6, pp. A1–11.

Mencher, Melvin. 1997. *News Reporting and Writing.* 7th ed. Dubuque, Iowa: Brown and Benchmark.

Metzler, Ken. 1989. *Creative Interviewing: The Writer's Guide to Gathering Information by Asking Questions.* 2d ed. Englewood Cliffs, N.J.: Prentice-Hall.

Nathanson, D. L. 1987. *The Many Faces of Shame.* New York: Guilford.

Nader, Kathleen. 1997. "Treating Traumatic Grief in Systems." In Charles R. Figley, Brian E. Bride, and Nicholas Mazza, eds., *Death and Trauma: The Traumatology of Grieving.* Washington, D.C.: Taylor and Francis.

National Television Violence Study. 1997. Thousand Oaks, Calif.: Sage.

Nesaule, Agate. 1995. *A Woman in Amber: Healing the Trauma of War and Exile.* New York: Soho Press.

Ochberg, Frank. 1987. "The Victim of Violent Crime." *Radio-Television News Directors Association Communicator,* December, p. 12–13, 41.

——. 1993. "Post-Traumatic Therapy." In John P. Wilson and Beverley Raphael, eds., *International Handbook of Traumatic Stress Syndromes.* New York: Plenum.

——. 1996. "A Primer on Covering Victims." *Nieman Reports* 50 (3): 21–26.

Ochberg, Frank, ed. 1988. *Post-Traumatic Therapy and Victims of Violence.* New York: Brunner/Mazel.

Overholser, Geneva. 1989. "American Shame: The Stigma of Rape." *Des Moines Register,* July 11, p. 6A.

——. 1990. "A Troubling but Important Set of Stories." *Des Moines Register,* February 25, p. 1C.

Painter, Brian. 1995. "Emotional Recovery Varies, Expert Says." *Daily Oklahoman,* May 29, p. 8.

Pinsky, Mark I. 1993. "Covering the Crimes." *Columbia Journalism Review,* January–February 1993, pp. 28–30.

Quarantelli, E. L. 1989. "The Social Science Study of Disasters and Mass Communication." In Lynne Masel Walters, Lee Wilkins, and Tim Walters, eds., *Bad Tidings: Communication and Catastrophe.* Hillsdale, N.J.: Erlbaum.

Quarantelli, E. L., ed. 1978. *Disasters: Theory and Research*. Beverly Hills, Calif.: Sage.

Quindlen, Anna. 1991. "A Mistake." *New York Times*, April 21, p. E17.

Raine, Nancy V. 1998. *After Silence: Rape and My Journey Back*. New York: Crown.

Ramsey, Martha. 1995. *Where I Stopped: Remembering Rape at Thirteen*. New York: Putnam.

Ricchiardi, Sherry. 1999. "Confronting the Horror." *American Journalism Review*, January–February 1999, pp. 35–39.

Rosenblatt, Roger. 1983. *Children of War*. Garden City, N.Y.: Anchor/Doubleday.

——. 1994. "Rwanda Therapy." *New Republic*, June 6, 1994, pp. 14–16.

Rynearson, E. K. n.d. "The Story of a Trauma: Collage or Chronicle?" Unpublished manuscript.

Scanlon, Joseph. 1998. "The Search for Nonexistent Facts in the Reporting of Disasters." *Journalism and Mass Communication Educator*, Summer 1998, pp. 45–53.

Scherer, Migael. 1992. *Still Loved by the Sun: A Rape Survivor's Journal*. New York: Simon and Schuster.

Schlosser, Eric. 1997. "A Grief Like No Other: Parents of Murdered Children." *Atlantic Monthly*, September, pp. 37–67.

Schorer, Jane. 1990. "It Couldn't Happen to Me: One Woman's Story." *Des Moines Register and Tribune*, February 25–29.

Shapiro, Bruce. 1995. "One Violent Crime." *Nation*, April 1995, pp. 445–52.

Shay, Jonathan. 1994. *Achilles in Vietnam: Combat Trauma and the Undoing of Character*. New York: Maxwell Macmillan International.

Simpson, R. A. and J. G. Boggs. 1999. "An Exploratory Study of Traumatic Stress Among Newspaper Journalists." *Journalism and Communication Monographs* 1 (1): 1–26.

Sitarski, Kathy. 1996. "The Wheel of Violence." *Humanist*, May, p. 23.

Sloan, William David and James D. Startt, eds. 1996. *The Media in America*. 3d ed. Northport, Ala.: Vision Press.

Smith, Carol. 1998. ""Witness to War: World War I Left Its Enduring Mark on the Life of Laura Frost Smith and Generations of Women." *Seattle Post-Intelligencer*, September 24, pp. A1, E5.

Stanush, Michele. 1994. "The Test of Fire." *Austin American-Statesman*, September 4, sec. G, p. 1.

Staub, Ervin. 1989. *The Roots of Evil: The Origins of Genocide and Other Group Violence*. New York: Cambridge University Press.

Stevens, Jane Ellen. 1994. "Treating Violence as an Epidemic." *Technology Review* (August–September): 23–30.

Terr, Lenore. 1990. *Too Scared to Cry: Psychic Trauma in Childhood*. New York: Harper and Row.

——. 1994. *Unchained Memories: True Stories of Traumatic Memories, Lost and Found*. New York: Basic.

Walters, L. M., Lee Wilkins, and Tim Walters, eds. 1989. *Bad Tidings: Communication and Catastrophe*. Hillsdale, N.J.: Erlbaum.

Witt, Howard and Hugh Dellios. 1995. "Local TV Disagrees with Tabloids." *Daily Oklahoman*, April 30, p. 20.

Ziegenmeyer, Nancy, with Larkin Warren. 1992. *Taking Back My Life*. New York: Summit.

Index

Accident, defined, 60
Achille Lauro, 25
Acute Stress Disorder, 27
Adams, Eddie, 134, 142–43
Aiken, Charlotte, 45
American Red Cross, 64–65
Anderson, Dan and Pat, 37, 109, 114
Anger, 37
Anxiety (PTSD symptom), 33
Argo, Jim, 213
Armenian genocide, 200
Avoidance (PTSD symptom), 31

Balakian, Peter, 200
Baldwin, Diana, 213, 214
Bartlett, David, 126
Benedict, Helen, 159, 169–70, 173
Beverly Hills (Kentucky) supper club
    fire, 70
Biagi, Shirley, 195
Bloom, Sandra, 5, 26, 27, 36, 190
Boggs, James G., 47–51
Borden, Sandra, 88
Bosnia, 103
Bragg, Rick, 3, 12, 75–77
Brownmiller, Susan, 168
Buchanan, Edna, 7
Bunyan, Clytie, 213, 217
Burgess, Ann, 168

Butterfield, Fox, 170–71
Byrd, Joann, 2, 13

Cambodian genocide, 205
Carey, James, 72
Casey, Ginger, 46
Centers for Disease Control and Pre-
    vention, 9
Challenger explosion, 112, 136, 188
Children and trauma, 36, 185–98, 230;
    and denial, 196; guidelines, 191–98;
    parents' role, 193–94; patterns of
    response, 189–91; "poster child,"
    195–96
Chung, Connie, 61, 220
Civil rights movement, 201
Cohen, Steven, 137
Collins, Patricia Hill, 167
Combat fatigue, 24
Community panel, in murder trial, 16
Compassion fatigue, 49
Convergence, 61
Coté, William, vii, 31, 33
Coverage, disaster planning, 56–60
Cronkite, Walter, 104
Crutchfield, Jim, 121

Daily Oklahoman (Oklahoma City),
    39, 45, 54, 61, 212–21

Dart Award for Excellence in Reporting on Victims of Violence, 235–36
Dart Center for Journalism and Trauma, ix
Dart Foundation, ix
Day, Allison, 212
De La Cruz, Ralph, 116, 121
Debriefing, 53
Dellios, Hugh, 219
Deppa, Joan, 28, 60
Des Moines Register, 157–60
Dezern, Craig, 118
Disaster, defined, 60; myth of victim behavior, 71–72, stages of, 73
Dissociation, 26, 190
Dobson, Lynne, 12, 113, 145–52, 153
Domestic violence, 200–201, 208–10, 231–32
Dunblane (Scotland) school shooting, 65, 197
Durner, Fran, 113
Dwyer, R. Budd, 132–34

Embelton, Gary, 120
Emotions, 25–27
Empathy, 49–50, 89

Fadiman, Anne, 206
Families and Friends of Victims of Violence, 14
Figley, Charles, 49
Fink, Michelle, 220
Fischer, Henry W. III, 70–71
Flashbacks, 29
Forgetfulness, 32–33
Fort Worth (Texas) church shooting, 192
Freeway suicide (Los Angeles), 136–37
Fussell, Paul, 201

Gaffney, Donna, 190
Galveston, Texas, 72–73
Gans, Herbert, 85
Gassaway, Bob, 45

Genocide, 25, 205–7, 231
Goldstein, Tom, 136–37
Goleman, Daniel, 25–26, 59
Gordon, Margaret, 164–66
Gradney, Jeff, 12, 102–4

Haile, John, 118
Hansen, Jon, 219, 220
Harrigan, Jane, 68
Herald (Everett, Washington), 13
Herman, Judith Lewis, 25, 26, 161, 162, 164, 172, 199, 200, 208–9
Higgins, Marguerite, 43, 83–84
Hight, Joe, 212
Hiley-Young, Bruce, 39, 216
Hillsborough soccer stadium (Liverpool, England), 70
Hindenburg, 136
Hinton, Carla, 122
Hippocrates, Cratis, 120
Hodges, Curt, 63–64
Holmstrom, Lynda, 168
Holocaust, 205
Homosexuality and violence, 210–11
Hover, Rebecca, 16
Hurricane Andrew, 68–69
Hurricane Gilbert, 70–71

Ignatieff, Michael, 86
International Society for Traumatic Stress Studies, 176
Interviews, 83–101, 225–27; anniversary, 97–98; control, 95; "death knock," 93; emotional responses, 96; gender issues, 90; ground rules, 95; history, 83; "informed consent," 88–89; location, 98; not doing, 9–10; questions, 94; reasons for, 86; reporter-subject relationships, 100–101; stopping, 38

Jacobson, Walter, 126
Jonesboro (Arkansas) school shooting, 63, 67, 76, 223
Jonesboro Sun, 63, 66

Journalism and Trauma Program (UW), viii, 238
Journalists and trauma, 232–33; exposure to auto crashes, 48; ways of coping with trauma, 51–55; witnesses to violence, 47

Kansas City, Missouri, skybridge collapse, 57–58
Kelley, Ed, 213, 217
KING-Channel 5 (Seattle, Washington), 104
KJRH-Channel 2 (Tulsa, Oklahoma), 103
Klaas, Marc, 93
Kobe (Japan) earthquake, 71
Kotlowitz, Alex, 196
Kotlowitz, Robert, 204
Kuralt, Charles, 104
Kurtz, Howard, 126

Lachowicz, Steve, 55
Lansing State Journal, 32, 111
Leach, Hugh, 111
Ledingham, John, 73
Lewis, John, 200
Libow, Judith, 193–4
Lichty, Lawrence W., 141
Lippmann, Walter, 87
Littleton, Colorado (Columbine High School shootings), 1, 63, 72, 190
Loan, Nguyen Ngoc, 142–3
Lockerbie, Scotland, 1, 23, 25, 28, 60–61, 125
Loma Prieta earthquake, 1, 59, 68
Lyons, Memyo, 90

McCoy, Roger, 57–8
McKinney, Debra, 12, 90–91, 113, 116, 118, 175, 177–80
McVeigh, Timothy James, 218
Maass, Peter, 44
Marine Barracks Bombing (Lebanon), 24

Melbourne (Australia) school shooting, 65–66
Mencher, Melvin, 114–15
Michigan Victim Alliance, 30, 108
Mothers Against Drunk Driving (MADD), 37
Murrow, Edward R., 104

Nader, Kathleen, 188, 197
Nation magazine, 39
National Center for Post-Traumatic Stress Disorder (U.S. Veterans Administration), 39
National Press Photographers Association, 144
National Television Violence Study, 6
Nesaule, Agate, 206
New York Times, 3, 75, 170–71
News Photographer magazine, 133, 138
Nichols, Terry, 218
North, Scott, 12, 13–17
Numbing, emotional (PTSD symptom), 30

Ochberg, Frank, vii, 24, 30, 32, 34, 35, 41, 88, 107, 108, 113, 128–29
Oklahoma City federal building bombing, 1, 4–5, 23, 50, 61, 62, 64–65, 77, 100, 103, 212–21
Overholser, Geneva, 157–58

Painter, Bryan, 212, 216
Papua, New Guinea tsunami, 1
"Parachute" journalists, 56
Peterson, Angela, 118
Peterson, David, 158
Photography, 123–144, 228–29; Anniston case, 131–32; Dwyer case, 132–34; equipment issues, 126–28; "flashbulb memories," 124; guidelines, 137–39; history, 129–35; images and horror, 128–29; in war, 139–44
Piedmont (Alabama) tornado, 78–82
Pinsky, Mark, 46–47

Post-Traumatic Stress Disorder (PTSD), 27, 29–36, 223–34; basic diagnosis, 29; and children, 188
Poynter Institute for Media Studies, 138
Press-Telegram (Long Beach, California), 121
Princess Diana, 125
Public-safety Personnel, 62

Quanterelli, E. L., 71
Queensland University of Technology, 120
Quindlen, Anna, 170–71

Radio-Television News Directors Association, 138
Raine, Nancy Venable, 162, 200
Ramsey, Martha, 176
Rape: defined, 160–61; false charges, 171; guidelines, 166; importance of privacy, 163; myths, 158–60; naming issue, 166–73; of children, 174–75; patterns, 158–60, 164–66; survivors' contributions to education, 159, 167–68; trial, 173–74
Rape trauma, 25, 161–64, 171–72, 229–30
Recovered Memory, 174–6
Refugees, 25, 44
Riger, Stephanie, 164–66
Rosenblatt, Roger, 51
Rwanda genocide, 205
Rynearson, E. K., 100

Safer, Morley, 141
Scanlon, Joseph, 59
Scherer, Migael, viii, 12, 162–63, 172
Schindler, Oscar, 207
Schlosser, Eric, 199
School shootings, explanations for, 72
Schorer, Jane, 158
Seattle *Post-Intelligencer*, 2
Shame, 37

Shapiro, Bruce, 39–41, 85, 88, 108, 113
Shay, Jonathan, 24, 202–4
Shell shock, 24
Shepard, Matthew, 210
Shine, Neal, 88
Simpson, Roger, viii, 47–51, 199
Sisney, Steve, 215
Sitarski, Kathy, 172
Smith, Carol, 204
Spielberg, Steven 201–2
Springfield, Oregon, school shooting, 65, 192
Stanush, Michele, 113, 115, 153
Staub, Ervin, 207
Steinke, Dale, 16
Stensrud, Nancy, 19–21
Stockholm Syndrome, 38
"Survivor's Psalm," 41
Sutter, Ellie, 212
Swissair 111, 23
Symonds, Martin, 92

Television, news, 7, 87; violence characteristics, 6
Terr, Lenore, 187, 194, 197
Thompson, Ken, 216
Torture, 25
Training, 237–38
Trauma: coping abilities, 34–35; defined, 22; employer responses, 53–54; heredity, 35; human violence, 22; journalists and, 42–54; natural disasters, 22; "organizing principle of society," 5; rape, 161–64; victims, 8; women's experience, 25
Tuttle, Hope, 59, 68, 73–74
TWA flight 800, 64, 65

Victims and the Media Program (MSU), vii, 108, 237
Vietnam, combat trauma, 24, 30–31, 36, 231; photography, 140–143; veterans' stories, 202–3
Violence, as epidemic, 9

Wallenberg, Raoul, 207
Walters, Lynne Masel, 73
War, 25
Washington Post, 2
Wenatchee World, 55
WESH-TV (Orlando, Florida), 11
Western Journalism and Trauma
    Conference (1996), 15, 113

Witt, Howard, 219
World Trade Center Bombing, 24
Writing trauma stories, 107–22,
    227–28; context, 120–22; details,
    111–12, 117–19; errors, 108–11; kicker,
    119–20; leads, 115–16; profiles, 114

Ziegenmeyer, Nancy, 158–60, 162, 172